C0-DAN-224

FOOD & WINE

MAGAZINE'S

official Wine Guide 2001

by Alice S. Feiring

American Express
Publishing Corporation
New York

FOOD & WINE
BOOKS

contents

FOOD & WINE

MAGAZINE'S

official Wine Guide 2001

by Alice S. Feiring

Editor in Chief **Judith Hill**
Art Director **Perri DeFino**
Managing Editor **Terri Mauro**
Project Director **Dana Speers**
Designer **Leslie Andersen**
Editorial Associate **Colleen McKinney**
Contributing Editor **Jack Robertiello**
Researchers **Sharon Kapnick,**
          Jamal Rayyis, Sarah Zwiebach
Production Coordinator **Stuart Handelman**

Senior Vice President, Publisher **Mark V. Stanich**
Director, Retail Sales & Services **Marshall Corey**
Marketing Manager **Sara Braun**
Marketing Coordinator **Richard Nogueira**
Business Manager **Keith Strohmeier**

Cover photograph **Mark Ferri**

Copyright © 2000
American Express Publishing Corporation
1120 Avenue of the Americas
New York, NY 10036

All rights reserved. No part of this book may be reproduced or transmitted in
any form or by any means, electronic or mechanical, including photocopying,
recording, or by any information storage or retrieval system, without permis-
sion in writing from the Publisher.   ISSN: 1522-001X

foreword
by Jacques Pépin

"No man has the right to inflict the torture of bad wine upon his fellow creatures," wrote Marcus Clarke in *The Peripatetic Philosopher* in 1869. And this is why all of us need *FOOD & WINE Magazine's Official Wine Guide*.

There is no meal without wine in my family. Wine is food, an integral part of our meal. From the farmer's simplest homemade potable that I drank as a young person in France to the great wines of the Côtes du Rhône or California, wine has always been a part of my daily repast. It is enjoyed throughout most of Europe as a component of daily living, not served only for special events. I believe that this way of life is taking hold in America as well.

Much has been said about the pairing of food and wine. If I had hundreds of bottles to choose from when planning a meal, I would select according to my mood and the food on that particular occasion. Eating the same meal at another time, I might try an entirely different wine. If my possibilities were limited to only two or three bottles, I would be happy to pick one of those, because, in my family, we must have wine. Even if the only available wine was a simple, homemade jug wine, I would enjoy a few glasses of it with my meal.

An extraordinary richness and variety of wines exists in our world. Most states in the U.S. produce wines, and delightful surprises to be explored for a modicum of money come from other countries, like Australia and New Zealand, Argentina and Chile in South America, and Portugal and Spain in Europe. The diversity in the sources of supply can quench the thirst of the most dedicated Bacchus.

"Wine, the most delightful of drinks, whether we owe it to Noah, who planted the vine or Bacchus, who first pressed juice from the grapes, dates from the childhood of the world," wrote Brillat-Savarin in 1826 in *The Physiology of Taste*. Wine is an essential part of most great cultures, and the enjoyment of wine is an international language that can cross barriers of tradition, religion, and nationality. The suspicious foreigner always looks more gentle and convivial over a glass of wine.

This wine guide is well organized and small, so you can slide it into your pocket and carry it with you. It will give you vintage charts for the greatest vinous pleasures of the last decade and inform you on the best buys and best wines available in the shops this year. It will help you handle a wine list and pair wine with food. It will even direct you to the top wine shops in the U.S. In a word, this exceedingly accessible and current little book will guide you to the most glorious nectar ever made by man.

list of boxes

Scattered throughout the text are information boxes to which you may want to refer again after coming across them once. They're alphabetized here by title or by main topic, when that's different from the exact title used in the book.

introduction
by Alice S. Feiring

Thousands of wines were tasted for this book and all were tasted without prejudice: When possible, bottles were wrapped in brown paper bags to insure anonymity. It is fair to say that whether it received one star or four, each of the wines in this book is a winner. You'll be able to see, from the ratings and the tasting notes, which ones are transcendent—just the right wines for high-state occasions—and which are perfect gems for tonight's informal dinner. Keep the book handy when shopping in stores or on-line, and do remember to take it with you to restaurants. Especially when there's no sommelier on duty, this is your secret agent to help guide you through pages of unfamiliar wines to make the choice that's right for you.

key to symbols

This guide is different from most: It's up to date. Our recommendations are for the exact wines being released for sale this year. Each recommendation includes the following symbols:

Type	🍷 / 🍷 / 🍷 red wine / white wine / rosé wine	
Quality	★★★★	**Outstanding** Worth a search
	★★★	**Excellent** Top-notch example of its type
	★★	**Very good** Distinctive
	★	**Good** Delicious everyday wine
Price	$$$$	$50 and up
	$$$	$25 to $50
	$$	$12 to $25
	$	$12 or less

NOTE Pronunciation guides for the names you are most likely to need to say in ordering or buying follow the first use of the name in the section where it is considered at most length.

guide to grape varieties

More than 1,000 different winemaking grape varieties are grown in the world. Some are little known outside their country of origin; others are world famous. Many of the latter group are so popular that they're called *international varieties* and are found almost everywhere that winemakers produce wine.

international white varieties

CHARDONNAY

Before Chardonnay was practically a brand name, people knew it as the white-wine grape of Burgundy and one of the three grapes permitted in Champagne. From tart, mineral-tasting Chablis to tropical-fruit–laden New World Chardonnays, the styles are widely disparate. Left on its own, with little oak overlay, its aromas are often of apples and melons.

CHENIN BLANC

In the Loire, the vigorously acidic, green-apple-scented Chenin Blanc performs its greatest acrobatics, making bone-dry whites, sparklers, and also unctuous dessert wine. It is grown elsewhere, most notably in South Africa and the United States.

RIESLING

A current darling of the wine world—lately heralded as the world's greatest white grape. Some may not agree, but the bottom line is that Rieslings are delicious. Fine examples are produced in Alsace, Germany, Austria, and New York's Finger Lakes, and increasingly in Australia. The flavors and aromas hint at peaches, apricots, flowers, and minerals. Styles range from steely dry to gorgeous dessert wines. Regardless of type, their acidity always makes them refreshing and ageworthy.

SAUVIGNON BLANC

Though it is an important white grape of Bordeaux, Sauvignon Blanc is most lionized in the Loire where it is coveted as Pouilly-Fumé and Sancerre. Acidic Sauvignon is marked by one of the more distinctive aromas in the grape world—a fresh-cut-grass scent. Tremendously food-worthy, it's grown all over the world. New Zealand and South Africa turn out stunning examples.

SÉMILLON

One of the important white grapes of Bordeaux, Sémillon gets top billing in that region's famous dessert wines as well as on its own or in tandem with Sauvignon Blanc in full-bodied dry whites. In other parts of the world, such as Washington State and Australia, it ends up alone or in Chardonnay blends.

international red varieties

CABERNET SAUVIGNON

Thick skinned and late ripening, this Bordeaux grape travels around the world and appears to be at home almost every-where. Cabernet often has aromas of black currants and cedar as well as green bell pepper and herbaceous qualities—a complex balance of fruitiness and earthiness. Concentrated tannin, which mellows with age, is an important part of its character.

MERLOT

Does any country *not* grow Merlot? In danger of suffering from overexposure, this variety is nevertheless one of the world's greats. Wine made from Merlot is considered easy to drink—low in acidity and tannin, with flavors of plum and chocolate.

PINOT NOIR

Before Pinot Noir was famed as an international varietal, it was known as the grape from which Burgundy is made. With heady aromas of roses, black cherry, and musk, Pinot Noir is one of the world's most seductive grapes. In its youth, the wine is lively and fruity; it develops complexity with age. Homes outside of Burgundy include New Zealand, South Africa, and the U.S.

SYRAH

Deeply colored and tannic, the Syrah grape produces full-bodied wines with intense berry flavor and black-pepper notes. Its happy home is the Northern Rhône, but it has found fame in the Central Coast of California as well and also, under the name of Shiraz, in Australia.

other popular grapes

BARBERA

The second most planted red grape in Italy is currently finding favor among California winemakers looking for the next new thing. Ironically, the dark grape with mellow fruit flavors was among the first vinifera grapes planted in California by Italian immigrants in the nineteenth century.

CABERNET FRANC

An important red grape of Bordeaux and the Loire Valley, Cabernet Franc is similar to Cabernet Sauvignon but makes wines that are lighter and more perfumed. It's gaining ground in California and on Long Island.

GEWÜRZTRAMINER

A flamboyant white grape with exotic apricot, litchi, rose, and spice aromas. Not only does it have heady aromas and assertive flavors, but it makes full-bodied, high-alcohol wines. It's especially important in Alsace and Germany.

MARSANNE

Now growing mostly in the South of France, this white grape that produces full-bodied wine is finding its way into the hearts of California wine growers. The Swiss like it, too.

MUSCAT

This is really a family of white grapes with similar floral, musk, peach, and orange aromas and flavors. It makes excellent dry and sweet wines.

NEBBIOLO

The noblest grape of Italy, Nebbiolo becomes the coveted and expensive Barolo and Barbaresco. Though winemakers are experimenting with it elsewhere, there is no doubt of its sovereignty in Piedmont. Lovers of the grape are drawn to the flavors of cherry, tar, tobacco, and violet as well as its full tannin.

PINOT BLANC

Makes medium-bodied, mildly flavored white wines. It's to be found in Burgundy, Alsace, Germany, Italy, and California but is most important in Austria, where it's called Weissburgunder.

PINOT GRIS

In Italy, Pinot Gris is known as Pinot Grigio and is made into light, brisk white wine. Elsewhere it generally produces full-bodied, nutty-flavored wines.

SANGIOVESE

Capable of developing cherry, pine, and leather tones and kept lively with plenty of acidity, there's no contesting that Sangiovese, which produces Chiantis and Brunellos, is Italy's most popular and well-known grape.

TEMPRANILLO

Grown all over Spain, Tempranillo is preeminent as Rioja. Wine made from the grape has spice aromas and full plummy flavors, and it's medium-bodied.

VIOGNIER

A peach- and floral-scented white grape, Viognier lived in obscurity in the northern Rhône until it recently became the rage in California.

ZINFANDEL

Red-wine grape with bold blackberry and spice flavors and lots of tannin. It has found its zenith in California.

shortcut to finding varietals

If you thought Riesling came only from Germany, guess again. Use this list to locate your favorite varietals and the (sometimes surprising) countries in which they are now being produced. You may be inspired to try something you never knew existed.

Cabernet Franc

California	193
Friuli-Venezia Giulia	101
Loire Valley	70
New York State	226
Washington State	220

Cabernet Sauvignon

Apulia, Campania, Sicily & Sardinia	94
Argentina	253
Australia	242
Bordeaux	34
California	192
Chile	257
Italy (other regions)	130
Portugal	148
South Africa	232
Spain	140
Tuscany	119
Washington State	218

Chardonnay

Australia	236
Austria	173
Burgundy	44
California	182
Chile	258
Friuli-Venezia Giulia	99

Italy (other regions)	130
New York State	224
New Zealand	247
Oregon	212
Piedmont	110
South Africa	231
Spain	141
Tuscany	121
Washington State	215

Chenin Blanc

California	190
Loire Valley	65
South Africa	231
Washington State	217

Gewürztraminer

Alsace	27
California	189
New York State	224
Oregon	212
Washington State	217

Merlot

Apulia, Campania, Sicily & Sardinia	94
Argentina	253
Australia	243
Bordeaux	34

California	196
Friulia-Venezia Giulia	100
Languedoc-Roussillon	60
Southwest France	89
Switzerland	179
Tuscany	120
Washington State	218

Muscat

Alsace	28
Austria	176
Italian Dessert Wines (Moscato)	284
Spain	143

Pinot Blanc

Alsace	27
Austria (Weissburgunder)	175
California	189
New York State	225
Oregon	211
Tuscany (Pinot Bianco)	121

Pinot Gris

Alsace	28
California	190
Friuli-Venezia Giulia (Pinot Grigio)	98
Oregon	210
Washington State	217

Pinot Noir

Austria (Blauburgunder)	175
Burgundy	47
California	198
New York State	226
New Zealand	249
Oregon	213
South Africa	232
Tuscany	119

Riesling

Alsace	27
Australia	238

Austria	173
Friuli-Venezia Giulia	99
Germany	162
New York State	224
New Zealand	248
Washington State	217

Sauvignon Blanc

Australia	238
Austria	176
Bordeaux	37
California	185
Chile	258
Greece	157
Loire Valley	67
New Zealand	246
South Africa	230
Washington State	216

Sémillon

Australia	238
Bordeaux	37
Washington State	217

Syrah

Argentina	253
Australia (Shiraz)	239
California	203
Languedoc-Roussillon	59
Rhône Valley	79
South Africa (Shiraz)	233
Switzerland	178
Washington State	221

Viognier

Argentina	255
California	187
Languedoc-Roussillon	58
New York State	225
Rhône Valley	80

Zinfandel

California	200

wine-style finder

Say you're serving trout, and you know you want a light white wine—this is the place to look to discover your options. Or maybe you order Beaujolais all the time and intend to stick with light-bodied red wine but would like a little variety. You'll find other possibilities in the same category here. And don't forget to consult this section when a recipe suggests something like, "Serve with a full-bodied red wine."

country	region	wines

light-bodied, dry white wines

country	region	wines
Austria		Riesling, 173
California		Chenin Blanc, 190; Sauvignon Blanc, 185
Chile		Sauvignon Blanc, 258
France	Alsace	Edelzwicker, 28; Pinot Blanc, 27
	Bordeaux	Bordeaux Blanc, 37; Entre-Deux-Mers, 38
	Languedoc-Roussillon	Costières de Nîmes, 58
	Loire Valley	Menetou-Salon, 67; Muscadet, 66; Quincy, 69; Sancerre, 67
Greece		Assyrtiko, 157
Italy	Friuli	Pinot Bianco, 99; Riesling, 99; Sauvignon Blanc, 100; Tocai Friulano, 99
	Latium	Frascati, 127
	Piedmont	Gavi, 110
	Trentino	Müller-Thurgau, 130
	Tuscany	Vernaccia di San Gimignano, 121
	Umbria	Orvieto, 131
	Veneto	Soave, 124
New York State		Pinot Blanc, 225; Riesling, 224
Portugal		Vinho Verde, 151
South Africa		Sauvignon Blanc, 230
Switzerland		Chasselas, 179
Washington State		Riesling, 217; Sauvignon Blanc, 216

medium-bodied, dry white wines

Australia		Riesling, 238; Sauvignon Blanc, 238; Semillon, 238
Austria		Grüner Veltliner, 173
California		Gewürztraminer, 189; Marsanne, 188; Pinot Blanc, 189; Pinot Gris, 190
Chile		Chardonnay, 258
France	Alsace	Gewurztraminer, 27; Pinot Gris, 28; Riesling, 27
	Bordeaux	Pessac-Léognan, 37
	Burgundy	Burgundy, 44
	Languedoc-Roussillon	Vin de Pays de Garde, 58; Vin de Pays de l'Hérault, 58; Vin de Pays d'Oc, 58
	Loire Valley	Pouilly-Fumé, 68; Savennières, 65; Touraine, 69; Vouvray, 64
	Rhône Valley	Côtes-du-Rhône, 81
	Southwest	Gaillac, 88; Jurançon, 87
Germany	Franken	Silvaner, 169
	Mittelrhein	Riesling, 169
	Mosel-Saar-Ruwer	Riesling, 162
	Nahe	Riesling, 169
	Pfalz	Riesling, 165; Scheurebe, 165
	Rheingau	Riesling, 166
	Rheinhessen	Riesling, 168
Greece		Mantinia Moscophilero, 157; Peloponnese Roditis, 157
Italy	Campania	Fiano di Avellino, 94
	Friuli	Pinot Grigio, 98
	Piedmont	Chardonnay, 110; Roero Arneis, 109
	Trentino	Chardonnay, 130
New York State		Chardonnay, 224; Gewürztraminer, 224
New Zealand		Chardonnay, 247; Riesling, 248; Sauvignon Blanc, 246
Oregon		Pinot Blanc, 211; Pinot Gris, 210
Portugal		Bucelas, 151; Dão, 151

country	region	wines

(medium-bodied, dry white wines, continued)

South Africa		Chardonnay, 231; Steen, 231
Spain		Albariño, 143; Penedès, 143; Rioja, 136; Rueda, 143
Washington State		Chardonnay, 215; Semillon, 217

full-bodied, dry white wines

Argentina		Viognier, 255
Australia		Chardonnay, 236
California		Chardonnay, 182; Rhône-style, 187
France	Alsace	Gewurztraminer, 27; Pinot Gris, 28
	Burgundy	Premier and Grand Cru, 44
	Rhône Valley	Châteauneuf-du-Pape, 84; Condrieu, 80

lightly sweet to moderately sweet white wines

Germany	Mosel-Saar-Ruwer	Riesling, 162
	Pfalz	Riesling, 165; Scheurebe, 165
	Rheingau	Riesling, 166
	Rheinhessen	Riesling, 168
New York State		Vidal, 225
South Africa		Steen, 231

light-bodied red wines

Austria		Zweigelt, 176
France	Burgundy	Beaujolais, 54
	Loire Valley	Anjou Rouge, 71
Italy	Abruzzi	Montepulciano d'Abruzzo, 126
New York		Pinot Noir, 226

medium-bodied red wines

Argentina		Cabernet Sauvignon, 253; Merlot, 253; Syrah, 253
Austria		Blauburgunder, 175
California		Cabernet Franc, 193; Merlot, 196; Pinot Noir, 198; Sangiovese, 203
Chile		Cabernet Sauvignon, 257; Merlot, 257

country	region	wines

(medium-bodied red wines, continued)

France   Bordeaux   Bordeaux Supérieur, 34; Canon-Fronsac, 36; Graves, 36; Haut-Médoc, 35; Margaux, 35; Pomerol, 34; St-Émilion, 34; St-Estèphe, 35; St-Julien, 34

Burgundy   Burgundy, 46

Languedoc-Roussillon   Corbières, 60; Costières de Nîmes, 62; Coteaux du Languedoc, 58; Côtes du Roussillon and Côtes du Roussillon-Villages, 60; Vin de Pays de l'Hérault, 59

Loire Valley   Anjou-Villages, 71; Bourgueil, 70; Chinon, 70; Côte Roannaise, 72; Menetou-Salon, 71; Saumur Champigny, 70; St-Nicholas-de-Bourgueil, 71

Rhône Valley   Côtes-du-Rhône and Côtes-du-Rhône Villages, 84; Crozes-Hermitage, 80; Lirac, 85; St-Joseph, 80

Southwest   Côtes du Frontannais, 88; Côtes de Gascogne, 87

Italy   Friuli   Cabernet Franc, 101; Pinot Noir, 101; Refosco, 101

Lombardy   Oltrepò Pavese Barbera-based, 128

Marches   Rosso Piceno, 129

Piedmont   Barbaresco, 103; Barbera, 108; Gattinara, 107; Nebbiolo delle Langhe, 106

Tuscany   Carmignano, 117; Chianti, 112; Morellino di Scansano, 117; Other Sangiovese-based wines, 117; Pinot Noir, 119; Rosso di Montalcino, 115; Vino Nobile, 117

New York State   Cabernet Franc, 226

New Zealand   Pinot Noir, 249

South Africa   Pinotage, 232

Spain   Navarra, 141; Penedès, 142; Rioja, 135

Switzerland   Merlot, 179; Syrah, 178

Washington State   Bordeaux blends, 218; Cabernet Franc, 220; Merlot, 218

country	region	wines

full-bodied red wines

Argentina		Malbec, 253
Australia		Cabernet Sauvignon, 242;
		Grenache/Shiraz/Mourvèdre blends, 243;
		Shiraz, 239
California		Cabernet Sauvignon, 192; Meritage, 206;
		Rhône-style, 203; Zinfandel, 200
France	Bordeaux	Top Classified Growths, 34
	Burgundy	Grand Cru, 46
	Languedoc-Roussillon	Collioure, 61; Minervois, 59; Pic-St-Loup, 61;
		Roussillon, 59; Vin de Pays, 60
	Provence	Bandol, 74; Coteaux d'Aix-en-Provence, 74;
		Les Baux de Provence, 74
	Rhône Valley	Châteauneuf-du-Pape, 83; Cornas, 80;
		Côte-Rôtie, 80; Gigondas, 84; Hermitage, 79;
		Rasteau, 84; Vin de Pays d'Ardèche, 84
	Southwest	Cahors, 88; Madiran, 88; Marcillac, 88
Italy	Apulia	Primitivo, 94
	Basilicata	Aglianico del Vulture, 127
	Marches	Rosso Conero, 128
	Piedmont	Barolo, 103
	Sardinia	Cannonau, 95
	Tuscany	Brunello, 115; Super Tuscans, 119
	Veneto	Amarone, 124
South Africa		Cabernet Sauvignon, 232; Shiraz, 233
Spain		Priorato, 140; Ribera del Duero, 138

how to handle a wine list

judging the list

Wine-list sins include usurious markups, an overload of common brands, and a simple varietal listing that excludes blends. All of these deserve contempt. What you should get is a good range of prices including at least one reasonably inexpensive choice around $20 and an interesting assortment of grapes and wines. If you find something like Grüner Veltliner (see "Grüner Who?," page 173), you know you're in good hands.

deciding on the price range

Taste one of the house wines by the glass as an aperitif. If it's good, you can feel confident in ordering the cheapest wine on the list. If not, go for the mid-range.

asking for help

Do speak to the sommelier, wine buyer, or someone familiar with the list. Don't be shy. Wine people thrive on wine talk. State your preferences, dislikes, and price range. Feel absolutely free to ask which are the best values.

sending a bottle back

If a wine smells so bad you don't want to even taste it, don't. Tell the server you're not sure about the wine and want to wait a few minutes to see if the bad smell dissipates. If it's still there after a pause, send the wine back. If a waitperson is rude, be polite but hold your ground. Life is too short to drink—and pay for—bad wine.

"Corked" wine smells moldy. This is the most prevalent wine flaw—affecting about three percent of bottles. It's often due to molds that can infest the bark from which corks are made. Other flaws are linked to the winemaking process. The most common smells you should not tolerate in wine are: rotten eggs, garlic, geranium, burned rubber, sauerkraut, skunk, sulfur, and vinegar.

france

The long-standing supremacy of France in the wine world has been challenged over the past twenty years by the increasing success of other winemaking countries. Challenged, but not toppled. No one doubts that *la belle* France still occupies winedom's pinnacle. After all, this is the land of the big three: Bordeaux, Burgundy, and Champagne.

grapes & styles

With a wealth of regions—and regions within regions—and a variety of microclimates that range from cold and wet to hot and dry, France obviously grows many grape varieties and produces a wide assortment of wine styles. You could spend a lifetime drinking nothing but French wines and never experience palate fatigue. Though French styles are imitated throughout the world, they are rarely equaled. The wines stress *terroir*, the character that seeps into the grapes from the environment where they're grown: the soil, climate, topography, the slope of the vineyard (which determines how it catches the sun), and a host of other factors.

No other country has such explicit wine laws. The Appellation d'Orígine Contrôlée (controlled name of origin) was instituted in the 1930s and became the world's model. This organization protects the French wine names by controlling myriad details, including the varieties of grapes that can be used, how they're grown, even when they can be harvested.

Many of today's wine drinkers prefer wines that differ from the traditional—primarily fruitier styles. To a degree, that market can be satisfied working within the strict French wine laws. However, some vintners are staging a quiet revolution by making wine in any way they please; they ignore the laws even though that means their wines can only claim one of the least prestigious classifications (see "On the Label," opposite).

Featured Wine-Growing Regions

Nord-Pas de Calais

Normandy (high)

Picardie

Normandy (low)

PARIS •

Île de France

Lorraine

Champagne-Ardenne

Bretagne

Alsace

Centre

Loire

Burgundy

Franche-Comté

Poitou-Charentes

Limousin

Auvergne

• LYON

Rhônes-Alpes

• BORDEAUX

Bordeaux

Midi-Pyrénées

Provence-Alpes-Côte d'Azur

• MARSEILLE

Languedoc-Roussillon

The traditional geographic regions of France

on the label

The Appellation Contrôlée (short for Appellation d'Origine Con-trôlée) categories, from highest to lowest:

Appellation d'Origine Contrôlée (AOC or just AC)

The designation given when all of the requirements for wines pro-duced in a given area are met. The specific geographic name will usually appear on the label in the middle of the classification, such as Appellation Anjou Contrôlée. Most of the French wines avail-able in the United States fall into this category. AOC also refers to the system of classification and to the organization that con-trols the wine laws.

Vins Délimités de Qualité Supérieure (VDQS)

Translates as *wines of superior quality from a specific area*, and applies to only a tiny group of wines. The qualifications are pretty much the same as for the highest level, but not quite so strict on some rules, such as the permitted grape yields per hectare.

Vins de Pays Literally *country wines*. The least number of hurdles must be passed to receive this place-name classification. On labels, the geographic name is usually at the end, as in Vins de Pays de Languedoc. Some terrific wines get dumped into this category because they defy the restrictions of the system (see "Grapes & Styles," page 22).

Vins de Table These are simple "table wines" that can claim no specific geographic area—except France. The label includes neither grape variety nor vintage.

alsace

With their heady aromas and clear fruit flavors, Alsace wines stand among the most drinkable of beverages, and are also among the most versatile with food. Try the wines of Alsace as a felicitous antidote to Chardonnay fatigue. The strong-minded Alsatians maintain a strict view of winemaking; their wines rarely see new oak. Therefore, Alsace wines taste of pure fruit in their youth, but many of them are made to last. Buy them to drink now, or hold onto the best of the Rieslings, Gewurztraminers (written without the umlaut in France), and Pinot Gris for five to fifteen years.

grapes & styles

Alsace is white-wine territory. Riesling, Gewurztraminer, Pinot Gris, and Pinot Blanc hold sway here and are bottled as varietals. The smaller players—Sylvaner, Chasselas, and Auxerrois—often go into the traditional blend called Edelzwicker; while this name doesn't always appear on the bottles that are imported to the United States, you can safely bet that any bottle without a grape name is a blend.

Although the wines of Alsace are aromatic, dry is the defining style—often bone dry. Alsatian dessert wines, of course, are sweet and are excellent (see "Dessert Wines of Alsace," page 274). A light-bodied Pinot Noir is the region's only red variety and accounts for about 10 percent of Alsace's wine production.

on the label

For the most part, rather than labeling its wines by place like the rest of France, Alsace identifies the bottles according to the name of the grape. You may also see Grand Cru on the label—about fifty vineyards in the region have Grand Cru status—but, due to the politics behind the conferring of that distinction, it's not the guarantee of quality that one might hope. In fact, some Alsatian producers of great reputation refuse to include Grand Cru and the specific vineyard to which that designation was given on the label, preferring to use their own house name.

what to buy ALSACE

1994	1995	1996	1997	1998	1999
★★★★	★★★	★★★	★★★	★★	★★★

RIESLING

Alsace produces some of the world's great Rieslings. They are dry and powerful, with a floral scent, and aromas and flavors of citrus zest, peaches, and minerals. With age these wines develop a classic petrol aroma, which is considered to be a positive characteristic.

at the table

Riesling's acidity slices right through cream sauces, or any other rich food, to refresh the palate. For a treat, try it with fettuccine Alfredo. The same tartness brings out the flavor of almost any fish and also of chicken. In fact, poultry is a traditional Alsatian match for Riesling.

the bottom line You can find some excellent Rieslings out there even at the $12 price point, but they get grander and more complex in the $25-and-over category.

GEWURZTRAMINER

Some people take to Gewurztraminer immediately, while others are put off by it. The wine's aromas are certainly intense; perfume comes to mind. When Gewurztraminer is well made, it can have an intoxicating clove and rose-petal aroma and lots of lychee on the palate.

at the table

Powerfully flavored Gewurztraminer can take on strong-flavored foods. You can try either contrasting the wine's perfumed quality with something pungent, like a smelly Alsatian Muenster cheese, or matching its exotic flavor with not-too-spicy Northern Indian dishes like Chicken Tikka Masala or Mattar Paneer. Then again, with its fruit-and-spice character, Gewurztraminer makes a great choice for Thanksgiving turkey with cranberry sauce.

the bottom line It's not difficult to find a Gewurztraminer for under $15, but the quality will be much better at around $30.

PINOT GRIS

Wines from this grape are full-bodied with nut, smoke, peach, and apricot flavors but only moderate acidity and little aroma.

at the table

Pinot Gris and choucroute garnie form a traditional Alsatian combination. The smoky, nutty, and summer-tree-fruit flavors also complement other dishes that include pork and are good with veal as well. Pinot Gris makes an ideal aperitif wine.

the bottom line Very little Pinot Gris is produced in Alsace, and so prices are relatively high. Good wines can be found for $18, and they top out around $50.

PINOT BLANC

Medium-bodied Pinot Blanc combines a fresh-orange taste with nut undertones. You'll enjoy these wines most when they're young; they're rarely aged.

at the table

When confronted with an unfamiliar wine list, the Pinot Blanc is a safe and wise choice. With its moderate acidity and fruity flavor, Pinot Blanc is a good middle-of-the-road wine. It makes an excellent aperitif, and it's an especially good match for many traditional dishes of the region; try it with onion tart, braised pork dishes, and hard mountain cheeses.

the bottom line Alsace Pinot Blancs are food friendly and kind to the pocketbook. Good values abound in the under-$10 range, and more complex wines are worth the extra money. They'll still be under $30.

recommended producers & their wines

DOMAINE WEINBACH ★ ★ ★ ★ $$-$$$$

One of the best and most respected winemakers in all of Alsace, Weinbach has been around for centuries. The wines are remarkable for their perfect balance of sweetness, acidity, alcohol content, and intense flavor. These are wines that are made to last. LOOK FOR the spectacular Rieslings and Gewurztraminers.

CHÂTEAU D'ORSCHWIHR ★ ★ ★ ★ $-$$$

Very low vineyard yields lead to wines that are ready to drink right out of the gate but are even more fantastic with a few years of age on them. LOOK FOR the peachy Pinot Blanc Bollenberg, the mild Gewurztraminer Hueben Steinbach, the Riesling Grand Cru Kessler, and the Riesling Grand Cru Pfingstberg.

TRIMBACH ★ ★ ★ $$$-$$$$

Subtle, gorgeous wines with good acidity and strong mineral qualities characterize this producer. The basic wines, vinified in stainless steel, are great—but it's the reserve wines, fermented in large oak casks, that generate goosebumps. Give them time to develop. LOOK FOR the basic Gewurztraminer as well as the Cuvée des Seigneurs de Ribeaupierre, Riesling Cuvée Frédéric Émile, and Clos Ste-Hune.

DOMAINE ZIND-HUMBRECHT ★ ★ ★ $$$-$$$$

Lovers of Zind-Humbrecht tend to be passionate about its intense, concentrated wines. When first bottled, they're a little lopsided toward sweetness, but they balance with age. LOOK FOR anything you can find, although the Rieslings are the most exciting.

DOMAINE MARCEL DEISS ★ ★ ★ $$-$$$$

Few of Marcel Diess's wines come into the United States, and that's really a shame because they're so good! We're talking about powerful wines here; let them rest in your cellar until they're ready. LOOK FOR the basic cuvées labeled Bergheim, the Riesling Grand Crus Altenberg and Grasberg, and the Gewurztraminers.

LUCIEN ALBRECHT ★ ★ ★ $-$$$$

If you like traditional Alsatian wines with the tightrope balance of sweetness, acidity, and flavor that comes from excellent winemaking, Albrecht is your guy. LOOK FOR the stony and smoky Domaine Albrecht Riesling, the Auxerrois Cuvée "A" de Albrecht Riesling '98, the Tokay Pinot Gris Vieilles Vignes, and the subtle Gewurztraminer and Pinot Blanc.

ALBERT BOXLER ★ ★ ★ $$$

Though Boxler can be inconsistent—when he hits, he hits big. LOOK FOR the producer's best-known offerings: the slightly metallic Rieslings, the distinctly nutty Pinot Gris, and the delicious Edelzwicker.

DOMAINE PAUL BLANCK ★ ★ ★ $$-$$$

Lovely and aromatic wines that you won't need to take out a mortgage to buy. LOOK FOR the Schlossberg Tokay Pinot Gris and Rieslings. Paul Blanck also makes some yummy Gewurztraminers and Pinot Noirs from the Furstentum vineyard.

MARC KREYDENWIESS ★ ★ ★ $$-$$$

A little bit old, a little bit new: Kreydenwiess is famed for applying biodynamic methods to wacky, one-of-a-kind blends. LOOK FOR the Klevner Kritt (Pinot Blanc) and the Riesling Kastelberg.

JOS MEYER ★ ★ ★ $-$$$

The aromas of these wines tend to be subtle yet seductive; the flavors can be intense. LOOK FOR the floral Rieslings Vin d'Alsace and Le Kottabe, the lychee-flavored Gewurztraminer Cuvée des Folastries, and the Tokay Pinot Gris. Definitely try the interesting blend Alsace L'Isabelle—it's perfumey, with a subtle note of Belgian beer.

OTHER TOP-NOTCH PRODUCERS

J. B. Adam *(Pinot Blanc, Riesling Kaefferkopf, and Jean Baptiste bottlings)*, Léon Beyer *(Gewurztraminer)*, Domaine Bott-Geyl, Ernest Burn *(Gewurztraminer, Tokay-Pinot Gris, and Muscat, all from their wholly owned Clos St-Imer within the Goldert Grand Cru)*, Hugel et Fils, André Kientzler *(Auxerrois K— Alsace's finest, Grand Cru Rieslings Geisberg and Osterberg)*, Albert Mann *(Riesling Schlossberg and Gewurztraminer Hengst)*, Domaine Julien Meyer *(any and all)*, Mittnacht-Klack *(Riesling Schoenenbourg, Gewurztraminer Rosacker, both Grand Cru)*, Muré *(Clos St-Landelin Riesling and Gewurztraminer)*, André Ostertag *(Sylvaner Vieilles Vignes, Tokay-Pinot Gris Muenchberg, Riesling Muenchberg)*, Rolly-Gassmann *(Muscat Moenchreben, Auxerrois Moenchreben)*, Bernard Schoffit *(Chasselas, Gewurztraminer Harth, and Tokay–Pinot Gris Clos St-Théobald)*, Albert Seltz *(Sylvaner and Pinot Blanc)*, Pierre Sparr *(Pinot Gris Prestige, Gewurztraminer Mambourg Grand Cru, and Riesling Schlossberg)*

bordeaux

All over the world, the serious collector looks to Bordeaux first for important reds. Even in America, where Meritage, the Bordeaux wannabe from California, enjoys great respect, red Bordeaux has never lost its cachet. Though the reds are better-known, the region also boasts lovely whites, as well as the show-stopping dessert wines Sauternes and Barsac (see "Dessert Wines of France," page 274).

finding good value

Bordeaux is a three-tiered market. At the top are the investment-grade wines. The obvious choices here are the famous names from the star appellations of the Right and Left Banks—Pomerol, St-Émilion, St-Julien, St-Estèphe, Pauillac, Margaux. But don't overlook the less obvious appellations of Fronsac on the Right Bank and Listrac and Moulis on the Left; they suffer from lack of name recognition and therefore offer superb value.

Within appellations, the great individual châteaux make supposedly the best wines of all. Here you should look for something known as *second labels*. These are made from grapes that are not quite up to the standards the châteaux set for their *grands vins*, but the second wines should not be thought of as second-class. They can be terrific values. You won't ever see the words *second wine* on a bottle, but when a château name, or part of it, is included in the name of a wine, that's a good hint. For example, Château Latour's second label is Les Forts de Latour; the second label of Château Haut-Brion is Bahans-Haut-Brion; and Château Lafite-Rothschild's is Carruades de Lafite. (See "10 First-Rate Second Labels," page 30.)

In the middle tier are the social climbers, which are made in the style of the big guys but don't have the reputations to score inflated prices. Serious wines at affordable prices can be found in this group. Look for bottles that are labeled Médoc or Haut-Médoc, rather than the well-known smaller appellations within these districts, and also for less familiar districts, such as the Côtes—Côtes de Bourg, Côtes de Blaye, and Côtes de Castillon.

At the bottom of the hierarchy are the table wines, and those from a good vintage, like the '98s that should be creeping onto the

29

market this year, offer a real live bargain for everyday drinking. They are marked simply Bordeaux or Bordeaux Supérieur, or, for whites, Entre-Deux-Mers (the reds from this large area between the rivers are not allowed to carry the Entre-Deux-Mers appellation and so are also labeled Bordeaux or Bordeaux Supérieur).

10 FIRST-RATE SECOND LABELS
(and their pricier "first-label" counterparts)

1. Bahans-Haut-Brion, $45
   (Château Haut-Brion, $177)
2. Carruades de Lafite, $34
   (Château Lafite-Rothschild, $194)
3. Château Haut-Bages-Avérous, $27
   (Château Lynch Bages, $51)
4. Clos du Marquis, $39
   (Château Léoville-Las Cases, $175)
5. Fiefs de Lagrange, $26
   (Château Lagrange, $37)
6. Les Forts de Latour, $50
   (Château Latour, $232)
7. Lady Langoa, $20
   (Château Langoa-Barton, $35)
8. Pavillon Rouge du Château Margaux, $43
   (Château Margaux, $282)
9. Les Pensées de Lafleur, $100
   (Château Lafleur, $198)
10. Sarget de Gruaud-Larose, $25
    (Château Gruaud-Larose, $55)

the lay of the land

The fifty-seven appellations of Bordeaux are naturally divided into three major groupings according to where they stand in relation to the area's major waterways: the Dordogne River, the Garonne River, and the Gironde Estuary into which the two rivers flow. The stars of **the Right Bank** (right of the Dordogne and then the Gironde Estuary) are the appellations Pomerol and St-Émilion. The wines here are Merlot-based and therefore mellow due to moderate tannin. **The Left Bank** (left of the Garonne River and the Gironde Estuary) houses the districts Médoc and Graves. In the Médoc, the famous appellations are St-Julien, St-Estèphe, Pauillac, and Margaux. The Graves produces mostly Sauvignon Blanc-based white wines in the south, and both reds and whites in the north. The northern Pessac-Léognan makes the most notable wines of the Graves, producing both reds and whites of excellent quality. The Left Bank red wines are Cabernet Sauvignon-based and thus more tannic and longer-lived than their Merlot-based cousins. Between the rivers is **Entre-Deux-Mers** (literally *between two seas*), which is known for its inexpensive red and white wines.

St-Éstephe
St-Julien
Gironde
Médoc
Pauillac
Haut-Médoc
Listrac
Margaux
Moulis
BORDEAUX
Graves
Blaye
Bourg
Fronsac
Pomerol
St-Émilion
Côtes de Castillon
Entre-Deux-Mers
Dordogne River
Garonne River
Southwest Region

Featured Wine-Growing Regions

red wines of bordeaux

More than 70 percent of the region's wine production is red, and the best of it is the benchmark for complex red wine of exceptional quality. At this high end of the spectrum of Bordeaux wines are the Classified Growths (or *crus*). These were chosen and graded into first down to fifth growths in 1855, thanks to an interested Napoleon III. A classified wine from a good year practically guarantees a sublime experience. However, just because a bottle is not marked with a classification or as a Grand Cru Classé doesn't mean it isn't great. The exquisite and exceedingly expensive Château Pétrus, after all, is not a cru wine.

grapes & styles

To appreciate Bordeaux, forget the current obsession with single-grape wines. Bordeaux is all about blends. On the Right Bank, where the clay soil is ideal for Merlot, fragrant Cabernet Franc is often cast in an important supporting role. Both these Merlot-based reds and their Cabernet Sauvignon-based counterparts on the Left Bank use small percentages of inky Malbec to add color and perfumed Petit Verdot to increase aroma. The art and personality of Bordeaux wines lie in the way that the grapes are combined.

But don't be in a big hurry to drink these reds. High-quality Bordeaux, especially those from the Left Bank, can be unpleasantly tannic when young. (This is probably the basis of the rumor about some rich wine novices sacrilegiously watering down their Château Margaux with Sprite.) Most of the top wines require a couple of decades to show themselves in all their glory. The subtlety and depth of flavor that comes only from an aged Bordeaux is worth the wait.

at the table

Red Bordeaux is perfect for those on a high-protein diet—the conventional pairings here are steak or lamb chops. Why? Protein and fat tame Bordeaux's tannin. A bite of meat, a sip of wine, and bingo; the tannin recedes, and you can taste the gorgeousness of the wine. But what if you don't want a steak or a chop? Other, leaner red meats, such as buffalo or venison, will also do nicely. They're fine with an older, less tannic wine, too.

Or, with a mellow aged Bordeaux, try braised meat; rich fish like salmon, perhaps in a red-wine sauce; or even a woodsy, wild-mushroom risotto.

the bottom line Despite a less than stellar '97 vintage, Bordeaux remains more pricey than ever. The wines at the top of the Bordeaux status sheet are within reasonable reach only of dot-com moguls. They're generally hundreds of dollars per bottle. If you do buy in this category, remember to pay attention to the vintage and to lay down your bottles for at least ten to fifteen years. Second labels as well as the lesser growths generally fall in the $35 to $60 category. A good wine that does not have growth status will fetch $17 to $40, and the table wines should be under $12. While in other regions a great winemaker can still produce a great wine in a bad year, this seems less true in Bordeaux. Many people who are now drinking their '82s with delight are dismally disappointed in their '79s. With some exceptions, skip the '97s and go directly to the '98s.

what to buy BORDEAUX RIGHT BANK

1989	1990	1991	1992	1993	1994
★★★★	★★★★	0	★	★★	★★★

1995	1996	1997	1998	1999
★★★	★★★★	★★	★★★★	★★★

what to buy BORDEAUX LEFT BANK, EXCLUDING GRAVES

1989	1990	1991	1992	1993	1994
★★	★★★★	★	★	★★	★★★

1995	1996	1997	1998	1999
★★★★	★★★★	★★	★★★	★★★

what to buy RED GRAVES

1989	1990	1991	1992	1993	1994
★★★★	★★★★	★	★	★★★	★★★

1995	1996	1997	1998	1999
★★★	★★★	★★★	★★	★★

recommended wines

1998 Château Beauregard, Pomerol ♥   ★ ★ ★ ★ $$$$

A beautiful, complex wine. Aromas are powerful, sweet, and plummy. On the palate, the full-bodied wine shows some mint, earth, cedar, blackberry, and cassis, with a dusting of cocoa. If you can find this château's second label, Benjamin du Beauregard, you're in for a big treat at less than half the price.

1997 Château Bellisle Mondotte, St-Émilion ♥   ★ ★ ★ ★ $$$$

If you usually drink California Cabernet Sauvignon and want to experiment with Bordeaux, start here with this terrific, full-bodied wine. It's got depth of flavor and lots going on—grilled red fruits, cedar, spices, roasted coffee beans, white chocolate, and a tiny suggestion of green bell pepper. The taste of coffee lingers in its long, long finish.

1997 Le Carillon de l'Angélus, St-Émilion ♥   ★ ★ ★ ★ $$$

Starts with a complex nose of ground coffee, violet, and damp earth. On the palate, there's an explosion of sweet, fully ripe fruit, restrained by a dusting of chalk. The complexity grows exponentially as the wine aerates; if you drink it now or in the next two years, decanting is a good idea.

1998 Château Gaillard Grand Cru, St-Émilion ♥   ★ ★ ★ ★ $$

Deep ruby in color, with hints of cedar and toasty oak on the nose, this wine comes on lush with velvety texture and black-fruit flavor. Substantial but gentle tannin completes the complex picture.

1997 Château Lagrange, St-Julien ♥   ★ ★ ★ $$$

Except for seriously velvety tannin and a seriously full-bodied mouth-feel, this is a wine that's slow to reveal itself. With vigorous swirling, though, it becomes compelling—plummy and deliciously drinkable, even at this young age.

1997 Les Fiefs de Lagrange, St-Julien ♥   ★ ★ ★ $$

A potent wine, with an anise aroma, good tannin, and depth of flavor—an almost granite stoniness and the spiciness of cinnamon and cloves.

1997 Château Reignac Speciale de Reignac, Bordeaux Supérieur ♥   ★ ★ ★ $$

This one packs a wallop and is a prime example of the kind of stellar wines that can come out of lowly appellations. Jammy, oak-empowered black fruit, along with flavors of walnut, coffee, and chocolate.

1998 Château Les Ricards, Premières Côtes de Blaye ♥   ★ ★ ★ $$

Bargains like this are ripe for the picking in lesser-known parts of Bordeaux. The wine is all about powerful tannin balanced by full black-fruit flavors. An intense and elegant performance.

1998 Château Bellegrave, Pomerol ▼ ★ ★ $$$$
There's a strong whiff of alcohol on the nose, but then the grape reveals itself with concentrated flavors—roasted coffee and hints of earth. The wine is far from ready-to-drink right now, but the finish goes on for miles. Should become a beauty.

1997 Château Lafon-Rochet Grand Cru Classé, St-Estèphe ▼ ★ ★ $$$$
You can drink this one tonight or lay it down and wait for the flavors to become smooth and deep. If you opt for popping the cork, you'll find a classic, medium-bodied Bordeaux with moderate tannin and gentle aromas and flavors of black cherry and black pepper with touches of cedar, clove, and pencil shavings.

1997 Le Bahans du Château Haut-Brion, Pessac-Léognan ▼ ★ ★ $$$
There's the familiar Pessac-Léognan earth and violets, but here it has intensity in spades. The main flavors are backed up by notes of hybrid black-cherry/raspberry, a touch of jasmine, and a pinch of smoky tea.

1997 Château La Galiane, Margaux ▼ ★ ★ $$$
A Merlot-based Margaux from an estate that hand-picks its grapes. The wine has a strong dose of oak on the nose, but the nice berry flavor comes through well, with a little bit of cocoa bitterness on the finish.

1997 Clos Mazeyres, Pomerol ▼ ★ ★ $$$
Plums and figs, with notes of firestone and soil, in a full-bodied, smooth and mellow wine.

1997 Phélan Ségur, St-Estèphe ▼ ★ ★ $$$
Right now, this wine has full blackberry and cherry flavors, with a dusting of allspice. The tannin is subtle.

1997 Smith-Haut-Lafitte Grand Cru Classé Graves, Pessac-Léognan ▼ ★ ★ $$$
Hello, oak! This vintage has tons of it, but it's also got voluptuous fruit flavors—cherry, plum, and black currant—along with a bit of cedar and caramel on the finish.

1997 Château La Vieille Cure, Fronsac ▼ ★ ★ $$$
A wine that shows the kinder, gentler side of Bordeaux. Look for gentle tannin, a gentle aroma of coffee beans, gentle berry flavor. It won't ever take your breath away, but it's a good, solid wine.

1997 Château Beaumont, Haut-Médoc ▼ ★ ★ $$
Blueberry and cherry aromas and meaty, mushroomy flavors in a silty-textured, medium-bodied wine.

1998 Château La Cheze, Premières Côte de Bordeaux ♥ ★ ★ $$

The first impression is of a beautiful texture, as smooth as silk. After that, the wine shows a core of cherry-like sweetness and a dusting of cinnamon. At the end, there's a touch of caramel and oak on the lengthy finish.

1997 Château de Cruzeau, Pessac-Léognan ♥ ★ ★ $$

A solid and earthy wine with great body and a touch of licorice. It's overly tannic now and probably needs about another year to become balanced.

1998 Château La Marche-Canon, Canon-Fronsac ♥ ★ ★ $$

This is a powerful wine that will only taste better in a few years. Right now it's concentrated and silty on the tongue, with undertones of earth, black olive, black currant, and cassis. The whole package finishes with a defiant touch of tar and tobacco. Nice.

1997 Château Moulin de Curat, Puisseguin-St-Émilion ♥ ★ ★ $$

Deep, dark, and intriguing, this full-bodied wine has a musty, mineral quality. The fruit flavors are almost spicy but lead to a flowery finish.

1998 Château Puy Guilhem, Canon-Fronsac ♥ ★ ★ $$

Earth and tar aromas, full body and lots of tannin, and subtle blackberry and cassis flavors.

1998 Château St-Galier, Graves ♥ ★ ★ $$

There's a slight taste of green pepper and a good bit of plum. If we fault anything, it's the lack of tannin. So enjoy it right now. We've drunk more important wines that we didn't like as much.

1998 Château St-Sulpice, Bordeaux ♥ ★ ★ $

The negative way to describe this wine would be generic, or you could say it's typical. It has a lovely herbal quality and medium body. A satisfying wine, it can age a few years in the bottle.

BORDEAUX SOUND BITE

During the negotiations for their companies' mega merger, Time Warner Chairman Gerald Levin jetted off to AOL Chairman Steve Case's home for dinner. For the main course, Case popped a bottle of 1990 Château Léoville-Las-Cases. The choice not only showed his impeccable taste but also his foresight and investment savvy. When he bought the wine, it retailed for about $40; now it retails, if one can find it, for $325.

white wines of bordeaux

Bordeaux white wines are usually Sauvignon Blanc and Sémillon blends. The styles range from primarily Sauvignon Blanc wines—herbaceous, acidic, light-bodied, ready-to-drink—to full-bodied, ageworthy wines made from varying proportions of the two. Look to Entre-Deux-Mers or the Graves for satisfying everyday whites. You'll also find Graves wines with more pomp and circumstance. Many makers of more costly whites seem to be going through a California phase, trying to make their wine taste like Chardonnay.

at the table

The tart Sauvignon Blanc-based wines complement a first course of raw shellfish, or acidic dishes like goat-cheese tart and salade niçoise. At the main course, they pair well with simply prepared lean fish or chicken. The more complex, buttery whites from the Graves can take on richer, more complex dishes, like chicken with a creamy sauce or turkey with oyster stuffing.

the bottom line
Both Graves and Entre-Deux-Mers make lovely Sauvignon Blanc-based wines under $10. Upper-end whites from the Graves are quite pricey—$30 and up.

recommended wines

1998 Château Couhins-Lurton, Pessac-Léognan ★ ★ ★ $$$
Full body and refreshing flavor are the winning combination here. Floral aromas flow into lemon flavor for a taste of springtime.

1998 Les Arums de Lagrange, St-Julien ★ ★ ★ $$
No doubt about this one: It's way too young. But we're willing to bet that five years or so will balance its fruitiness, acidity, and sweetness to perfection.

1998 Château Smith-Haut-Lafitte, Pessac-Léognan ★ ★ $$$
A full-bodied wine with New World-style flavors of pineapple and lots of vanilla, and also some refreshing lemon. One for the cellar.

1998 Excellence de Haut Rian, Bordeaux ★ ★ $$
A lovely example of restrained oak aging in a 100 percent Sémillon white Bordeaux. Full-bodied with a mineral and citrus taste and finish.

1999 Château Bonnet, Entre-Deux-Mers 🍷 ★ ★ $
Always a great buy, this medium-bodied wine is fragrant, earthy, and herby, with a nice dose of lemon and a touch of honey and honeydew.

1998 D & H Signature Blanc, Bordeaux 🍷 ★ ★ $
Simple, fruity, and easy to drink, with lots of grapefruit tempered by some honeysuckle and a touch of grass.

1999 Château Haut Rian Bordeaux Blanc, Bordeaux 🍷 ★ ★ $
Mostly Sémillon, this refreshing wine has some nice melon on the finish and classic yet subtle Sauvignon Blanc acidity.

1998 Château Coucheroy, Pessac-Léognan 🍷 ★ $
A delicate and subtle wine, with vegetal notes in the aroma and a bit of grapefruit—some bitterness, too, like a tiny bit of grapefruit rind. The finish is a little woody and very dry. Thanks to its healthy acidity, the wine is highly food-worthy.

1999 Sauvignon Blanc des Tourelles, Bordeaux 🍷 ★ $
A great price for a solid everyday Bordeaux Sauvignon. Fruity, grassy, pungent.

BORDEAUX FACTS

1. Bordeaux is the largest fine-wine producing area in the world.
2. The region devotes 250,000 acres to grapevines.
3. Bordeaux has 57 appellations.
4. Roughly 13,000 producers make wines here.
5. More than 70 percent of all Bordeaux wine is red.
6. The five primary grapes for red wine are: Merlot, Cabernet Sauvignon, Cabernet Franc, Petit Verdot, and Malbec.
7. The Left Bank's gravelly soil is ideal for Cabernet Sauvignon, which is the base of its wines.
8. Merlot thrives on the Right Bank and is the predominant grape in its wines.
9. St-Émilion produces more wine than any other Right Bank district.
10. The two primary grapes for Bordeaux whites are Sauvignon Blanc and Sémillon.

burgundy

Lovers of Burgundy seem to enjoy complaining about their big disappointments as much as waxing poetic about their sublime finds. But is it frustrating for most of us that the same region produces dogs as well as amazing beauties? Very. Part of the problem is the less-than-ideal weather: Hail and rain often ruin a harvest. Then there's recent history to overcome. During the '60s and '70s, farmers overworked and over-fertilized the soil, and these mistakes showed in the bottle. For the past decade, however, Burgundy's wine production has been in turnaround mode. Many growers have gone organic, or *biologique* as the French say. The soil is healing. Techniques are being modernized. Still, finding a bottle that meets, let alone exceeds, expectations takes patience and study. There are a welter of tiny individually owned vineyards to sort through, rather than the relatively easy-to-learn huge estates of Bordeaux. But when you hit a great Burgundy, it's ecstasy.

grapes & styles

Learning all there is to know about Burgundy may take a lifetime, but remembering the grapes of the region? That's a cinch. With little exception, if it's red, it's Pinot Noir; if it's white, it's Chardonnay. Burgundy is the starting and ending point for lovers of these two wines. Though the bold flavors of California Chardonnay or Oregon Pinot Noir seduce many drinkers, they often come back to Burgundy. Reds range from summer-weight to medium, velvet-bodied wines. The flavors include truffles and earth, red and black berries, and cherries. Rosé is also produced; just a few cases make it to the United States from the Marsannay area at the top of the Côte d'Or. They can be delicious, gently berried wines. White Burgundy dances from lean and mean Chablis to full and sensual Meursault, touching all possibilities in between. Whites fermented and aged in wood are long-lived, and the best of them need the age. Flavors and aromas can be flamboyant with the essence of apple, pineapple, and pear. But the market is also filling up with whites trying to be buttery and huge, the kind of over-manipulated wine that leaves you wondering—where's the fruit? Beaujolais is odd man out in Burgundy. Though it's part of the region, geographically it belongs more logically to the Rhône. The grape of Beaujolais is Gamay.

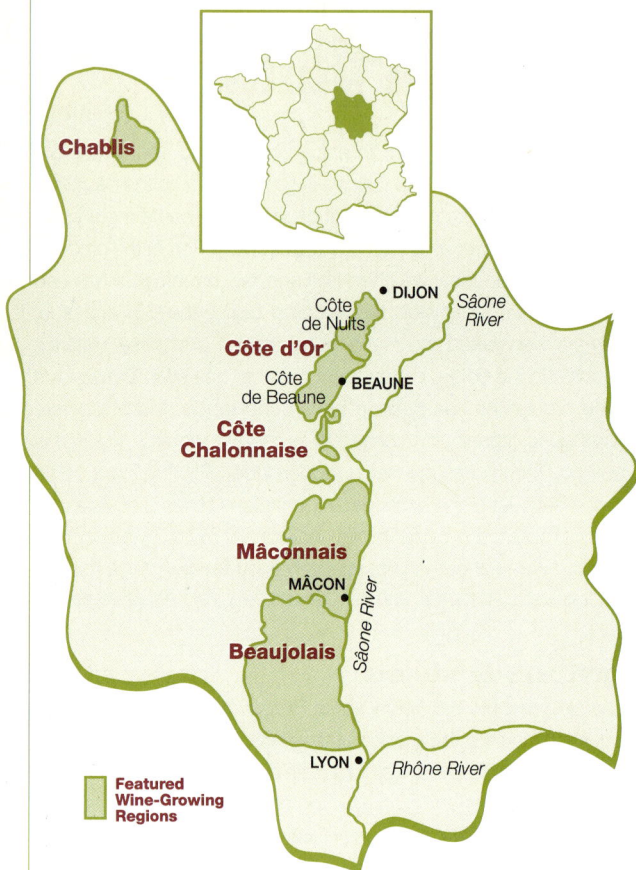

Chablis

Côte
de Nuits

Côte d'Or

• DIJON

*Sâone
River*

Côte
de Beaune

• BEAUNE

**Côte
Chalonnaise**

Mâconnais

MÂCON

Sâone River

Beaujolais

LYON •

Rhône River

Featured
Wine-Growing
Regions

the lay of the land

There are five major districts in Burgundy: Chablis, the Côte d'Or
(including the Côte de Beaune and the Côte de Nuits), the Côte
Chalonnaise, the Mâconnais, and Beaujolais. Different from Bordeaux, individual vineyards, not châteaux or estates, receive
Premier Cru or Grand Cru status.

on the label

What follows are the classifications of Burgundy, in ascending
order. As the rating goes up, the area that can use the designation becomes more focused, from the whole region of Burgundy
to a sub-region to a village to (for the top two) a single, specially
selected vineyard.

Regional Bourgogne, the name of the whole region, is the designation that is given to generic Burgundy. You'll see Bourgogne Rouge and Bourgogne Blanc on the bottle—or more likely these days, to cater to the U.S. market (as well as the changing worldwide market), Bourgogne Pinot Noir or Bourgogne Chardonnay. Whenever the main name on the bottle is, or starts with, Bourgogne, the wine is of this most basic level.

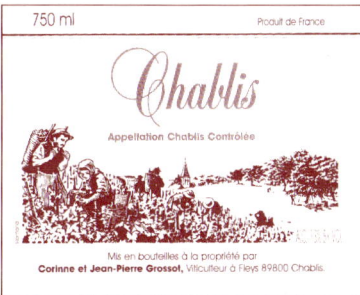

Sub-region The next step up from the basic regional wines is to those bottles that are labeled with the name of one of Burgundy's sub-regions, such as Beaujolais, Chablis, or Mâcon, instead of just the more general Bourgogne. Rather confusingly (in light of the fact that there is a Village category, see below), the word *villages* is often appended, as in Chablis-Villages, but if there is no village name on the label, the wine is of this second-level category.

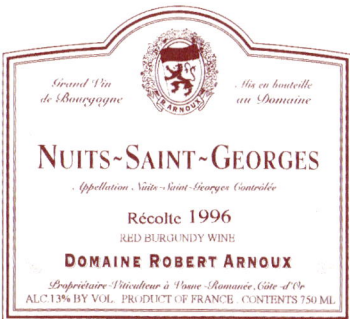

Village Within Burgundy's sub-regions lie certain villages that are especially lauded for the quality of their wines. Only about one quarter of the wine that is bottled in Burgundy can be labeled with the name of its village.

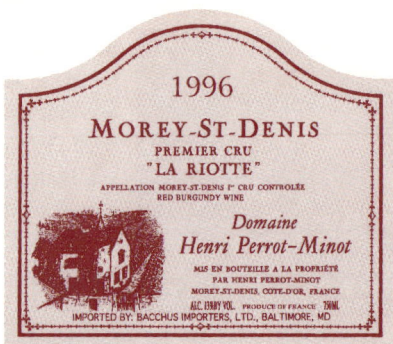

Premier Cru This distinction is conferred on only 561 of the four thousand vineyards in Burgundy. Premier Cru wines are labeled with the name of the village followed by the name of the vineyard. In the above example, Morey-St-Denis is the village and La Riotte is the specific vineyard where the grapes for the wine were grown. When a bottle is marked Premier Cru but has only the village name with no vineyard, then the wine is a blend of grapes from two or more Premier Cru designated vineyards.

Grand Cru Only thirty-two of the vineyards in Burgundy have this exalted status, and all but one of them is in the Côte d'Or. The vineyard name stands alone on the label. It's something like Cher—first name recognition. The exception is the lone Chablis Grand Cru, which is labeled with the district, Chablis, as well as the vineyard. Possible confusion lurks in the fact that a few French villages with Grand Cru vineyards have added the names of the famous vineyards within their boundaries to their original names. For instance, the village of Chambolle has become Chambolle-Musigny. Le Musigny on the label means the wine is Grand Cru. Whereas, Chambolle-Musigny is a village-level wine.

at the table

When in doubt, choose Pinot Noir—this is especially true of French Burgundy. It pairs well with nearly everything: vegetables, fish, poultry, meat. The best aged Burgundies sometimes develop a gaminess that makes them sure shots to match with pheasant, hare, and even venison. A younger version will be relatively less complex, suggesting fish steaks, chicken, duck, veal, or pork. For vegetable pairings, stick with the aromatic, herbaceous, or earthy, such as fennel, fiddlehead ferns, or mushrooms. Burgundy Chardonnays are markedly more food friendly than New World Chardonnays with their high alcohol content and gobs of oak. White Burgundy complements chicken or shellfish beautifully.

finding good value

Our best advice is first to find a producer whose wines you like and only secondarily to check into the ratings of its vineyards. In Burgundy, this approach works far better than the opposite (starting with specific vineyards). Though the region's rating system appears to provide a guarantee of excellence, we've been disappointed by Premier and Grand Cru wines, and had regional-level wines that were superb. The producers are critical. Most of them make a Bourgogne Rouge or Blanc as well as their more exalted offerings, and, especially for a good vintage, the basic wines from the best producers represent excellent value. Bad vintages offer good value, too, because the prices for the whole year are generally depressed. But in a bad year, you'll want to reverse the choice: Go for wine from the best vineyards, the Premier and Grand Cru.

the bottom line Burgundies are expensive. Regional and district wines start at $15 and go to $35. Village wines can also start low but go up to about $50. Premier Crus range from $35 to $65, and the Grand Crus zoom up from there.

chablis

Chardonnay is the only grape that goes into Chablis. Yet the cool weather and limestone soil of Chablis make a Chardonnay like no other—light-bodied, stony, very dry, and bracing.

what to buy CHABLIS

1995	1996	1997	1998	1999
★★★★	★★★★	★★★	★★★	★★★

recommended producers & their wines

JEAN-MARIE RAVENEAU ★★★★ $$-$$$$

Probably the most celebrated estate in Chablis, Raveneau's vineyard sites are so excellent that he doesn't even produce a basic wine. He ferments all his wines in stainless steel and then ages them in barrels for a year, though his style is never over-oaked. The wines are gorgeous, but they can be harshly acidic in their youth. LOOK FOR anything you can find. His wines are quite rare, and you're most likely to encounter them on restaurant wine lists.

JEAN-PIERRE GROSSOT ★★★ $$-$$$$

Though Grossot is one of the more undervalued Chablis producers around to-day, that will change once the word gets out. LOOK FOR the basic Chablis as well as the delicious Premier Cru wines Vaucoupin and Les Fourneaux.

JEAN-MARC BROCARD ★★★ $$-$$$

The specialty here is wines with a perfect lemony, creamy Chablis character. LOOK FOR the Chablis Les Clos and Bougros (Grand Cru) and the Montmains and Fourchaume (Premier Cru).

WILLIAM FÈVRE ★★ $$-$$$$

While Fèvre claims to have cut down on the new oak, the reduction is rather hard to notice. The wines will definitely appeal to lovers of oaky California Chardonnay, though. LOOK FOR the Premier Crus Montée de Tonnerre and Montmains.

DOMAINE LAROCHE ★★ $$-$$$$

This producer admits to having over-oaked its wines in the '80s, but these days Laroche is pulling back and producing absolutely reliable, beautifully brisk Chablis. The wines are best drunk within the first six years. LOOK FOR the Les Clos and the Blanchot. In special vintages, this house makes a wine from selected parcels in Blanchot called Réserve de l'Obediencerie.

OTHER TOP-NOTCH PRODUCERS

Billaud-Simon, Domaine Jean Dauvissat, Olivier Leflaive, Domaine de la Mala-dière *(William Fèvre)*, Château de Maligny, Albert Pic & Fils, Verget

CHABLIS & OYSTERS

The idea behind the old-standby combination of Chablis and raw oysters is twofold. First, the best addition to shell-fish is a bit of acidity, whether it comes from lemon juice, vinegar, or the accompanying wine. A young Chablis has just the right amount of tartness. Secondly, oysters have lots of minerals from the sea, and the soil of Burgundy is also full of minerals, the flavors of which show up in the wine. The acidity complements, the minerals match. It's a grand marriage. Though other wines, like a Muscadet or Sancerre from the Loire, stand in for Chablis quite effec-tively, you can't beat the elegance of the classic match.

the côte d'or

Revered for its luscious reds and long-lived, full white wines, the Côte d'Or consists of two lobes, the Côte de Nuits and the Côte de Beaune. Here is where the most famous Burgundy villages and Premier and Grand Cru vineyards are.

Côte de Nuits This is the sweet spot for reds. When these wines peak, they've got a fierce bouquet of cherries and roses, sometimes with a wonderful undercurrent of earthy, barnyardy, smoky, some people call it bacon-fatty yumminess. The most famous villages are Gevrey-Chambertin, Morey St-Denis, Chambolle-Musigny, Vougeot, Vosne-Romanée, and Nuits-St-Georges.

Côte de Beaune Many would say that the best Chardonnays in the world are from the Côte de Beaune. Whites rule here; red Beaunes have fallen somewhat out of fashion, and as a result they are a tad more reasonably priced than they used to be. So much the better for those of us who love them. They're deli-ciously aromatic and tend to be ready for drinking sooner than those of their lofty neighbor, Côte de Nuits. The most famous vil-lages in the area are Savigny-lès-Beaune, Aloxe-Corton, Beaune, Pommard, Volnay, Meursault, Chassagne-Montrachet, Puligny-Montrachet, and Santenay.

what to buy CÔTE D'OR RED WINES

1996	1997	1998	1999
★★★	★★★	★★★	★★★

recommended producers & their red wines

DOMAINE SYLVAN CATHIARD ★★★★ $$$-$$$$

A domaine on the rise. LOOK FOR anything you can get your hands on from the '98 vintage, especially the velvety Chambolle-Musigny Premier Cru Clos de l'Orme, the Vosne-Romanée Premier Cru Les Murgers, and the Nuits-St-Georges.

DOMAINE DUJAC ★★★★ $$$-$$$$

Always to be found on top ten lists, Dujac wines are classics for a reason: These are sensuous wines that have wonderful perfume, succulent red-fruit flavors, and a silky texture that's helped along by the use of new wood. Though the wines are good in their youth, they're really built to age. They develop an extra complexity because the producer does not remove the stems from the grapes. LOOK FOR Chambolle, Clos St-Denis, Clos de la Roche, and Bonnes Mares.

GEORGES ROUMIER ★★★★ $$$-$$$$

Full-bodied wines with deep red-berry flavors are Roumier's specialty. The house keeps new-oak usage to 30 percent, and so the style strikes a balance between new and old. The wine needs time in the bottle to develop. Don't pick up a '98 and expect it to sing the way it will in a few years. LOOK FOR wines from the village of Chambolle-Musigny, especially the Grand Cru Bonnes Mares.

CAMILLE GIROUD ★★★★ $$-$$$$

Excellent, old-fashioned wines that give pure fruit flavor without new-oak enhancement. LOOK FOR anything you can find from Giroud at any price point, but the Beaunes and Chassagne-Montrachets are great deals. The Corton-Languettes are sublime.

CHÂTEAU GÉNOT-BOULANGER ★★★★ $$-$$$

Here's a house with powerful wines, and the '98s are all great. If you're willing to invest the time to age them, by all means grab some of these still-a-little-underpriced bottles. LOOK FOR anything you can find, but especially Savigny-lès-Beaune and the strongly tannic Beaunes Grèves Premier Cru.

BOUCHARD PÈRE ET FILS ★ ★ ★ $$-$$$$

It seems as if Bouchard just keeps getting better. Its '98s are full of flavor. Thanks to judicious use of new oak, the wines can be drunk now, as well as later. LOOK FOR the Le Corton, the Beaune Clos de la Mousse, and, as usual, their prize Beaune Les Grèves Vigne de l'Enfant Jésus.

NICOLAS POTEL ★ ★ ★ $$-$$$

It's on a rapid path to fame, but Potel still has a problem with spotty quality. Nevertheless, what's good is very good, and even the simple Bourgogne Rouge, with its touch of caramel, can be yummy. LOOK FOR the Volnays, from simple to Premier Cru.

GASTON ET PIERRE RAVAUT ★ ★ ★ $$-$$$

Sure, they produce the popular Aloxe Corton and Côte de Nuits-Villages, but it's Ravaut's Ladoix that's the show-stopper. It will need aging. LOOK FOR two Premier Cru Ladoix: Bois Roussot and Basses Mourottes.

ANTONIN RODET ★ ★ $$$-$$$$

New winemaker Nadine Gublin has really turned Rodet around. She's got a New World, flavor-packed approach to wine, so if your tastes run to the California style, this is a house you'll want to explore. LOOK FOR the Monthélie, the Gevrey Chambertin Estournelles St-Jacques, the Musigny, and the full-of-fresh-ground-coffee-intensity Echézeaux from Rodet's Domaine des Perdrix.

DOMAINE DE L'ARLOT ★ ★ $$$

Strong earthy and bacon-like smoky flavors mark these wines. LOOK FOR the excellent Nuits-St-Georges, especially the Clos des Forêts, Clos de l'Arlot, and Clos des Forêts St- Georges.

DOMAINE CHANDON DE BRIAILLES ★ ★ $$$

Many of the wines from this mostly organic house are big and beefy, yet silky in texture with some dynamite herbal and violet intensity. LOOK FOR the Pernand-Vergelesses Premier Cru Île des Vergelesses, the Savigny-lès-Beaune, and the Corton.

ROBERT ARNOUX ★ ★ $$-$$$$

From the basic up to the Grand Cru, Arnoux's wines are full-bodied, tannic, and earthy with pure fruit flavors. LOOK FOR his excellent Bourgogne Pinot Noir and Nuits-St-Georges in both Premier Crus—Corvées Pagets and Poisets. Also, his reputation in Vosne-Romanée as well as Échézeaux is long established, and his Vougeots are excellent.

OLIVIER LEFLAIVE ★ ★ $$-$$$$

In recent years, Leflaive has gone organic and biodynamic, and the wines have gotten much better. LOOK FOR the luscious Santenay (a best deal), Chassagne-Montrachet, and Monthélie Premier Cru. The Rully is lovely, as is the Pommard.

HENRI PERROT-MINOT ★ ★ $$-$$$$

A house that receives consistent kudos, Perrot-Minot is known for its fragrant floral style. LOOK FOR Gevrey-Chambertin, Morey-St-Denis, En la Rue de Vergy, Charmes, and Chambolles.

OTHER TOP-NOTCH PRODUCERS

Domaine Bertrand Ambroise *(Bourgogne Rouge)*, Jean-Claude Belland *(Santenays)*, Domaine Jean Boillot *(Volnay Chevrets Premier Cru and Beaune Les Epenottes)*, Domaine des Comtes Lafon *(Volnay)*, Domaine Heretzyn *(Bourgogne Rouge)*, Louis Jadot *(Bourgogne Rouge and Beaunes—especially from Clos des Ursules)*, Domaine Robert Jayer-Gilles *(anything from basic wine to Échézeaux)*, Domaine des Lambray *(Morey-St-Denis)*, Mommesin *(Clos de Tart)*, Joseph Roty *(Marsannay Rosé)*

what to buy CÔTE D'OR WHITE WINES

1996	1997	1998	1999
★★★★	★★★	★★★	★★★

recommended producers & their white wines

DOMAINE MICHAEL TESSIER ★ ★ ★ ★ $$$-$$$$

If you're looking for oaky, California-style wines, look elsewhere. But if pure Meursault, with its full-bodied texture and deep nutty flavors, is what you're after, go for Tessier. LOOK FOR any Meursault you can find, but we especially love the Premier Cru Genevrières.

BOUCHARD PÈRE ET FILS ★ ★ ★ $$-$$$$

The '98 whites from this house are great crowd pleasers, full-bodied and powerful. LOOK FOR the Bourgogne Blanc and Puligny-Montrachet as well as the Corton-Charlemagne. Beaune Clos St-Landry is also an excellent choice.

HENRI CLERC ★ ★ ★ $$-$$$$

With some of the best parcels of land in Puligny-Montrachet, Henri Clerc excels at producing wines that are full-bodied and complex. LOOK FOR his Puligny-Montrachet and Bâtard-Montrachet.

MARC COLIN ★ ★ ★ $$-$$$$

The wines from Marc Colin are extremely full-bodied. The use of oak ranges from subtle to in-your-face, but all the wines are supremely satisfying. LOOK FOR the Montrachet.

SYLVIN ET NATHALIE LANGOUREAU ★★★ $$-$$$

Look to this producer for the Premier Cru St-Aubin made in the New World style with lots of new oak. Also LOOK FOR the other excellent Premier Crus: Les Frionnes and En Remilly.

DOMAINE BERNARD MOREY ★★★ $$-$$$

There's lots of powerful oak in this wine, but it's balanced by full tropical-fruit flavors. LOOK FOR Chassagne-Montrachet Les Embazées and Chassagne-Montrachet Morgeot.

JEAN-MARC BOILLOT ★★ $$-$$$$

The '98 wines are outstanding. Many have a perfume-like, dried-apricot appeal. LOOK FOR Puligny-Montrachet and Bâtard-Montrachet.

DOMAINE HUBERT LAMY ★★ $$-$$$$

Wine drinkers in France consider the wine from the St-Aubin area to be one of modern Burgundy's most seductive. Lamy, with its toasty, fruity wines, is one reason why—particularly if the wines have been aged in oak for five years. LOOK FOR the wines from En Remilly, Les Murgers des Dents de Chien, and Les Frionnes.

OLIVIER LEFLAIVE ★★ $$-$$$$

Known for its good prices and its high-quality wines, Leflaive is one of the great white-wine producers of Burgundy. LOOK FOR the Meursault, Charmes, Corton-Charlemagne, and Criots-Bâtard Montrachet.

ANTONIN RODET ★★ $$-$$$$

Many of Rodet's New World, oaky-style wines are extremely tasty. LOOK FOR Bourgogne Blanc, Meursault, and Puligny-Montrachet.

DOMAINE GUY BOCARD ★★ $$$

Bocard's awe-inspiring wines are rarely obscured by oak. LOOK FOR Meursault from Narvaux.

CHÂTEAU GÉNOT-BOULANGER ★★ $$-$$$

Known for its reds, Génot-Boulanger also produces powerful whites. LOOK FOR the Meursault, the Meursault Clos du Cromin, the Chassagne-Montrachet Premier Vergers, the oaky and full-bodied Corton, and the fruity Savigny-lès-Beaunes.

OTHER TOP-NOTCH PRODUCERS

Bonneau du Martray *(Corton-Charlemagne)*, Louis Carillon et Fils, Fontaine-Gagnard, Gagnard-Delagrange, François Jobard, Domaine Comtes Lafon, Domaine Leroy, Domaine Maroslavac-Leger, Marc Morey, Michel Niellon, Paul Pernot, Étienne Sauzet

recommended producers & their rosé wines

JOSEPH ROTY ★★ $$-$$$$
Known for its red wines from Gevrey-Chambertin, Roty also produces a deliciously fragrant and yummy rosé from Marsannay. It's a bit hard to find but definitely worth the search.

MARC BROCOT ★★ $$
Try Brocot's refreshing rosé from Marsannay. Its subtle aroma hints at honeysuckle and roses.

côte chalonnaise

Known as the poor-man's Côte d' Or, the Côte Chalonnaise produces wines that vary in quality—but some are excellent, and they certainly sport lower price tags than bottles from more prestigious areas. Most whites are nicely fruity and are meant to be drunk young, though those of Rully can reach a lush Meursault-like fullness. Bouzeron turns out the one non-Chardonnay white of Burgundy, the tart Aligoté. Do not overlook the reds, which actually make up the bulk of the Côte Chalonnaise's production, especially those from Mercurey and Givry.

recommended producers & their wines

CHÂTEAU GÉNOT-BOULANGER ★★★ $$-$$$
In 1994, this producer began dramatically improving its wines, and now they are first class. Génot-Boulanger makes terrific Mercureys, both red and white. LOOK FOR the flowery Les Bacs whites, and grab anything you can in the Mercurey reds. If you have cellar space, try the Premier Cru Les Saumonts, which is strongly tannic when young, but well worth aging.

PAUL COUEDIC ★★★ $$
Properties owned by Couedic produce some very exciting wines. LOOK FOR Mercurey Blanc, a buttery white with nutty undertones.

CHOFFLET-VALDENAIRE ★★ $$$

Especially in good years, like 1997 and 1998, Chofflet-Valdenaire is a source of excellent Givry. LOOK FOR Clos Jus Premier Cru, which could pass for the Côte d'Or's more expensive Morey-St-Denis, a flavorful red wine that's light on the tannin.

ANTONIN RODET ★★ $$-$$$

As usual, Rodet is producing good wines all over Burgundy. LOOK FOR the Château de Chamirey and the powerful Château de Rully.

JACQUES DURY ★★ $$

Sample Dury's wines in a blind tasting and you'd swear they're from Meursault, the renowned home of full-bodied, nutty whites. LOOK FOR the Rully la Chaume.

PERROT-MINOT ★★ $

Primarily known for Côte d'Or whites, Perrot-Minot also produces a refreshing, lemony Aligoté made from Côte Chalonnaise grapes. LOOK FOR the Aligoté.

OTHER TOP-NOTCH PRODUCERS

Domaine Jean-Marc Joblot *(Givry Clos du Cellier aux Moines)*, Michel Juillot *(white and red Mercureys)*, Louie Max *(Mercurey les Rochelles)*

THE NÉGOCIANT & THE FARMER IN BURGUNDY

The role of négociant has always been important everywhere in France but most of all in Burgundy where the split between grower and merchant was especially clear-cut. Traditionally, farmers grew the grapes, and négociants purchased grapes or grape juice from various sources, made wine, put their name on it, and sold it. Sometimes they bought ready-made wine and put their house label on the bottles. This still goes on, of course, but over the last decade, the old way of doing business has turned upside-down. Négociants are becoming growers, and growers are becoming négociants.

Seeking more control over the end product and more independence from the growers, négociants started in the '90s to invest heavily in Burgundy vine land. They're making more and more of their wines from the vineyard up. Conversely, some small growers, who want to make their own wine but are frustrated by their inability to get more land, are buying grapes from their neighbor's vineyards, vinifying it in their own style, and marketing it themselves.

mâconnais

Light, uncomplicated white wines—which often represent fantastic Chardonnay bargains—come from the Mâconnais. Try the well-regarded but lesser-known St-Véran. And of course, the famous and more powerful Pouilly-Fuissé.

what to buy MÂCONNAIS

1996	1997	1998	1999
★★★★	★★★	★★★	★★★★

recommended producers & their wines

DOMAINE ANDRÉ BONHOMME ★★★ $$
One of the Mâcon's most famous producers, known especially for his Mâcon-Viré, with its clear fruit flavor and endless finish. LOOK FOR Mâcon-Viré.

VERGET ★★★ $$
This firm produces medium-to full-bodied wines with low acidity that are great for early drinking, at a good price. LOOK FOR the St-Véran, the Pouilly-Fuissé, and the Mâcon-Villages Tête de Cuvée.

CHÂTEAU FUISÉE ★★ $$-$$$
Meticulous practices in the field as well as in the winery show: Fuisée's wines are full-bodied and satisfying. LOOK FOR the Le Clos and the Cuvée Vieilles Vignes as well as their best deal, the St-Véran.

CHÂTEAU VITALLIS ★★ $$-$$$
These wines always seem to have a wash of apple touched with spice. LOOK FOR the lively Pouilly-Fuissé.

DOMAINE THOMAS ★★ $-$$
Well-made wines that surprise with their complexity. LOOK FOR the St-Véran Vieilles Vignes.

JEAN TOUZOUT ★★ $
Sometimes a basic Mâcon-Villages knocks your socks off, and you could swear it was a much more expensive wine. LOOK FOR the basic Mâcon-Villages Vieilles Vignes.

OTHER TOP-NOTCH PRODUCERS
André Bonhomme, Domaine des Chazelles, Deux Roche, Georges Dubouef *(Mâcon-Villages)*, Guffens-Heynen, Domaine Guillemot-Michel, Mâcon-Lugny, Domaine Manciat-Poncet, Prissé, Domaine de Roally *(Henri Goyard)*, Robert-Denogent, St-Denis, Thévenet, Domaine Valette, Domaine de Vieux St-Sorlin *(Olivier Merlin)*

beaujolais

Often maligned as a frou-frou wine, Beaujolais is nevertheless the wine of choice in bistros all across France. Most of it is intended to be lighthearted—though certainly there's more serious Beaujolais, too.

on the label
Virtually all Beaujolais is made from Gamay grapes and falls into one of four categories:

Beaujolais Nouveau Always released on the third Thursday of November, just a few months after the harvest. To be drunk within six months of release.

Beaujolais The basic stuff, and not terribly interesting.

Beaujolais-Villages Now we're getting more interesting. These wines must come from one of thirty-nine select villages.

Cru Beaujolais When people dismiss the Gamay grape, a mention of Cru Beaujolais is just the thing to stop them in their tracks. From ten of the best villages, it can be ageworthy wine with serious mineral and earth components. The villages are St-Amour (order it on Valentine's Day!), Juliénas, Chénas, Moulin-à-Vent, Chiroubles, Fleurie, Morgon, Regnié, Côte de Brouilly, and Brouilly.

at the table
Beaujolais is a good sipping wine and a handy, flexible, inoffensive food wine. It's not big on intensity or acidity or tannin, so don't challenge it too much. It goes well with comfort food. Roast pork, chicken, macaroni and cheese, or a turkey burger—why not?

recommended producers & their wines

CLOS DE LA ROILETTE   ★ ★ ★ ★ $$
Twenty-five-year-old vines and clay and manganese soil contribute to the concentrated black-currant color, restrained nose of crème de cassis, and earthy flavor of these wines. LOOK FOR the Fleurie and the Morgon.

DOMAINE BERROD   ★ ★ ★ ★ $-$$
The winery is modern, but the techniques used are artisanal. If you don't think Beaujolais can age, lay some of these down and see what happens. Though they're delicious right away, the wines develop a Burgundian lushness with time and will forever change how you feel about Beaujolais. LOOK FOR the Nouveau, the Beaujolais-Villages, the Fleurie, and the Moulin-à-Vent.

LOUIS JADOT   ★ ★ $-$$
In addition to its famed Côte d'Or bottles, this house also produces reliable, powerful, and full-bodied oak-aged Beaujolais. LOOK FOR the Beaujolais-Villages, the Morgon, the Fleurie, and especially the five single-vineyard estates within Moulin-à-Vent—Clos de Rochegrès, Clos des Thorins, La Roche, Champ de Cour, and Clos du Grand Carquelin.

TRENEL FILS   ★ ★ $-$$
The wines from this producer offer silky texture and big red-fruit flavors. The winery even makes a delicious Nouveau. LOOK FOR the Chiroubles, the Morgon, the Moulin-à-Vent, and the Nouveau.

GEORGES DUBOEUF   ★ $-$$
Here's the man who put a Beaujolais in every wine store in America. His flamboyant, flower-labeled wines are always refreshing and fruity, while those bottled under individual estate names have a bit more complexity. LOOK FOR the Flowers in Juliénas and St-Amour. Under Duboeuf's domaines, look for Jean Descombes and Domaine des Versauds (Morgon) and Domaine la Rosiere (Moulin-à-Vent).

OTHER TOP-NOTCH PRODUCERS
Guy Bréton *(Morgon)*, Château de la Chaize *(Brouilly)*, Louis-Claude Desvignes *(Morgon Côte de Py and Javernières)*, Durdilly *(Beaujolais Nouveau and Beaujolais Les Grandes Coasses)*, Paul Janin *(Moulin-à-Vent)*, Jacky Janodet *(Moulin-à-Vent)*, Château de Juliénas *(Juliénas)*, GAEC René et Christian Miolane *(Beaujolais-Villages)*, Château de Raousset *(Chiroubles, Fleurie, and Morgon)*, Joël Rochette *(Brouilly and Régnié)*, Domaine des Terres Dorées, Michel Tête *(Beaujolais-Villages, Brouilly, Juliénas, and Juliénas Cuvée Prestige)*, Jean-Paul Thévenet *(Morgon Vieilles Vignes)*

BURGUNDY FACTS

1. Five districts make up Burgundy: Chablis, the Côte d'Or, Côte Chalonnaise, Mâconnais, and Beaujolais.

2. The thirty-mile Côte d'Or is divided into two major areas: Côte de Nuits and Côte de Beaune.

3. Nearly always, red Burgundy=Pinot Noir and white Burgundy=Chardonnay.

4. Savigny-lès-Beaune whites often aren't 100 percent Chardonnay; some Pinot Blanc may be added.

5. Beaujolais, made from Gamay, is a Burgundy wine, though legally it's in the department of the Rhône.

6. Though the land devoted to vineyards in Burgundy is about half that of Bordeaux, Burgundy is divided into 669 appellations versus Bordeaux's fifty-seven.

7. La Romanée is the smallest of Burgundy's appellations. It produces about 300 cases a year from barely a couple of acres of vines.

8. An average Burgundy grower owns around ten acres.

9. Of the region's 4,000 vineyards, 561 are Premier Cru.

10. Only thirty-two are Grand Cru vineyards.

languedoc-roussillon

After too many decades of producing lousy wine, the Languedoc-Roussillon, a sun-baked crescent of land that hugs the Mediterranean, is on a blue streak of self-improvement. And now, here come the Rothschilds of Bordeaux, moving in to make a super-premium. There goes the neighborhood; no more $4 bottles here. We do sometimes miss those rock-bottom prices of yore, but Languedoc wines still won't break the piggybank, and they're better than ever.

grapes & styles

The Carignan grape dominates the traditional wines of the Languedoc-Roussillon. While it's true that this variety isn't terribly exciting, when it's mixed with other traditional red grapes that have been approved for the region—such as Grenache, Cinsault, Syrah, and Mourvèdre—the wines that result can be agreeably bold and spicy.

Costière de Nîmes borders the southern Rhône Valley, and produces wines that are similar in style. Big improvements in quality have been made over the last few years, and the area now offers some great bargains for lovers of Rhône-style wines. The Côtes du Roussillon and Collioure areas are best known for their intense Port-like wines, called Vins Doux Naturels, from the areas Banyuls and Maury.

The whites of the Languedoc-Roussillon, made from the likes of Maccabéo, Muscat, Marsanne, Roussanne, Grenache Blanc, and Picpoul, are not the region's strong suit, but are certainly drinkable, and some have charm. Many vineyards are being replanted with international favorites such as Chardonnay, Sauvignon Blanc, and Viognier.

on the label

The most general designation that appears on labels is Vin de Pays d'Oc, which covers the entire region of Languedoc-Roussillon. A step above this basic classification is Vin de Pays (van duh peh-yee) with the name of a *departement* (like a county), such as Vin de Pays de l'Hérault or Vin de Pays de l'Aude. Many wines at this level are good, and they're great bargains.

The Institut National des Appellations d'Origine gives the right to use a more specific place name on the label only to wines made with traditional grapes. These blended appellation wines are improving rapidly.

In the appellation Coteaux du Languedoc are twelve smaller appellations important enough to use their names alone as identification on the label. Look especially for Montpeyroux, Pic-St-Loup, Faugères, Cabrières, and St-Chinian. The Coteaux du Languedoc is also home to a cluster of vineyard areas that can use their own village names appended to the Coteaux du Languedoc designation. Look particularly for these village names on the bottle: Pic-St-Loup, Montpeyroux, St-Georges-d'Orques, and La Clape. In the southern part of Languedoc, Minervois,

Corbières, and Fitou are the top appellations. The less-known Cabardès produces wines made from a blend of Bordeaux and Mediterranean varieties. The best unfortified red wines from the Côtes du Roussillon appellation will be marked as Côtes du Roussillon-Villages.

THE LANGUEDOC-ROUSSILLON REBELS

Some Languedoc-Roussillon winemakers have rebelled against the appellation system by growing nontraditional international favorites like Chardonnay, Merlot, and Cabernet Sauvignon, even though the varietal wines made from these grapes get the bottom-of-the-heap designation Vin de Pays (VdP). These anarchic boutique winemakers don't give a hoot about tradition or about having appellation status, and, somewhat ironically, they've gained big reputations by flouting the rules and making the wines of the moment, winning important awards and attracting press notice.

at the table

The generally full red wines from the Languedoc-Roussillon work well with roasted or grilled meats and vegetables. These wines can take on garlic or hot pepper, as in the traditional cassoulet or Mexican black beans. And they're also a shoo-in for a Moroccan tagine. Sausages, curries, duck, beef, lamb—as long as you think hearty, you can't go too far wrong. The white wines of the region are, for the most part, pleasant and easy-to-drink, and they pair nicely with creamy pasta dishes. Try a Languedoc-Roussillon rosé with Southern fried chicken or alongside a basic turkey sandwich.

bottom line Good buys abound in the $8 to $15 category. Higher prices are attached to the very best bottles, and they're worth the expenditure.

what to buy LANGUEDOC-ROUSSILLON

1996	1997	1998	1999
★★	★★	★★★★	★★★★

recommended white wines

1999 Domaine Deshenrys Alliance, Vin de Pays de Coteaux du Languedoc 🍷 ★★★ $
Imagine the earth of Sauvignon Blanc, the fruit and body of Marsanne and Roussanne, and the flower power of Viognier and Muscat, and you've got a foolproof remedy for Chardonnay fatigue. The above five grapes are blended to make a wacky, fruity, flowery, earthy wine of perfect balance. Impressive.

1999 Château Calabre, Montravel 🍷 ★★ $$
Very complex and subtle for the price. The wine has a strong blend of grapefruit and honeysuckle, and just a lick or two of licorice.

1999 Mas de Daumas Gassac Blanc, Vin de Pays de l'Hérault 🍷 ★★ $$
Peachy on the nose with highly concentrated floral aromas and tastes. Beautifully intense.

1999 Domaine des Cantarelles Viognier, Vin de Pays de Garde 🍷 ★★ $
A bargain Viognier that's extremely floral, with a combo of rosewater and jasmine. Impossible without food; fascinating with shellfish.

1999 Mas Carlot Cuvée Tradition Marsanne, Costières de Nîmes 🍷 ★★ $
Light-bodied with a nice lemon tang as well as a bit of anise and lavender.

1999 Château de Campuget Viognier, Vin de Pays de Garde 🍷 ★ $
An excellent entry-level Viognier. If you want to check out the possibilities of the grape without taking out a mortgage, try this wine—just a touch of a tang and a bit of flowery perfume.

1999 Grange des Rouquette Réserve Le Pelican, Vin de Pays d'Oc 🍷 ★ $
With 60 percent Marsanne and 40 percent Viognier, this tangy, tart, even puckery wine has a little lift of orange in the finish. Fun!

recommended red wines

1995 Peyre Rose Clos de Cistes, Coteaux du Languedoc 🍷 ★★★★ $$$
With aromas and flavors of berries and violets picked right from the sweet summer earth, this wine is compellingly delicious and complex.

1998 Domaine Sarda-Malet, Roussillon 🍷 ★★★★ $$$

Everything from Sarda-Malet is fantastic, but this wine in particular is stunning. It doesn't have the typical roasted fruits of the region's hot-weather wines but is filled instead with perfectly ripe blueberries and blackberries, obvious tannin, and incredible body.

1998 Château Bousquette, St-Chinian 🍷 ★★★★ $$

A whole lot of violets here, as well as herbs, gaminess, musk, and serious tannin. This is not for everyone, but it's great for those who can deal with a wine that's on the wild side.

1998 Château d'Oupia, Minervois 🍷 ★★★★ $

Shows what the lowly Carignan grape can do. The wine has an intense aroma of sweet fruit, like a mess of ripe plums shoved under the broiler, with an undercurrent of strong, wild herbs, like big bushes of rosemary. It will please both the wine nerd and the newcomer.

1998 Mas de Daumas Gassac, Vin de Pays de l'Hérault 🍷 ★★★ $$$

The '98 vintage is yet another in a string of stellar years for a winery that's achieved fame. This wine is rich in carnation aromas and is dusty and earthy with tannin that can use a few years to mellow. You can drink it now in its sturdy stage or hold it a few years and be rewarded for your patience.

1998 Abbot's Cumulo Nimbus Shiraz, Minervois 🍷 ★★★ $$

Powerful, with lots of concentrated earthiness, like licorice and tobacco; a little coffee and cocoa; and a bit, just a bit, of clove.

1998 Domaine Les Aurelles Solen, Coteaux du Languedoc 🍷 ★★★ $$

There are few aromas in this wine, except very subtle berries and licorice. Nevertheless, the first sip hits you with a blast of dark cherries—refreshing, clear fruit flavor.

1998 Domaine Deshenrys La Closerie de l'Abbaye Sylva Plana, Faugères 🍷 ★★★ $$

Almost everything Domaine Deshenrys produces is exceptional; they believe in the power of the blend, and we say more power to them. This wine—made up mostly of Carignan, with Syrah, Grenache, and Mourvèdre thrown in as well—is full bodied, with intense black fruits, a touch of Earl Grey tea, and a creamy, luscious finish.

1998 Mas Champart, St-Chinian 🍷 ★★★ $$

Excitement on the nose is balanced with excitement on the palate. The color is like that of crushed blackberries, which repeat in the taste, along with earthiness, a touch of gaminess, herbs and spices, and a leathery finish.

1997 Mas des Chimères, Coteaux du Languedoc 🍷 ★ ★ ★ $$

If you like a full-bodied, tannic wine with lots of strong flavors, this one is for you. A gorgeous blend of Syrah and Grenache, it's got a licorice-root taste along with its fruitiness. Sun-dried black cherries lurk underneath.

1997 Domaine Fontareche, Coteaux du Languedoc 🍷 ★ ★ ★ $$

If one believes that bottling with the phases of the moon and other biodynamic techniques help to make beautiful wine, this one might be offered as proof. Made from Carignan, Grenache, and Cinsault, its dominant aroma is of black fruit. Take a quick swallow and more fruit and spicy flavors explode in the mouth.

Mommessin Pinot Noir/Syrah, Vin de Pays d'Oc 🍷 ★ ★ ★ $

This is astonishingly tasty and satisfying, even though it's not too serious. The amount of oak is perfect, and there's just enough acidity to make the wine food friendly.

1998 Château Prat de Cest, Corbières 🍷 ★ ★ ★ $

Ah, Prat de Cest—we go back a long way with this wine. There's a bit of bottle variation, but when you hit a good one, it's sensational, a charming wine that gushes aromas and flavors of berries and violets. The finish is a little rough, making it perfect for food.

1998 Château St-Martin de La Garrigue Bronzinelle, Coteaux du Languedoc 🍷 ★ ★ ★ $

A full-bodied wine with substantial but smooth tannin carrying concentrated earth and spice flavors. Quite a mouthful.

1998 Abbot's Cirrus, Cabardès 🍷 ★ ★ $$$

No surprise that a blend of Merlot, Shiraz, Cabernet, Grenache, and Malbec would make a complicated little wine. But it all melds together with just a hint of mint on the nose, earthy notes, and a bit of toast on the long, long-lingering, primarily caramel finish.

1998 La Chance de Saint-Luc, Côtes du Roussillon 🍷 ★ ★ $$

These days, lots of wineries are buddying up to play. La Chance is a joint venture between Jean-Luc Colombo and Étienne Montes. The wine they've produced is 50-50 Grenache and Syrah—rough, big, and beefy, with a touch of tomato jam and subtle garigue flavors leaving an acidic tang in the finish. Just the kind of wine to have with a grilled steak.

1997 Château de l'Engarran Cuvée Quetton St-Georges, Coteaux du Languedoc de St-Georges d'Orques 🍷 ★ ★ $$

With its 80 percent Syrah, this is one of the more subtle wines from the area. Relatively low in acid and big in other flavors, it delivers intense meaty, smoky, peppery tastes and a bit of berry. Though it's oak-aged, only a quarter of that oak is new, and so it functions more as a body builder than a flavor enhancer.

1996 Château Lerys, Fitou ♥   ★ ★ $$

An inky mix of dense fruit and earth, this wine succeeds where many Fitou these days leave us cold. Eucalyptus and sage enliven a tannic wine that has a full dark-cherry center.

1997 Parcé Domaine du Mas Blanc, Collioure ♥   ★ ★ $$

Much more subtle and complex than the Casa Blanca (below)—but also more expensive—this wine has a more focused flavor of dried fruit and roasted meat along with herbs and menthol. The wine's weight is medium to full.

1998 Mas Amiel Le Terroir,
Vin de Pays de Côtes Catalanes ♥   ★ ★ $

Complexity rules here. Port-like aromas dominate at first, but then there are aromas and flavors of cinnamon, licorice, and cooked plums, and in the end a fine, dry finish. Definitely a crowd pleaser.

1998 Domaine de la Casa Blanca, Collioure ♥   ★ ★ $

Here's a nice, simple wine. It has little in the way of fragrance, some suggestion of licorice and plum flavors, and subtle tannin. This is one that goes down easy.

1998 Domaine de la Rectoire Le Seris, Collioure ♥   ★ ★ $

The blend is a typical one, Grenache and Carignan, but the result is super. Super silky, super earthy, and super yummy.

1996 Château la Roque, Pic-St-Loup ♥   ★ ★ $

A floral lily-like aroma and similar taste, along with ripe fruit, like sun-baked blackberries. The texture is velvety.

1998 Château de Caladroy, Côtes du Roussillon ♥   ★ $$

A tannic wine, but at the same time full-bodied and mulberry-flavored, with some taste of juicy sun-ripened figs.

1998 Grenat Domaine l'Aigueilère, Montpeyroux ♥   ★ $$

An earthy and gamey mid-weight wine, well-positioned to take on spicy food.

1998 Domaine des Blagueurs Syrah, Sirrah,
Vin de Pays d'Oc ♥   ★ $

California winemaker Randall Grahm went to Languedoc, and all we got was this Syrah, which is quite enough really. In fact, it's pretty darn good—spicy and peppery, with a silky texture and inky color. Then there's the wild-looking label.

1998 Mas de Bressades Cabernet/Syrah,
Vin de Pays de Gard ♥   ★ $

There's lots of complexity here. The wine first attacks with licorice and tar, but underneath that rough exterior is a mess of prunes and deep-purple plums. A big wine for little money.

1997 Château de Campuget, Costières de Nîmes ☖   ★ $

Good little everyday wine with a suggestion of strawberry flavor and fine notes of vanilla.

1998 Chevalière Réserve Syrah, Vin de Pays d'Oc ☖   ★ $

Be prepared for a subtle, dusty nose. In the mouth, this is a full-bodied, pruney wine, with the added taste of cherries. It finishes tart. All in all, an enjoyable choice for informal food.

1995 Château St-Martin de la Garrigue, Vin de Pays d'Oc ☖   ★ $

At first, there's a touch of cedar on the nose, counterbalanced in the mouth with fresh and baked plums. The wine finishes with touches of clove and allspice.

1998 Réserve St-Martin Merlot Val d'Orbieu, Vin de Pays ☖   ★ $

When an interesting Languedoc varietal turns up at a good price, we pay attention. This is a Merlot with an almost neutral nose, but a very pleasant raspberry flavor and good food-friendly acidity. We'll go for that second glass.

recommended rosé wines

1998 Mas Jullien, Coteaux du Languedoc ☖   ★ ★ ★ $

Without looking, you might ask yourself: Is this a rosé or a red wine? Honey-dew on the nose, with a bit of bacon and dark fruit flavors.

1999 Château Grand Cassagne Rosé, Costières de Nîmes ☖   ★ $

Melons and roses in a pretty rosé that somehow, though it's got a lot going on, remains remarkably delicate.

loire valley

Wines from the Loire have been hot for a couple of years, and there's no indication that interest is flagging. The region's refreshing whites, smooth reds, delicious rosés, and unctuous, age-defying dessert wines are the sort that give both the everyday drinker and the expert sommelier goosebumps.

lay of the land

The vineyards of the Loire flow along the river for some 375 miles, so you'd expect diversity—in weather, topography, and soil, and therefore in grapes and styles of wine. And you do get variety, but actually the Loire Valley is one of the easier regions to understand. It divides conveniently into four sections, and four grapes dominate.

Starting at the ocean, the Nantais is known for its dry whites made from Muscadet. Anjou-Saumur grows the most important Loire grape, Chenin Blanc, and also its star red, Cabernet Franc. Next door in Touraine, the same grapes rule the vineyards. From this district come the famous wines of the Vouvray area. And finally, in the Centre, Sancerre and Pouilly are famed for their Sauvignon Blancs.

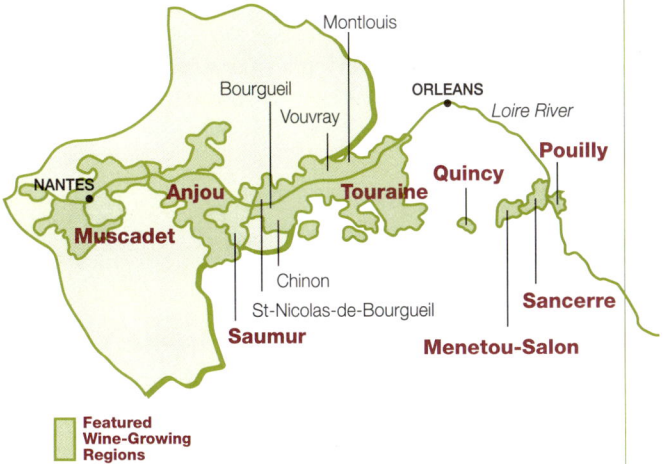

Montlouis

Bourgueil

Vouvray

ORLEANS

Loire River

Pouilly

Quincy

NANTES

Anjou

Touraine

Sancerre

Muscadet

Chinon

St-Nicolas-de-Bourgueil

Saumur

Menetou-Salon

Featured Wine-Growing Regions

white wines of the loire

CHENIN BLANC

The Loire's magic grape, Chenin Blanc, makes superior dry, sparkling, and dessert wines, and, because of its crackling acidity, it ages beautifully. Its aroma is of honey-sprinkled Granny Smith apples, with perhaps a whiff of apricot and pineapple. Nutty aromas and flavors develop with a little age.

on the label

The level of sweetness is often indicated on the bottle: *sec* (dry), *demi-sec* (off-dry), or *moelleux* (medium to very sweet). If the wines are from Vouvray, or its neighbor Montlouis, and there's no indication of sweetness, assume that there is some.

at the table

Pike with beurre blanc is the traditional Loire Valley match for young, dry Chenin Blanc, but the same acidity that makes the wine complement the fish and cut through the rich sauce allows it to work well with oily fish, such as mackerel, sardines, or bluefish, and also with shellfish.

bottom line
Right now, more quality Chenin Blancs are coming out of Savennières than Vouvray. Some can be ridiculously cheap, with quality wines starting at $12 and staying under $20 for the most part. Vouvrays will go up from there to around $25.

what to buy DRY CHENIN BLANC

1995	1996	1997	1998	1999
★★★★	★★★★	★★★	★★★	★★

recommended wines

1998 Marc Brédif, Vouvray 🍷   ★★★ $$
Here's an easy-to-understand and easy-to-drink wine. It has hints of pear, a subtle taste of honeysuckle nectar, and a lingering mineral quality in the finish.

1998 Domaine du Closel Clos de Papillon, Savennières 🍷
★ ★ ★ $ $

There's a formidable concentration of green apple as well as a little honey-suckle in this ageworthy Chenin, but it's the slatey mineral flavors that keep you interested in another glass.

1999 Domaine du Vieux Pressoir, Saumur 🍷
★ ★ ★ $

Perfect for summer, this fruity, easy-drinkin' wine has wonderful grapefruit aromas and solid acidity. Such a deal!

1998 Vincent Raimbault Sec, Vouvray 🍷
★ ★ $ $

Many Vouvrays just don't cut the mustard these days, but this producer is a throwback to the time when Vouvray was king of the Loire. The wine is packed with flavor and has a tangy finish.

1998 Domaine Le Peu de la Moriette, Vouvray 🍷
★ ★ $

Though the wine has a very typical lemony Chenin nose, the flavor is more of pear with a touch of coconut.

1999 Benoit Gautier de Gautier, Vouvray 🍷
★ $

A bit less subtle and sweeter than Gautier's very dry Cuvée Clos la Lanterne, but quite lovely in its own right.

MUSCADET

Also known as Melon de Bourgogne, the Muscadet grape has an almost neutral aroma and flavor and good acidity, though it's not so zingy as the other whites of the Loire. Because of the unobtrusive-ness of the grape, this always dry wine reveals the land on which it's grown, with a distinct mineral finish that is most refreshing.

on the label

Look for *sur lie*, which means the wine was aged on the lees (the sediment left after fermentation). This method gives the wine a slight, appealing sparkle, or *pétillance*. It also preserves the wine's vibrancy and enhances it with a nutty note.

at the table

Raw oysters with Muscadet is a local passion. Other shellfish and mild finfish, whether from river, lake, or ocean, are equally good matches. Grilled and raw vegetables, including vinaigrette-dressed salads work, too, and Muscadet also makes a fine aperitif on its own.

the bottom line Don't be put off by the low price, which will generally be in the $6 to $12 range. Muscadet is largely either overlooked or mistakenly looked down upon by the buying public, but it's one of the current darlings of many who work in the wine biz.

recommended wines

1998 Luc Choblet Clos de la Sénaigerie, Muscadet Côtes de Grandlieu 🍷 ★ ★ ★ ★ $
On the nose, this wine is bursting with mineral aromas. On the palate, it's refreshing, something like a basketful of fall apples that have been sprinkled with a little earthy yeast.

1998 Luneau-Papin Clos des Allées Sur Lie Vieilles Vignes, Muscadet de Sèvre-et-Maine 🍷 ★ ★ ★ ★ $
Old vines make this wine the Big Boy of Muscadet. Full aromas and flavors of apple, pear, and almond, along with strong mineral complexity, make it stand out from the crowd.

1999 Domaine de L'Ecru Sur Lie, Muscadet de Sèvre-et-Maine 🍷 ★ ★ ★ $
This organic producer has just switched over to vinifying *sur lie*, giving the wines a yeasty flavor that gives an added dimension to their complexity. There's a bit of pine and lemon on the nose, lots of apple on the palate, and a touch of mineral chalkiness.

1999 Domaine les Hautes Noëlles, Muscadet Côtes de Grandlieu 🍷 ★ ★ ★ $
Put this one in the easy-drinking category. The apple and herbal aromas and flavors are subtle, and the wine's stony mineral quality adds just the right amount of interest.

1998 Domaine de la Pépière Clos de Briords Sur Lie, Muscadet de Sèvre-et-Maine 🍷 ★ ★ ★ $
A boutique Muscadet that's low in fruitiness, high in minerality, and rich in nutty flavors.

1999 Domaine de la Pépière Sur Lie, Muscadet de Sèvre-et-Maine 🍷 ★ ★ $
Here's a perfect example of the kind of tartness that makes Muscadet a classic, refreshing match for seafood. The wine has a slight effervescence, great acidity, and a good, fruity finish.

SAUVIGNON BLANC

Smack in the middle of France, the Centre sub-region of the Loire makes Sauvignon Blanc that's as good as it gets. As with many Loire whites, it's light and refreshing. Grassy, gooseberry, and citrus flavors stand out as its hallmarks, along with plenty of mouthwatering acidity.

on the label

If the label on a white wine indicates the town name Quincy, Menetou-Salon, or Sancerre, or if the wine is marked Pouilly-Fumé (from the town Pouilly-sur-Loire), then you can be sure that it's a Sauvignon Blanc.

at the table

A good, crisp Sauvignon Blanc is practically indestructible. The wine is fine on its own as an aperitif; it can stand up to vinegar or asparagus (both notoriously difficult to match); and it's right at home with an herbed omelet or anything herbal or vegetal due to its grassy character. Traditional and ideal is a glass of Sauvignon Blanc and a piece of goat cheese from neighboring Chavignol.

the bottom line Sancerres are going up in price, with the simpler ones selling for $16 and up. Pouilly-Fumé is not as fashionable as in the last decade, so the prices may be a couple of dollars lower. For less expensive wines, look to Quincy and Menetou-Salon.

recommended wines

1999 Domaine de Châtenoy, Menetou-Salon ♥   ★ ★ ★ ★ $ $
It may be from the other side of the border, but this powerful Sauvignon Blanc, with its lush fruit and refreshing acidity, outshines the Sancerres from Sancerre. Nobody does it better.

**1999 Philippe Raimbault Apud Sariacum,
Sancerre** ♥   ★ ★ ★ ★ $ $
Fruity and easy to drink, this Sancerre has mouthwatering aromas of honeysuckle and apple. Grass, earth, and star-fruit flavors, along with good acidity, bring it almost to perfection.

1999 Thomas-Labaille Chavignol Les Monts Damnés, Sancerre ★★★★ $$
No wild aromatics here—perhaps a hint of tarragon. This is a full-bodied wine, with just enough acidity to make your mouth water.

1998 Didier Dagueneau En Chailloux, Pouilly-Fumé ★★★ $$
Not exactly what you'd expect from a Sauvignon Blanc—but after all, this wine's from Dagueneau, the bad boy of the Loire. Peaches and nectarines meet tropical mangos and papayas. The wine has great flintiness, and the refreshing acidity balances the ripe fruit to make a pretty intriguing package.

1999 Dominique Guyot, Pouilly-sur-Loire ★★★ $$
A Loire wine with a lot of sophistication but a non-sexy appellation equals one very appealing bargain. This one is subtle and restrained, with faint grassiness and mouthwatering acidity.

1999 Jean-Paul Picard, Sancerre ★★★ $$
Every year, Picard succeeds with a totally classic Sancerre that's filled with fig and apple flavors as well as typical grassiness and refreshing, cleansing, grapefruit-like acidity.

1999 Domaine Michel Thomas Chant du Merle, Sancerre ★★★ $$
A Sancerre that's less sharp than is typical, filled with pears and apples rounded out with a hint of grass and a tad of stony minerals.

1998 La Poussie, Sancerre ★★ $$$
Gentle gooseberry, fig, grapefruit, and pear aromas and a nice minerality—this is a classy Sancerre that finishes with a sharp bite.

1999 Henri Bourgeois Les Bonnes Bouches, Sancerre ★★ $$
Gooseberry and grapefruit aromas melt into a full-bodied wine with palate-cleansing acidity.

1999 Domaine A. Cailbourdin Les Cris, Pouilly-Fumé ★★ $$
Save for a bit of peach skin and pear, this light-bodied Fumé is higher on stony, flinty minerals than fruit.

1998 Domaine Girard La Garenne, Sancerre ★★ $$
A hint of licorice, a moderate amount of grassiness, and a whole lot of fruitiness mark this Fumé.

1998 Pascal Jolivet La Grande Cuvée, Sancerre ★★ $$
A dry wine with a toasty taste. This Sancerre is also chock-full of minerals that continue to proliferate as the wine aerates. It's delicious.

1999 Jean Tatin Domaine du Tremblay, Quincy ★★ $
A kicker of a Sauvignon Blanc with plenty of apple taste and acidity and a dusting of green herbs, especially tarragon.

1998 Marc Brédif, Pouilly-Fumé ★ $$
A light-bodied wine full of chalky, silty mineral qualities, along with spring-blossom flavors. Delightful.

1998 Cazin, Cheverny ★ $
A fairly straightforward Sauvignon Blanc with lovely citrus aromas, soil-rich minerality, and zippy acidity.

1999 Domaine Délétang, Touraine ★ $
It's citrusy, with good acidity—but this wine is also on the flowery side, which makes it a Sauvignon with a difference.

red wines of the loire

CABERNET FRANC

If Cabernet Franc were an ice cream, it would be called Very Berry. Strawberries, especially, are evident in the aroma, along with raspberries and currants. There's often a note of bell pepper, too. Fruitiness, medium body, tangy acidity, mellow tannin—altogether an easy wine to love.

on the label

Look for the appellations Chinon, Bourgueil, St-Nicolas-de-Bourgueil, Anjou-Villages, and Saumur-Champigny. Chinon and the Bourgueils tend to be a bit more bell-peppery than the others, Anjou more herbal, and Saumur-Champigny (an appellation on the rise) more fruity. The top wines come from single vineyards, and the bottles carry the name of the particular site as well as that of the larger area.

at the table

The first time we tried a Cabernet Franc with lime pickle in an Indian restaurant, we were sold on its versatility. It's a good wine for Indian or Asian dishes, especially when there are peppers involved, either sweet or hot. And it's also fine, even excellent, with good-old, simple American home cooking. Use it as a safe wine (like a Pinot Noir) when there are many flavors and choices on the table. At Thanksgiving, it will work with the turkey as well as the trimmings.

the bottom line Loire Cabernet Francs are among the best deals around. Prices start at about $12. Many of the top cuvées come in at $25, and they go up to $40.

what to buy CABERNET FRANC

1995	1996	1997	1998	1999
★★★★	★★★★	★★★	★★★	★★

recommended wines

1997 Charles Joguet Les Varennes du Grand Clos, Chinon ▼ ★★★★ $$
A bottle full of riches. The wine seems a little dull at first, and then the acidity and tannin take hold and ride you through the cherry core to the lovely finish.

1996 Olga Raffault Les Picasses, Chinon ▼ ★★★★ $$
Aged in old oak and chestnut barrels after stainless steel fermentation, this is a spicy wine with black pepper, a touch of sandalwood, and loads of raspberry juiciness—everything you want from a Cabernet Franc. A must have.

1997 Domaine des Roches Neuves Marginale, Saumur-Champigny ▼ ★★★ $$
Nothing marginal about this Marginale. If you're looking for a great big, full-bodied Cabernet Franc and prefer a little oakiness to your wine, this one's for you. There's a core of raspberry and cherry wrapped up in a velvety texture. The finish keeps going on and on.

1997 Pierre-Jacques Druet Grand Mont, Bourgueil ▼ ★★ $$
A full-bodied wine, with smooth and delicious fruit flavors and definite hints of strawberry. The tannin is smooth, the experience satisfying.

1998 Domaine des Roches Neuves Terres Chaudes, Saumur-Champigny ▼ ★★ $$
These are always subtle wines. Just a bit of raspberry aroma. A sip reveals deep raspberry flavor and a velvet texture.

1998 Taluau Cuvée du Domaine, St-Nicolas-de-Bourgueil ♥ ★ ★ $$

Black cherries and red berries come together with a touch of green bell pepper—on the nose, not the palate. The finish delivers a good dose of tannin. This wine warrants aging a few years.

1998 Clos de Coulaine Rouge, Anjou-Villages ♥ ★ ★ $

Cabernet Sauvignon is blended with Cabernet Franc here, and the two varieties add up to a full-bodied wine with slight earthiness and a lot of lovely roasted-fruit flavor.

1998 Domaine Fouquet, Saumur-Champigny ♥ ★ ★ $

A great little Cabernet Franc—simple, mainly fruity with a hint of black tea.

1998 Alain Lorieux, Chinon ♥ ★ ★ $

Earth outranks fruit in this new vintage, but the earth is like sweet black licorice, and the wine has lovely medium tannin giving a texture as smooth as washable silk.

1998 Domaine Delesvaux Rouge, Anjou ♥ ★ $

A ripe concoction of red fruits and green bell pepper on the nose, melting into fruitiness on the palate.

other red wines & rosés of the loire

There are some very good red wines coming out of the Loire Valley that are made from less important grape varieties like Pinot Noir and Gamay. The same grapes are also responsible for some excellent rosés.

recommended red wines

1998 Domaine de Châtenoy, Menetou-Salon ♥ ★ ★ ★ $$

If you find one of these, grab it. It's one of the best Pinot Noir deals around. When young, this silky wine has fresh cherry flavors. As it ages, lovely dried-cherry and rose-petal flavors surface.

1998 La Poussie, Sancerre 🍷 ★ $$$

A gentle, light-bodied Pinot Noir with touches of rose petals, earth, and pine nuts and a generous sprinkling of pepper on the finish.

1999 Domaine du Pavillon, Côte Roannaises 🍷 ★ $

Made entirely of Gamay grapes, this is a wine that's fruity and meant to be drunk young—just like Beaujolais. Strawberry-ish is the description that comes to mind.

recommended rosé wines

1999 James Paget Azay-le-Rideau Sec, Touraine 🍷 ★★★★ $

A gorgeous wine, full of cherry blossoms and rose petals.

1999 Jean Reverdy et Fils Domaine Des Villots, Sancerre 🍷 ★★ $$

Refreshing, vibrant fruit in the aroma. Layers of chalk and subtle currant are laced with a pleasant, food-friendly bitterness. This is a wine that really makes us happy.

provence

Even if the closest you've gotten to Provence is your spice rack, you probably have an image of the region that includes lots of sun, the Riviera, the beautiful people on the beach . . . and mediocre rosé, right? Well, the notion of the wine is wrong. Many of those rosés have improved dramatically, and some truly great reds come from Provence.

grapes & styles

The important red grapes that grow in Provence are about the same as the ones that grow in the Southern Rhône—Carignan, Cinsault, Grenache, Mourvèdre, and Syrah—but there are also increased plantings of Cabernet Sauvignon. All of these grapes go primarily into rosés and bold reds.

red wines of provence

Bandol is the only area in France where the Mourvèdre grape rules. Wines that are labeled Bandol must contain at least 50 percent of the grape (many of the best wineries use even more). And a growing number of the vineyards practice organic farming. Furthermore, by law, all of the grapes must be handpicked, and red wine must spend at least eighteen months in barrel. Bandol is a fine, full wine with strong tannin and flavors of herbs, nutmeg, truffles, blackberries, and leather. The wines are good on release, and yet they have what it takes to improve over ten years or more.

Les Baux de Provence The other star appellation of Provence is Les Baux de Provence. Here, among sharp cliffs and stunted pines, up and away from the sea, the temperature drops. As a result, the grapes develop more slowly, which in turn results in deep flavors, especially those of cherry and plum. Not quite so power-packed as Bandol, these wines, ideally, should be aged five to ten years.

at the table

We think a Bandol is indestructible. Actually, it's the food you have to worry about—this forceful wine will simply overpower delicate flavors. So pick your basic ingredient, whether it's game, lamb, chicken, or a vegetable, and have fun with a Provençal sauce that is redolent of garlic, rosemary, and olives. Bandol, some herbed olives, and smoked mozzarella or an aged, salty cheese like Cabrales or Parmesan make a good combination as well. The reds of Les Baux de Provence can go with the same big food, but also with more simply prepared dishes like plain roasted or grilled meat.

the bottom line

Bandols have always been expensive. The best of them range from $20 to $50. Considering how good they are and how crazy wine prices have become, those numbers don't seem so outrageous anymore. For the full experience, ask for an "old-style" Bandol with at least 70 percent Mourvèdre. Expect to pay from $12 to $30 for a red from Les Baux de Provence.

what to buy BANDOL

1995	1996	1997	1998	1999
★★★	★★★	★★★	★★★★	★★★

what to buy LES BAUX DE PROVENCE

1995	1996	1997	1998	1999
★★★	★★★	★★★	★★★★	★★★

recommended wines

1998 Mas de la Dame Coin Caché, Les Baux de Provence ♥   ★★★★ $$$

Simply put, this wine, based on the Grenache grape, is delicious. It tastes and smells like pure sun-baked raspberries, with a strong hint of apricots, too. The wine is wonderfully luxurious in the mouth—both full in body and silky smooth in texture.

1997 Domaine Le Galantin, Bandol ♥   ★★★★ $$

A wine that's two parts musk and one part fruit, due to the whopping amount of Mourvèdre included. It's full-bodied, with a nice bit of floweriness. Deep black plum and blackberry flavors lurk underneath the strong tannin. This one will age deliciously.

1997 Terra Door, Coteaux d'Aix-en-Provence ♥   ★★★ $$$

A lot of new oak, but in a very subtle package. Lots of Provençal herbs, like lavender and rosemary, in a wine that screams for the company of something hearty that's been cooked on the grill.

1997 Domaine de la Tour du Bon, Bandol ♥   ★★★ $$

Though it's way too young right now, at this point the wine is already marked by wonderful violet and licorice aromas. This one is for lovers of hearty Mourvèdre.

1998 Mas du Gourgonnier Rouge, Les Baux de Provence ♥   ★★★ $

Always a reliable wine, but this vintage in particular knocked us out. If we described it as tarry, with a definite muskiness and tongue-coating tannin, you might think it undrinkable—but the fact is that it's nothing short of delicious, with ripe purple fruit, a subtle undercurrent of stewed prune, and a floral carnation-like quality.

1998 Domaine Sorin, Côtes de Provence ☥   ★★★ $

The usual Rhône suspects turn up here, with the addition of 10 percent Cabernet. The result is a deep-purple wine that's full-bodied, with a peppery black-cherry bouquet and mellow tannin.

1997 Domaine de la Tour du Bon Sainte Ferreol, Bandol ☥ ★★ $$$

It's all gussied up in new oak, but the wine has yummy masses of ripe, but not overripe, fruit. Buy now and give it a year or two; five would be even better.

1997 Château de Pibarnon, Bandol ☥   ★★ $$

Tannic and a bit barnyardy. The wine needs some time, though it's already laced with licorice and the aromas of wild Provençal herbs.

1997 Château Ste. Anne, Bandol ☥   ★★ $$

Bandols are never quiet and gentle, but this one comes close. It's an elegant wine, with a touch of rosemary.

1997 Domaine Terres Blanches, Les Baux de Provence ☥   ★★ $$

We like this one with at least five years of age on it, so let it stay in the cellar for a year so that the delicate fruit flavor deepens. If you open it now, you'll find a medium-bodied, nicely tart wine with a subtle smell of cherries and dust.

1998 Château de Roquefort Les Mures, Côtes de Provence ☥   ★★ $

Roquefort wines, whether a basic bottling like this or an intense old-vine type, are powerful-tasting. This one's laden with licorice, cassis, and pepper flavors.

rosé wines of provence

Rosé was certainly the drink of choice when Gatsby-era socialites and literati charged the Provençal beaches. The wine was chic and looked so good against their white clothes. And now rosé is fashionable again, although a lot of Americans aren't aware of it yet. This time around, the wine is better. Where Provence rosés generally used to be neutral to insipid, they are now likely to be dry and packed with strawberry and anise flavors. Most are based on Cinsault, Grenache, and Mourvèdre, with other Southern grapes mixed into the blend as well. As a rule, rosés should be consumed within a year or two of the vintage. If you haven't been a rosé drinker, this is the time to start.

at the table

Chilled pink wines are always appealing as an aperitif, but they also work beautifully with food. Certainly try them with salmon, but also with a fragrant bouillabaisse with *rouille* (rosés from Provence stand up to garlic remarkably well) or with a basket of fried clams.

the bottom line Many picnic-friendly wines are available for less than $10, but there are also more rosés coming to market at the $15 to $20 price range—and often worth it.

recommended wines

1999 Château de Roquefort Corail, Côtes de Provence 🍷 ★★★ $
Here's an easygoing rosé with a nice bite of tartness on the palate and a peach-skin fuzziness to the texture.

1998 Domaine le Galantin, Bandol 🍷 ★★ $
The nose is subtle at first, but then a whole lot of licorice and fennel come in, along with wild Provençal herbs, and a tart finish balanced with a bit of candied peach and kumquat.

1999 Mas du Gourgonnier, Les Baux de Provence 🍷 ★★ $
Here's one to drink with a bowl of steaming mussels. It's a low-fruit, acidic to the point of puckeriness kind of wine that can take what the sea can throw at it and refresh your palate at the same time.

rhône valley

The U.S. is falling in love with wines from the Rhône. In the past, there have been flirtations with Shiraz (the Australian name for the Rhône grape Syrah) and with the Rhône-like wines from the California Rhône Rangers, but now the combination of the great 1998 vintage and decent prices have encouraged us to go for the real thing in a big way.

Wines of the Rhône Valley split stylistically between the North and the South. Think of it this way: Northern = elegant and Southern = lusty. The production up north is tiny, only five percent of total Rhône wine production. Both areas are known for their bold red wines. The Northern Rhône has one rare and coveted white, Condrieu, while the South has a noted white dessert wine, Muscat de Beaumes-de-Venise (see "Vins Doux Naturels," page 279).

Featured Wine-Growing Regions

Rhône River

LYON

Côte-Rôtie
Château-Grillet
Condrieu

St-Joseph
Hermitage
Crôzes-Hermitage
St-Péray
Cornas

Coteaux du Tricastin
Côtes du Vivarais
Rasteau
Vacqueyras

Gigondas

Côtes-du-Rhône
Villages

Tavel
Côtes du Ventoux
Châteauneuf-du-Pape
Rhône River
Lirac

lay of the land

The small northern section of the Rhône Valley vineland enjoys a Mediterranean-accented continental climate, whereas the Southern Rhône ranges from continental to true Mediterranean. The soils of the two are also dissimilar, and so it's no surprise that the grapes that thrive in the two areas differ. Many think of the North and the South as two distinct regions that lie close together along the Rhône River.

northern rhône

grapes & styles

If it's red Rhône from the North, it's Syrah. This is the region's only red grape. In its youth, the wine can be harsh. With five to ten years' aging, the wines turn intensely flavorful, with the taste of black currants and plums and a certain smokiness. In the white category, it is the floral, exotic Viognier, grown only on a handful of acres, that creates all the excitement. Viognier is also added to a few of the appellation's red wines, contributing a seductive aroma and taming the tannin so they're ready to drink earlier. The white grapes Marsanne and Roussanne end up in blends.

Côte-Rôtie The Syrahs in this appellation are silky, smoky, and bursting with berry aromas. With age, the wines become almost Bordeaux-like, but fruitier. The addition of up to 20 percent Viognier is allowed.

Condrieu The star white grape Viognier flourishes in this Lilliputian appellation. With a potent perfume of apricots, peaches, and honeysuckle but low-ish acidity, the wines are the kind you'd almost as soon sniff as drink. Condrieu is supposed to be ageworthy, but from too many disappointments, we advise to drink it while it's young.

St-Joseph and Crôzes-Hermitage From these appellations come the lightest Syrahs of the Northern Rhône. The wines often include Viognier, and they can be drunk younger than the other reds of the district.

Hermitage This appellation's red wines are usually 100 percent Syrah and deliver a beautifully complex flavor combining earth, fruit, anise, and black pepper. Lay them down for a minimum of five years. White Hermitage is usually a blend of Roussanne and Marsanne.

Cornas In a traditional producer's hands, a full-blooded young Cornas is terrifically tannic and needs many years to mellow and expose its fruit and smoke flavors. However, some producers, like Jean-Luc Colombo, make the newer, oaked style. These 100 percent Syrah wines have a center of black cherry and an overlay of spice and leather, and they need less bottle aging.

at the table

Full wines like most of the Syrahs from the Rhône meet their match in meaty and gamey food—whether vegetable or animal. Think about wild mushrooms, steak, or venison. An older wine will be gentler but will still stand up to simply roasted beef or lamb. Poultry, pork, and veal love the lighter St-Joseph and Crôzes-Hermitage. Just sip Viognier on its own, or try it with risotto or fairly plain shellfish so its perfume won't be overwhelmed by a strong sauce.

the bottom line Reds from St-Joseph and Crôzes-Hermitage are priced from under $15 to $35. In the 19th century, red Hermitage was more expensive than wines from top Bordeaux estates. Oddly enough, the reds of Hermitage are undervalued in today's marketplace. With the small number that get to the shops, it's best to buy them on sight. Expect them to be $30 to $65. The Côte-Rôtie and Cornas are replete with compelling red wines, but availability is tight and prices for the most sought-after start high, generally at $35. However, the quality for the money is definitely there. Château-Grillet is a rare one-vineyard appellation, and, as you'd expect, their Viogniers carry hefty price tags. Worth the outlay? That's debatable. Condrieu is a tad less expensive at $30 to $60, and, for many people, one of the best white wines in the world.

what to buy NORTHERN RHÔNE REDS

1995	1996	1997	1998	1999
★★★★	★★★	★★★	★★★	★★★

recommended red wines

1997 E. Guigal, Hermitage ♀   ★★★★ $$$$

Just a baby, but what a beauty. A little earthy violet, as well as a tiny bit of coffee, the gentlest taste of plum and blackberry, and moderate tannin. Drink now, or enjoy it even more after cellaring.

1998 Paul Jaboulet Aîné La Chapelle, Hermitage ♀   ★★★★ $$$$

The heat wave of '98 shows in this silky Hermitage. At first, the wine smells a little like a smoky tomato sauce, but then it blooms with seductive grilled-fruit aromas of cherry, currant, and cranberry.

1998 Domaine Alain Voge Vieilles Vignes, Cornas ♥ ★★★★ $$$
If you like big, monster wines with grace as well as power, check out this Cornas. We're talking blockbuster here. The wine is saturated, every molecule bursting with flavors of herbs, menthol, bittersweet chocolate, black olive, and cherries.

1997 Domaine Jamet, Côte-Rôtie ♥ ★★★ $$$
Restrained, sophisticated, delicious. Give it a few years for the tannin to mellow and you'll think you're drinking a Premier Cru Bordeaux, though you really have to appreciate the flavors of violet and earth to love this wine. It's medium-bodied.

1997 Domaine Clusel-Roch, Côte-Rôtie ♥ ★★★ $$
A fairly light-bodied Côte-Rôtie packed with delicious raspberry flavor, with a touch of cayenne, the slightest hint of cumin, and a musky animal quality.

1998 Alain Graillot, Crôzes-Hermitage ♥ ★★★ $$
A smoky wine with black-cherry flavor, notes of roasted almonds and cocoa, and a touch of tar.

1998 Jacques Frelin, Crôzes-Hermitage ♥ ★★★ $
Sun-baked fruit with a lingering touch of coffee ice cream on the finish. Sounds like an odd combination, but it's delicious. Silky tannin.

1997 George Vernay, Côte-Rôtie ♥ ★★ $$$
A smoky aroma. The wine is mellow and earthy with discernible notes of cedar and licorice, but it's not ready to drink yet.

1997 Domaine Alain Paret Rochecourbe, St-Joseph ♥ ★★ $$
If you suspend your preconceived notions of what a St-Joseph is supposed to be (tannic with dark-fruit and black-pepper flavors), this one is quite good—full-bodied with no harsh tannin, a little taste of coffee, and subtle hints of vanilla.

recommended white wines

1998 E. Guigal, Condrieu ♥ ★★★★ $$$-$$$$
A mélange of pear, honeysuckle, gardenia, jasmine, and fennel compete for attention and make this full-bodied wine a heady experience.

1998 Alain Voge Cuvée Boisée, St-Péray ♥ ★★★★ $$
St-Péray is the southernmost point of the Northern Rhône. It produces some killer white wines that are undervalued because people say "Where's St-Péray?" However, this one knocked our socks off. Made mostly of the Marsanne grape, it's a stunning piece of liquid art, a full-bodied wine bursting with honey, tropical fruits, and unctuous lusciousness.

1999 E. Guigal, Côtes-du-Rhône 🍷   ★ ★ ★ $

Think of this as a kinder, gentler Condrieu—an excellent example of wine power without wood. All sorts of subtle white flowers such as gardenia and jasmine (yes, there's some Viognier in here) waft from the glass. On the palate, there's also a pleasant hint of tarragon. Good with food, easy to drink all by itself.

1998 Jean-Luc Colombo les Figuières, Côtes-du-Rhône 🍷   ★ ★ $ $

A Condrieu taste-alike at half the price. The wine is refreshing and brisk, and Viognier perfumes the peachy, nutty, pear-like Roussanne. Yum.

1998 Delas Frères St-Esprit, Côtes-du-Rhône 🍷   ★ $

An excellent entry-level white Rhône. It's a full-bodied wine with quite a bit of guava and honey aroma and a hint of cedar flavor. It finishes bone-dry.

recommended rosé wines

1999 E. Guigal, Côtes-du-Rhône 🍷   ★ ★ ★ $

If Guigal keeps on making wines like this, he might single-handedly restore the Rhône's failing rosé rep. With an almost neutral nose, a tad of raspberry on the tongue, and beautiful acidity, it's everything an under-$10 rosé should be.

1998 Château de Trinquedevel, Tavel 🍷   ★ ★ $ $

Not a simple, alcoholic substitute for soda pop, this orange-hued wine has compelling flavors of minerals, bitter herbs, and dried tangerine peel. Serve it alongside roasted chicken with lots of rosemary.

southern rhône

grapes & styles

Though Châteauneuf-du-Pape gets all the attention, the Southern Rhône offers a plethora of excellent wines at all price points. Most of the wine is red, and the Grenache grape in all its raspberry, herb, and spice splendor gets star, but not solo, billing. Carignan, Cinsault, the tannic Mourvèdre grape, and Syrah play major roles in Rhône blends. Châteauneuf-du-Pape and Gigondas are robust, spicy, and full-bodied. Lirac and Vacqueyras are also full but perhaps not quite so lusty.

Red wine is the overpowering theme down here, though the Southern Rhône is also known for full-bodied, fragrant, and bone-dry rosés from the area around the village of Tavel, for white Châteauneuf-du-Pape, and for the fortified dessert wine Muscat de Beaumes-de-Venise. The district is experimenting with some primo examples of Viognier—not so perfumed as the northern version, but not so expensive either.

on the label

Côtes-du-Rhône This designation on the bottle indicates basic wine of the Southern Rhône, which accounts for about 80 percent of all the wine produced here.

Côtes-du-Rhône Villages The next level up from basic Côtes-du-Rhône. Sixteen villages enjoy this status. If you see Côtes-du-Rhône Villages alone on a bottle label, that means it is a blend from more than one of the villages; otherwise a village name is attached, as in Côtes-du-Rhône Rasteau. Look especially for the villages of Cairanne, St-Gervais, Rasteau, Sablet, and Beaumes-de-Venise.

Crus At the top of the Rhône hierarchy are the five appellations allowed to label bottles with their name on its own, without Côtes-du-Rhône. They are: Châteauneuf-du-Pape, Gigondas, Lirac, Vacqueyras, and Tavel.

Satellite Appellations These are around the edges of the official boundaries of the Southern Rhône. They're additional cru-status appellations. Look especially for Côtes du Ventoux and Coteaux du Tricastin.

at the table

Food pairing with the red wines is a cinch: Go for earthy and gamey. Don't hesitate to add a bit of spice and heat to match the wines' spiciness. The likes of lamb kebabs, goat curry, braised hare, and spicy merguez sausages work well. If you're a vegetarian, think Moroccan vegetable tagines, dishes with preserved lemons, or pasta in a red-pepper sauce with pignolis and rosemary. Spare not the garlic. And a nice smelly French cheese works sublimely with red Côtes-du-Rhône. Fragrant white Châteauneuf-du-Pape or Viognier makes a good choice for bouillabaisse or chicken with mushrooms. Tavel's rosé complements pork perfectly.

the bottom line
We are passionate about the '98 vintage. If you haven't bought wines in quantity before—to drink through the year or to age for a few years—Southern Rhônes, right now, make a good starting point. Incredible deals are to be had at every price point; even as little as $7 will get you a good basic red. Village wines go for between $11 and $20. As the village Cairanne may soon be promoted to cru status, buy it up while the going is cheap. Look to the village of St-Gervais for sleepers. The five crus range from less than $20 up to $50. Gigondas, which had been the poor man's Châteauneuf-du-Pape, now starts at $20, no longer the bargain it was. However, quality is consistently high, much less spotty than that of Châteauneufs, which sell in the $25 to $50 range. Tavel's rosés hover in the mid-teens. Whites in each category are usually at the high end of the red range.

what to buy SOUTHERN RHÔNE REDS

1996	1997	1998	1999
★★	★★★	★★★★	★★★

recommended wines

1998 Domaine de Bois de Boursan, Châteauneuf-du-Pape ♟
★★★★ $$$
Every once in a while, you find a wine that gives you goosebumps. This is one of those wines. It's an old-fashioned Châteauneuf that offers no apologies for its incredible power. There's a gorgeous nose of violets and clove. The flavor is earthy, with some chalk and cocoa powder.

1998 Château des Tours Réserve, Côtes-du-Rhône ♟
★★★★ $$
So shockingly good, it's hard to believe that it's a lowly Côtes-du-Rhône. Caramelized raspberry, spice, and game flavors are intensely concentrated and complex in this full-bodied wine, and the tannin is strong.

1998 Domaine de Beaurenard, Châteauneuf-du-Pape ♟
★★★ $$$
Here's a Châteauneuf that pumps iron. Forget the game and musk that usually characterize a muscular wine. This is a powerhouse driven by fruit and spice, with pepper and allspice blanketing a whopping Bing-cherry core.

1998 Château La Nerthe, Châteauneuf-du-Pape 🍷 ★★★ $$$
Right now, this wine is more about having a full-bodied feeling in the mouth than about flavors and aromas. Give it a year, and the honeyed-pear aspects will come out loud and clear.

1998 Domaine Bressy-Masson Cuvée Paul Emile, Rasteau 🍷 ★★★ $$
Mostly Grenache, with Syrah and Mourvèdre thrown into the mix, this is a wine you can't accuse of lacking flavor. It's opulent with the darkest-of-black fruits seasoned with a smidgen of flowers and earth.

1997 Les Closières, Châteauneuf-du-Pape 🍷 ★★★ $$
The incredible aroma combines fruit, earth, smoke, and spice. Delicious undertones of dried fruits. This is a winner.

1998 Domaine du Pesquier, Gigondas 🍷 ★★★ $$
There's no removal of the grape stems at Domaine du Pesquier, and so you know you're in for a big, tannic ride. This is a whopping, concentrated, fruit-driven wine with strong game and violet notes, opulent blackberry, and fresh-roasted coffee.

1998 Domaine du Vieux Lazaret, Châteauneuf-du-Pape 🍷 ★★★ $$
An intense, vanilla-scented wine that's hopping with lively berry flavors and has a touch of musk and tar.

1998 Domaine du Vieux Lazaret, Châteauneuf-du-Pape 🍷 ★★★ $$
An aroma of peaches is a good thing in a wine, and this one has lots. In the mouth, the wine feels medium-weight; there's a touch of spice, as if from licorice root, and some luscious, tart gooseberries.

1998 Domaine Nôtre Dame Ardesc de Cousignac, Vin de Pays d'Ardèche 🍷 ★★★ $
A brilliant new, full-bodied wine with 80 percent Grenache and 20 percent Syrah. It's got lots of concentrated flavor—cocoa, black pepper, and full-throttle fruit, especially grilled plum.

1998 Bousquet des Papes, Châteauneuf-du-Pape 🍷 ★★ $$$
Powerful fruitiness in the middle of full-bodied, gamey flavors, with a hint of wild rosemary and lots of black pepper.

1997 Les Cailloux André Brunel, Châteauneuf-du-Pape 🍷 ★★ $$
An good old-fashioned red: full-bodied with peppered-blueberry flavor and a lively bite of tannin.

1997 Delas Frères Les Calcerniers, Châteauneuf-du-Pape ▼ ★ ★ $$

Seems on the light side at first, but the flavors deepen with a little air. Delicacy still rules, though: It's more raspberry than earth, more flower than game.

1998 Paul Jaboulet Aîné, Gigondas ▼ ★ ★ $$

A straightforward Gigondas with medium-strength cherry and currant flavors and a tiny taste of silt.

1998 Domaine de la Monadière, Vacqueyras ▼ ★ ★ $$

Vacqueyras reds aren't known for subtlety or sophistication, but this '98 has both, in spades. Flavors are of red berry, licorice, pepper, and earth.

1997 Oratorio, Gigondas ▼ ★ ★ $$

New World wine comes to the Rhône. This one has full body and intense fruit and earth flavors, buttressed with clove and caramel or butterscotch, and cherry on the finish.

1997 Domaine Santa Duc, Gigondas ▼ ★ ★ $$

Slight gaminess on the nose. Deep, cooked-cherry flavors bring Kirsch to mind. This is a good one.

1998 Jean-Luc Colombo Les Abeilles, Côtes-du-Rhône ▼ ★ ★ $

Refreshingly acidic and cherry-like—a perfect hot-summer-day wine at a great price.

1998 E. Guigal, Côtes-du-Rhône ▼ ★ ★ $

No new-fangled techniques for Guigal—just great grapes and sensible wine-making. This one's packed with old-fashioned goodness. Full, delicious, and spicy, with dark raspberries on the nose, lots of black pepper on the palate, and a tiny bit of coffee on the finish.

1998 Domaine St-Luc, Coteaux du Tricastin ▼ ★ ★ $

At its worst, this is a lovely table wine; at its best, it's like a full-bodied, silky, and spicy Châteauneuf-du-Pape. The '98 has an extra bit of everything—more clove, more smoke, more plum.

1998 Domaine Santa Duc, Côtes-du-Rhône ▼ ★ ★ $

There's a lot going on here: fennel, anise, leather. At the finish, spicy cooked cherries, pepper, and a little dryness on the tongue.

1999 Château de Ségriès Cuvée Réserve, Lirac ▼ ★ ★ $

A deeply flavored Grenache and Syrah blend from the Rhône Valley, with flavors of black raspberry, pepper, and a touch of earth. Savor now, and over the next five to seven years.

1998 Domaine André Brunel Cuvée Sommelongue, Côtes-du-Rhône ♟ ★ $
A lovely gamey aroma, a rosemary-and-fennel taste, a smooth texture—all for under $10. This is a sophisticated little wine.

1998 M. Chapoutier Belleruche, Côtes-du-Rhône ♟ ★ $
Simple, with full cherry flavor, this works well as an everyday wine.

1998 Delas Frères St-Esprit, Côtes-du-Rhône ♟ ★ $
A fairly simple, easy-to-drink wine with pignoli nuts on the nose, which are repeated on the palate and joined by a deep fruit flavor. Black tea on the finish.

1998 J. Vidal Fleury, Côtes-du-Rhône ♟ ★ $
Earth, tobacco, and tea are the predominate factors in this medium-bodied Côtes-du-Rhône. A simple, sturdy table wine.

1998 Rabasse-Charavin, Rasteau ♟ ★ $
Flavors and aromas here are straightforward; baked raspberries are prominent, with muskiness lying just beneath the surface.

southwest france

Scattered between Bordeaux and Languedoc-Roussillon and down to the Spanish border are the various wine-growing areas known collectively as the Southwest. They hold a treasure trove of inexpensive and individual wines from isolated villages and can give quite a bit of excitement to the taste adventurer. In addition, the town of Limoux claims to have discovered sparkling wine hundreds of years before the Champenoise.

grapes & styles
The range of types of wines in this collection of vineyard areas runs the gamut from traditionally powerful reds to new-style fruity offerings. And there are whites, sparklers, and dessert wines as well. The Southwest's two best-known wines are not exactly household names: Cahors and Madiran. Their grapes, Auxerrois (also known as Cot and Malbec) and Tannat, aren't either. Don't let that stop you, but be braced for intensity.

Cahors, based on Auxerrois, might be described as a rustic Bordeaux. Young Madiran can be a bit hard to take, almost scratching the tongue with its fierceness. As the name of its base grape, Tannat, suggests, the wine is tannic and takes a few years to mellow. Blanquette de Limoux, made of Mauzac, Chardonnay, or a blend of the two, is not to be overlooked. It's a bone-dry bubbly and a top value.

at the table

The reds of the Southwest are surprisingly versatile. Traditional, full wines stand up well to the dishes of the region, such as the hearty cassoulet. For the newer, stewed-fruity wines, you might think of rich fish or poultry, perhaps salmon in lemongrass broth or duck with fig or cherry sauce.

the bottom line
The Southwest is an excellent source for inexpensive and interesting wines. Bottles that cost as little as $8 can provide fine drinking. Cahors is generally in the $10 to $20 range. Madirans start a tad higher but also top out at about $20.

recommended white wines

1998 Domaine Alain Brumont, Vin de Pays des Côtes de Gascogne ♟   ★ ★ $
A simple and refreshing wine with a bracing flavor that makes us think of grapefruit juice.

1999 Plaimont Colombelle, Vin de Pays des Côtes de Gascogne ♟   ★ ★ $
A perennial summer favorite, this is a wine that never disappoints. It's lightly acidic and fully pleasing, with aromas of fresh-cut grass and fragrant honeysuckle, and a lovely limey edge. It's also dirt cheap.

1999 Domaine Castéra Sec, Jurançon ♟   ★ $
There's an initial skunkiness on the nose—that's the bad news. The good news is that this wine is so cheap and tasty we thought we should recommend it and leave the choice to you. We can tell you that once you get past that first whiff, the wine is fruity on the palate, with an apple taste and a bit of lemony acidity, some chalkiness, and a pleasant, ever-so-slight prickle of effervescence.

1999 Château Clement Termes Perlée, Gaillac 🍷 ★ $
With its aromas and flavors of grapefruit and tangerine, this is a honey of a wine. Setting it apart from the fruity pack is a fascinating stony finish and a little pettilance that tickles the tongue.

1999 Domaine du Mage,
Vin de Pays des Côtes de Gascogne 🍷 ★ $
Delicious, lemony, grassy, with a touch of honeysuckle and pepper—a perfect summer drink.

recommended red wines

1997 Château Lagrezette, Cahors 🍷 ★★★ $$
Lovers of Bordeaux will cozy up to this medium-bodied, tannic wine. Though it's full of subtle fruit, it owes more to allspice and pepper.

1997 Domaine Alain Brumont Château Boucassé,
Madiran 🍷 ★★ $$
Madirans are usually tannic brutes, but Brumont has set out to tame them—and has succeeded brilliantly. This wine is 65 percent Tannat and the rest is Cabernet Sauvignon and Cabernet Franc. The result is a wine you can drink right now. The nose is meaty, with a little bit of bacon fat; the taste is smoky, with lovely laces of licorice.

1997 Heart of Darkness, Madiran 🍷 ★★ $$
Another French entry from Californian Randall Grahm. The tannin is somewhat tamed, as Californians prefer, yet the wine remains powerful, with deep flavors of plums and blackberries.

1998 Jean-Luc Matha Rouge, Marcillac 🍷 ★★ $
Get ready for a great big hectare's-worth of earth in your wine. With this little number, it seems as if the grapes sucked up every bit of Marcillac soil they could and mixed it with subtle red-berry flavor. At first sip, the earthiness and pepper are a bit overpowering, but then paprika, violets, and carnations come in—and the texture is pure velvet.

1997 Château Bellevue-la-Fôret, Côtes du Frontannais 🍷 ★ $
Based on the Négrette grape, this is not too complicated, but pleasing nonetheless. It's full of roses and has a dash of cayenne.

1998 Domaine du Cros, Marcillac 🍷 ★ $
Rather strong herbal aromas of rosemary and tarragon, but the tart raspberry flavor and the tannin are gentle. The combo makes for a riveting wine.

1998 Domaine du Mage, Côtes de Gascogne ❦   ★ $
Earthy and mushroomy aromas lead to a wallop of flavor in the mouth—a lot
of complexity for an inexpensive wine that's mostly Merlot. That mellow grape
is bolstered with a local favorite, Tannat, and so the wine delivers good tannin
and powerful allspice and blackberry flavors.

10 GREAT PARTY WINES

A perfect party wine is easy to drink with or without food, is
in the $10 or under category, and yet is good enough to
impress wine-loving friends with your fine taste. All the
below fill the bill.

WHITES

1999 Jean Touzout Mâcon-Villages from Burgundy,
France (page 52)

1999 Domaine du Vieux Pressoir from the Loire Valley,
France (page 65)

1999 Marqués de Cáceres Blanco from Rioja, Spain
(page 137)

1999 Herzog Sauvignon Blanc from California (page 186)

1998 Seaview Sparkling Wine from Australia (page 271)

REDS

Mommessin Pinot Noir/Syrah from the Languedoc,
France (page 60)

1998 Domaine St-Luc from the Rhône Valley,
France (page 85)

1999 Cecchi Vino Nobile di Montepulciano from
Tuscany, Italy (page 117)

1995 Tinto da Anfora from Portugal (page 148)

1997 Vigil Vineyards Terra Vin from California (page 207)

italy

Though it's only about three-quarters the size of California, Italy produces not only a remarkable array of wine but also more of it than any other country in the world. Vastly different microclimates, stretching from the Austrian border almost to North Africa, allow Italy to grow some two thousand grape varieties. Until World War II, a large proportion of those grapes went into wines that were sold in bulk as the equivalent of jug wine, or worse. The past thirty years, however, have seen upgrades in almost every category.

grapes & styles

Think Italian wine, and you probably think red—and you're right to do so. Certainly the country's greatest wines are based on the indigenous Nebbiolo, Sangiovese, Corvina, and Aglianico grapes, all of which go into reds. Barbera, Dolcetto, and Montepulciano make good, somewhat lighter red wines. The most important white grape is Trebbiano.

But these days Italian wine means much more than those traditional grapes. Italy was in the vanguard of worldwide wine modernization, and now the new style (foreign varietals aged in new-oak barrels) coexists with the old (indigenous varietals aged in old-wood casks for long periods of time).

As we change over to the new millennium, we see some of Italy's avant-garde winemakers reverting back to tradition, though that's not to say they're going back to the old industrial-quality stuff. Italy is about to take another step forward, toward excellent wines that satisfy the international market but are more subtle than the current new-style oaky wonders.

Val D'aosta
Trentino-Alto Adige
Friuli-Venezia Giulia
Lombardia
MILAN
Veneto
VENICE
Piemonte
Emilia-Romagna
Liguria

Featured Wine Growing Regions

FLORENCE
Toscana
Marche
Umbria
Abruzzo
Lazio
ROME
Molise
Puglia
Campania
NAPLES
Sardegna
Basilicata
Calabria
Sicilia
Pantelleria

on the label

Like most of Europe, Italy stresses location over grape variety, and the labels reflect this: Chianti is from the Chianti area of Tuscany, Barolo from Barolo in Piedmont, Valpolicella from the Valpolicella area in Veneto, and so on.

Some labels announce both the primary grape and the place. So we get Brunello di Montalcino and Nebbiolo d'Alba—Brunello-based wine from the Montalcino area of Tuscany and wine based on Nebbiolo grapes from the Alba area of Piedmont. The grape variety is always first and the place second.

Friuli-Venezia Giulia, on the Austrian border, is the sole Italian region that uses only varietal labeling. Trentino-Alto Adige, with its strong German influence sometimes puts a German label on some bottles and an Italian one on others of the same wine.

apulia, campania, sicily & sardinia

For many, many decades, wine was not southern Italy's strong suit. Though there's still a lot of inferior stuff being made, the South is now a source of immensely satisfying reds, full rosés, and sturdy whites. What's even better is that value for money is holding solid.

grapes & styles

In Apulia, red wines made from the Negroamaro (literally *black bitter*) and Primitivo grapes are the most noteworthy. Negroamaro makes full and ageworthy wines. Primitivo goes into both reds and memorable rosés. Aglianico (ah-lee-AH-nee-co), the prime red grape of Campania, becomes Taurasi (tao-RAH-zee), one of Italy's greatest wines. Greco di Tufo and Fiano di Avellino are the two whites of interest; both are dry, distinctive, and ageworthy. Sicily boasts Marsala and sweet Moscato wine. Sardinia makes spicy red Cannonau (cah-noh-NAH-oh), called Grenache in France, as well as light herbal whites from the Vermentino grape.

apulia

Italy's heel, Apulia, never had trouble pumping out rivers of red wine; its problem was quality. Among other difficulties, grapes were over-cropped, and most of the fermenting tanks were outdoors with no temperature controls. But a great turnaround started in the '70s, and much of what is being made today is downright exciting.

Most of the wines made from Negroamaro grapes are from the Salice Salentino area. They're inky, velvety, and filled with sun-baked, dried-fruit flavors with a slight, pleasant bitterness. Primitivo is thought to be the same grape as Zinfandel. The Apulia marketing machine is already aiming at the U.S. customer, and some bottles actually come in labeled Zinfandel. But the wine doesn't need a California name to make it good.

campania

Better known for Neopolitan cuisine (e.g. pizza) and the charms of the Isle of Capri than for its wines, Campania nonetheless produces significant reds that are well worth exploring. Taurasi, made from Aglianico grapes, is rife with blueberry and raspberry flavors backed up with strong tannin. And, unusual for Italy, Campania's whites are equally important. Greco di Tufo has a wonderful stony finish after the fruit and almond flavors. Fiano di Avellino's peachy, nutty flavors become beautifully complex with age.

sicily & sardinia

Resting on the reputations of its Marsala and sweet Moscato and its two highly regarded brand-name wineries, Corvo and Regaleali (which deliver great value), Sicily has lagged behind the big changes evident in the rest of southern Italy. Sardinia, however, is gaining lots of fans for its improved wines made from grapes that aren't indigenous to the island—the reds Cannonau and Cabernet and the white Vermentino.

at the table

The full reds of Apulia, Campania, and Sardinia can sit in for each other as far as food is concerned. They're all wines that call out for meat and that can take as much garlic as you can. Apulia's rosés are excellent with grilled octopus, crab dishes, and all but the very strongest finfish—or alongside flavorful vegetable first courses like fava beans with sautéed greens. Among southern whites, Greco di Tufo is lovely with linguine and clam sauce. Think roast chicken or rich fish dishes with Fiano di Avellino, and possibly fish and fruit salsas for the light Vermentino.

the bottom line Southern Italy offers great punch for the dollar. Stock up on wines in the $10 range, but don't ignore those that are higher-priced. The ones around $20 are often worth the money, especially Salice Salentinos and Aglianicos. Buy them now; we predict that in three years or so prices will skyrocket.

recommended wines

1997 Montrevetrano Colli di Salerno, Campania ♥   ★ ★ ★ $$$$
With its mix of Cabernet, Merlot, and a touch of Aglianico, this is a powerful wine. You're unlikely to find it in stores, but do look for it on fine Italian wine lists. Chocolate is the first impression, then blackberry and leather. The wine finishes with a tannin wallop; it could definitely use a year or two more to settle down so that the tannin isn't overwhelming.

1997 Argiolas Costera, Sardinia ♥   ★ ★ ★ $$$
Deep aromas of fruit and spice that just leap up and grab your attention lead to full body and powerful earthy flavors.

1996 Feudi di San Gregorio Taurasi, Campania ♥   ★ ★ ★ $$$
Earthy and especially full-bodied, with lots of intense black-cherry flavor and some vanilla from new oak. Good tannin.

1997 Planeta Merlot, Sicily ♥   ★ ★ ★ $$$
Very lively aromas, including plum and black currant. The flavor is dusted with a sprinkling of allspice.

1995 Terre Brune, Sardinia ♥   ★ ★ ★ $$$
This is a powerful wine made from Carignan. There's more earth than fruit in the bottle right now, and the wine is gently tannic. Right underneath the musky, porcini, cave-like flavors are masses of luscious blackberries and strawberries just waiting to mature.

1995 Librandi Gravello, Calabria ♥   ★ ★ ★ $$
This is a full-bodied wine with vibrant black-cherry flavor and lots of delicious smokiness. It has good tannin and a welcome bit of bitterness on the finish.

1995 Ocone Aglianico del Taburno, Campania ♥   ★ ★ ★ $$
There's a smell of varnish and some cherry aroma. In the mouth, the wine becomes a blockbuster, with fresh fruit flavors and full body.

1998 Nicola Romano Fiano di Avellino, Campania ♥   ★ ★ ★ $$
We love this wine. It's old-fashioned—meaning nice and full in the mouth—with a lovely peach aroma and hazelnuts on the finish.

1998 Savese Terrarossa Pichierri Primitivo di Manduria, Apulia ♥   ★ ★ ★ $$
There's a bit of carnation-like aroma tempered by a kiss of chocolate mint on the nose. Flavors are complex and yummy, with luscious fruit, especially baked blueberry, but it needs a few years to become truly outstanding.

1995 Sella & Mosca Cannonau Riserva, Sardinia 🍷 ★★★ $$
Appealing smells start things off—nuts, blackberries, plums, and figs. The wine is full-bodied, as these fruit-packed numbers typically are, and it has the added value of nutmeg and allspice.

1993 Taurino Patriglione Rosso del Salento, Apulia 🍷 ★★★ $$
A consistently delectable wine—and one that always needs about a year after release to mellow. Right now, this is a beaut, and it should stay strong for another five years. It's made from dried grapes, and the result is a treat, a complex wine packed with plums, licorice, spicy nutmeg, and chocolate.

1995 San Pietro Brindisi Riserva, Apulia 🍷 ★★★ $
Try anything from this great, reliable producer; you'll be happy. This particular wine has a violet aroma, medium body, and sun-baked fruit and toffee flavors.

1995 Argiolas Turriga, Sardinia 🍷 ★★ $$$
New World flavors, with gobs of vanilla, black-cherry, and other dark, sweet fruits. It's a powerful wine; if you like the big California Merlots, try this baby.

1998 Regaleali/Tasca d'Almerita Cabernet, Sicily 🍷 ★★ $$$
Intense aroma of summery field greens, with a lot of super-ripe fruit flavors and a touch of caramelized sugar on the finish.

1998 Michele Caló Mjére Alezio Rosso, Apulia 🍷 ★★ $$
This is just a tad shy of full-bodied and boasts sun-baked fruits and a slight raisiny quality. It's less lusty than other vintages, but still delicious.

1999 Feudi di San Gregorio Falanghina del Sannio, Campania 🍷 ★★ $$
A mellow, nutty kind of wine with a creamy finish, full-bodied and smooth. There's lime on the finish, too. Amazing with Gorgonzola *dolce*.

1999 Feudi di San Gregorio Fiano di Avellino, Campania 🍷 ★★ $$
A bit of pear on the nose with some peach, a touch of honey, and gooseberry, too, in a delicious, refreshing wine with a bone-dry finish.

1998 Mastroberardino Falanghina Sireum Benventano, Campania 🍷 ★★ $$
Although subtle in aroma and flavor, this wine more than makes up for it in complexity. It's got a real mineral quality—you can almost taste volcanic ash.

1998 Mastroberardino Lacryma Christi del Vesuvio, Campania 🍷 ★★ $$
The fruit in this wine isn't intense, but it is very pleasant and just complex enough to draw you in with each sip. The subtle currant and the slightest suggestion of Concord grape are augmented by a hefty dose of tamed tannin.

1998 Mjére Bianco del Salento, Apulia ♆   ★★ $$
Bright sunny color, nutty aroma, and a strong lemony flavor finishing with a touch of cream. Ideal for a seafood platter.

1998 Terredora Loggia della Serra, Campania ♆   ★★ $$
Subdued yet clear aromas of spiced apple, mint, and hazelnut in a wine with a full, concentrated mouth-feel.

1999 Argiolas Costamolino, Sardinia ♆   ★★ $
Here's one to drink if you're suffering from Chardonnay fatigue. It's a bit prickly on the tongue, with hints of fennel seed, cumin, and lemon—perfect for serving with a salad.

1998 Botromagno Gravina, Apulia ♆   ★★ $
Probably one of the happiest white wines from the area, with a glorious quality-to-price quotient. Aromatic for sure, but not perfumey, its scents of lime, lemon, and honeysuckle are tempered by just a hint of fennel. On the palate there's a long, lingering, refreshing finish. Totally delicious.

1993 Botromagno Pier delle Vigne, Apulia ♆   ★★ $
Wines from the northern part of Apulia are consistently well-priced and complex. This one has subtle roasted fruit and also hints of wild mushroom, olive, and licorice. The tannin is nice and gentle. It can be a hard wine to find; grab up whatever you can.

1997 Taurino Salice Salentino, Apulia ♆   ★★ $
Full and tannic, with deep, satisfying, spicy flavors, a touch of tomato paste, and a long, lingering finish of red berries and roasted nuts.

1999 Cala Silente Vermentino di Sardegna, Sardinia ♆   ★ $$
The immediate impression is of lemons and honeydew. The wine has an almost oily texture and ends with a snappy taste of cracked pepper.

1998 Mastroberardino Aglianico d'Irpinia, Campania ♆   ★ $$
An immediate, intense tart-cherry flavor more than makes up for the less than slam-dunk finish.

1999 Planeta La Segreta, Sicily ♆   ★ $$
Here's a nicely tangy and tannic young wine, the kind that's great at a summer barbecue or with pizza. The wine is medium in body, and it has a subtle red-currant flavor.

1997 Soletta Firmadu Cannonau, Sardinia ♆   ★ $$
The wild, gamey flavors and the almost cherry-candy taste in this powerful wine don't seem to belong together. But once you get over the shock, it's a tasty wine, with good acidity.

1997 Apollonio Copertino, Apulia ♥ ★ $
Made mostly from Negroamaro, the wine has a characteristic full, rustic aroma of baked fruits. In the mouth, it's less typical; its fullness becomes smooth and complex—very unexpected.

1998 Corvo Bianco, Sicily ♥ ★ $
Mass-marketed, inexpensive—and good. In the mouth, it's dry and the flavor is stony, with a little nice honeysuckle. A super sipper, and a fine food wine.

1999 Donnaluna Fiano, Campania ♥ ★ $
One of the best-value table whites we've had in a long time. It's got a great nose—full of mineral, slate, and gooseberry—and a slightly creamy finish.

1997 Murgo Etna Rosso, Sicily ♥ ★ $
While it won't absolutely knock you out, this will totally do the trick for a tasty and quaffable everyday wine. It's medium-bodied, with a touch of spiced plum and berry flavor and good acidity.

1996 Santa Anastasia, Sicily ♥ ★ $
The aromas are inviting. Then there's lots of clear fruit flavors, including currants, raspberries, and plums, all with a slight dusting of cinnamon, in a full-bodied wine.

1998 Sella & Mosca Le Arenarie, Sardinia ♥ ★ $
A wine that smells like peach juice and tastes like a Bellini. Pretty one-note, but quite fun.

1999 Soletta Firmadu Vermentino di Sardegna, Sardinia ♥ ★ $
Banana, mango, and honeydew on the nose, following through on the palate, though with less intensity. The finish has a solid banana note.

friuli-venezia giulia

Bordered by Austria and Slovenia, Friuli-Venezia Giulia shows influences from both. Most obviously, this region makes primarily varietal wines à la the Germanic countries, just like Alsace in France. White wine is the norm, but the area produces small quantities of excellent red as well. The best whites and reds come from two hillside areas—Collio and Colli Orientali del Friuli.

white wines of friuli-venezia giulia

"World class" is the phrase that comes to mind when considering the whites of Friuli, as the region is usually called. The area is known particularly for its full-bodied Tocai Friulano (toh-KIE free-oo-LAH-no), but there are many other choices. The Pinot Grigio shows the rest of Italy that wines from that grape can be tasty. Great success has come from plantings of French and German grapes; seek out especially the Pinot Biancos, molto-herbaceous Sauvignon Blancs, and Rieslings. Even though Friuli is renowned for single varietals, attention is also being focused on the new white blends. Winemakers are coming up with all kinds of unexpected combinations that open possibilities to play with imaginative food and wine pairings.

at the table

Two good food-matching clues: Herbs grow all over the Friulian hills, and Adriatic fish are abundant throughout the region. Grilled fish flavored with rosemary is ideal. Friuli whites also complement simple pasta dishes, like spaghetti with olive oil, garlic, and sage. Vinaigrette-dressed salads work well, too, since most of these wines have good acidity.

bottom line There are great values here from below $10 to around $20, though some of the boutique blends can exceed $40.

recommended wines

1998 Jermann Pinot Grigio ♟   ★ ★ ★ ★ $$$
Though '98 wasn't the best year, this Pinot Grigio is gorgeous. Full of honeysuckle perfume, with some subtle flavors of five-spice powder and refreshing peach. A revelation for those who turn up their noses at this varietal.

1997 Walter Filiputti Ribolla Gialla ♟   ★ ★ ★ $$$
A mellow, easy-drinking wine that smells and tastes like apples sprinkled with nuts, cinnamon, and nutmeg.

1998 Ronco del Gelso Latimis Isonzo ♥ ★★★ $$$
Here's one of those crazy Friulian blends—the wine is mostly Tocai, with some Riesling and Pinot Bianco thrown in for good measure. The resulting aromas of peach and honeydew along with the wine's full-flavored complexity make it an excellent choice.

1997 Villa Aba Ribolla Gialla ♥ ★★★ $$
A medium-bodied wine that offers up some intense aromas of lemon, apricot, and hazelnut. It all comes to a creamy finish that hints of honeyed Golden Delicious apples.

1998 Ca' Bolani Opimio Aristos ♥ ★★ $$$
A delightful blend of Chardonnay and Tocai, this wine has beautiful clear flavors of lemon and clove along with a touch of earth and cedar. It's at its best with food.

1998 Livio Felluga Terre Alte ♥ ★★ $$$
It starts with a very, very vegetal nose, which then follows through on the palate. There are flavors of green grass and strong bitter licorice. Not for those who demand fruitiness, but we love it.

1998 Livio Felluga Tocai Friulano ♥ ★★ $$
Seductive aromas of peony and honeysuckle come together with a little acidity on the palate. The wine finishes with a touch of almond.

1995 Marego Holbar Bianco ♥ ★★ $$
Here's an oddball wine that's really tasty. It's 80 percent Riesling and 20 percent Chardonnay, aged in acacia wood. The result is a very full-flavored wine with complex aromas (sun-ripened apricots), spice on the palate, and mouth-watering acidity.

1998 Ronchi di Manzano Chardonnay ♥ ★★ $$
A very apple-y Chardonnay. The wine has a little spritz of effervescence on the tongue and a touch of chalk on the finish.

1999 Eno Friulia Pinot Grigio ♥ ★★ $
Intense honey on the nose, attractive hints of pears on the palate, and a straightforward steely finish.

1999 Pradio Pinot Grigio ♥ ★★ $
A lovely little Pinot Grigio, with refreshing acidity and a touch of pineapple on the palate.

1998 Schiopetto Collio Pinot Grigio ♥ ★ $$$
A little tingle on the tongue, and then a whole lot of refreshing minerals start dancing around the mouth. Definitely a food wine.

1998 Villa Russiz Sauvignon 🍷   ★ $$
A bracing wine that combines typical grassiness and atypical melon, finishing with mouth-puckering acidity.

1999 Livio Felluga Esperto Pinot Grigio 🍷   ★ $
An earthy nose meets lemon-lime flavor, with a dusting of almond powder and a note of honey.

red wines of
friuli-venezia giulia

Even though this is white-wine territory, the hills of Friuli retain enough heat to grow some red grapes, including the Bordeaux varieties Cabernet Franc, Cabernet Sauvignon, and Merlot. You'll find red single varietals and also some complex blends. Perhaps the most interesting reds, however, are from local grapes: tart Refosco; medium-bodied, violetty Schioppettino; and brawny, almost black Pignolo, which is considered particularly promising.

at the table
Use the Merlots and Cabernets as you would medium-weight Bordeaux; they work well with the usuál beef and lamb. Refosco and Schioppettino are good bets with chicken, veal, or pork dishes, while the fuller Pignolo is a shoo-in with flavorful, slow-cooked meats.

bottom line There are bargains in the international varietals, with sophisticated examples as low as $8. The trendy blends can be expensive, starting at $20. Local grapes like Pignolo will be higher, starting at $40, because the vines are low yielders.

recommended wines

1996 Livio Felluga Sosso Merlot 🍷   ★ ★ ★ $$$$
This full-bodied, delicious wine is layered with all the tannin new oak can give. Cherry and blackberry, tempered with tar and tea.

1997 Ronchi di Manzano Merlot Ronc di Subule ♥ ★ ★ ★ $$$

If you love Merlot, try some of the Friulian beauties. This one has plenty of cherry, cocoa, and espresso.

1997 Ronchi di Manzano Refosco dal Peduncolo ♥ ★ ★ ★ $$

Rhône wine lovers should check out this gamey red wine. It's medium-full in body and has lots of floral aromas and blackberry, plum, and tobacco flavors, along with touches of tar and leather.

1997 Puiatti Pinot Nero ♥ ★ ★ $$$

A summery-smelling candy-and-roses nose—and the taste seems perfect for hot-weather drinking, too. There's a lick of tar and earth on the long finish.

1995 Villa Aba Schioppettino ♥ ★ ★ $$

Underneath the vanilla-scented oak and the earth and tar aromas is a medium-bodied wine that has intense blackberry flavors.

1997 Schiopetto Collio Merlot ♥ ★ ★ $$

The fruit flavors here are so powerful. Underneath, there's a little taste of stem and a lot of spice, especially nutmeg. Lots going on here.

1999 Villa del Borgo Refosco ♥ ★ ★ $

At first, the wine seems to have a dusty sort of smell. A sip reveals a strawberry-ish, medium-bodied wine that's very tasty. It's almost like a Beaujolais from one of the serious producers.

1996 Krizia Cabernet Franc ♥ ★ $$

This medium-bodied wine bears touches of vanilla and baked raspberry flavors. While it doesn't offer a whole lot of complexity, it's an easy-drinking wine.

piedmont

Some of the most complex wines of Italy come from Piedmont. Though many of the traditional wines have been modernized over the past two decades, they're still a far cry from the fashionable fruit-in-your-face international style. Piedmont produces sparklers from Asti, a few still whites, and both plain and fancy reds, among which Barolo and Barbaresco make Piedmont the Italian region for wine lovers.

red wines of piedmont

Barolo & Barbaresco Barolos and Barbarescos come from neighboring areas and are made from the same grape, Nebbiolo. Often an individual winemaker may work in both areas and produce both wines; so it's easy to see why the differences between Barolo and Barbaresco can be subtle.

Barolo's strong tannin, full flavor, good acidity, and high percentage of alcohol make it the epitome of a powerful wine. By the time the vintner releases a traditional Barolo, the wine has already been aged for three years—two in the barrel and one in the bottle—and even longer if it's marked Riserva. At this point, the wine is like a child bound for a long life. As a youngster, it's so tannic that it's tough on the tongue, almost astringent. With age (ten to thirty years or even longer), the wine comes into its own: the tannin mellows to a manageable level, and the flavors mature to complexity. Barolos made from the grapes of a single vineyard, such as Cannubi and Brunate, are difficult to find but worth the effort—and the extra money. Though they're hardly light, Barbarescos are lighter-bodied than Barolos, and they need less aging—five to ten years.

at the table

Barolo and Barbaresco, Piedmont's quintessential wines, pair perfectly with the region's most famous comestible—white truffles. A whole roasted truffle and a glass of Barolo is heaven. Or try any game bird with truffles, pasta with truffles, truffled risotto, or truffles shaved over grilled polenta. If truffles are beyond your reach, perfume such dishes with white-truffle oil. Earthy morels, or any mushrooms, will also please your palate. The strength of the wines suggest full-flavored meats, such as venison, boar, or plain old beef. Or bring out one of these wines after dinner with a cheese course.

bottom line

The '95 to '98 vintages range from great to outrageously great, so stock up. Most producers make both a regular and a single-vineyard wine. They range in price from $25 a bottle for the most basic to about $175 for a top single-vineyard wine, but many Barolos and Barbarescos hover around the $80 price point.

what to buy BAROLO & BARBARESCO

1991	1992	1993	1994	1995
★★★	★★	★★★	★★	★★★★

1996	1997	1998
★★★★	★★★★	★★★

recommended producers & their wines

ALDO CONTERNO ★★★★ $$$$
In 1969, Aldo Conterno split with his brother, Giovanni, and left the family winery, Giacomo Conterno (below), to explore more innovative winemaking techniques. Neither strictly traditional nor thoroughly modern, Aldo's wines are hard to find but worth the search. His top cru—extremely expensive and even harder to find than the rest—is a blend of vineyards called Granbussia; Bussia Soprana is his trademark wine, produced only in good years. LOOK FOR Barolos from the vineyards Bussia Soprana, Vigna Caicala, and Vigna Colonnello.

GIACOMO CONTERNO ★★★★ $$$$
At least as difficult to find as the wines of Aldo Conterno (above), these godly nectars are complex due to longer-than-usual maceration. If you find one, buy it quickly—they'll sell out fast. LOOK FOR any Barolos, especially Monfortino, Monfortino Riserva, and Cascina Francia.

ANGELO GAJA ★★★★ $$$$
A legendary producer of Barbaresco, Gaja has received worldwide praise for pulling this wine out of the shadows. To that end, he pioneered the reduction of crop yields, the use of controlled fermentation temperatures, and the aging of wines in French barriques—and also created the first single-vineyard Barbarescos. Then, in 1988, he moved into Barolo and began making single-vineyard wines there as well. This year, though, the emphasis is back on Barbaresco Gaja—the wine produced by Angelo's father, grandfather, and great-grandfather. As a result, the Barolo estate wines Sperss and Conteisa and the Barbarescos Sorì Tildin, Sorì San Lorenzo, and Costa Russi will be labeled as Langhe Nebbiolo DOC from the 1996 vintage on. LOOK FOR the Barbarescos Sorì Tildin and Sorì Lorenzo and the Barolo Sperss.

ALBINO ROCCA ★★★★ $$$$
Rocca has a powerful yet velvety style, bringing the word *heaven* to mind. LOOK FOR Barbaresco Bric Ronchi.

MASSOLINO ★ ★ ★ ★ $$$-$$$$

Barolos produced by Massolino tend to be gentle on the tannin front and long on subtle flavor. LOOK FOR the licorice-and-baked-blackberry Margheria as well as the complex Parafada.

BARTOLO MASCARELLO ★ ★ ★ ★ $$-$$$$

A staunch traditionalist, Mascarello macerates (leaves grape skins in the juice) for a longer-than-currently-usual time and employs no new oak. And when you drink his wines, you'll wonder why anyone ever felt the need to invent those New World techniques anyway. If you've got the patience, waiting for one of these babies to age to perfection is definitely worth it. LOOK FOR Barolo—labeled simply that.

ROBERTO VOERZIO ★ ★ ★ ★ $$-$$$$

Voerzio's style is marked by the generous use of small new-oak barrels. The wines that result have great tannin and are full-bodied. LOOK FOR Barolos Cerequio and La Serra.

ALESSANDRO BRERO ★ ★ ★ ★ $$$

Brero may be a new producer, but he uses the best of Old World and New World techniques to make his amazing wines. Extremely low yields produce wines with highly concentrated, explosive flavors. You can't lose with Brero; even in notoriously bad years like '94, his wines were still extraordinary. And as he's still relatively unknown, the wines are fairly inexpensive. LOOK FOR anything you can find.

BRUNA GIACOSA ★ ★ ★ $$$$

Best described as an updated traditionalist, Giacosa macerates long, but not too long. He ages in large barrels, not the trendier barriques, but he does use new French oak, which definitely adds an oaky quality. The resulting wines are packed with yummy licorice and tar flavors. LOOK FOR Barolo from Villero and Falletto & Ricardo di Serralunga, as well as Barbarescos from Santo Stefano and Asili.

PAOLO SCAVINO ★ ★ ★ $$$$

A thoroughly modern producer in the best sense, Scavino uses new oak skillfully to produce excellent Barolos. LOOK FOR his basic Barolo as well as Cannubi and Bric del Fiasc.

CERETTO ★ ★ ★ $$$-$$$$

Ceretto believes that Barolos and Barbarescos should be drinkable right from the start, yet still be ageworthy. The '96 Barolos and Barbarescos are phenomenal—unusually flavor-packed and yummy—and should not be missed. LOOK FOR the Barolos Bricco Rocche and Prapo, and the Barbarescos Asili and Faset.

PRODUTTORI DI BARBARESCO ★ ★ ★ $$$-$$$$

Remarkable Barbarescos come out of this cooperative. LOOK FOR the single vineyards Asili and Rabajà.

FLAVIO RODDOLO ★ ★ ★ $$$

A new kid on the block, Roddolo is showing up some of the older guys with his glorious Barolos. Only small amounts have been coming into the United States, but they're worth seeking out. LOOK FOR the Barolo Bricco Appiani.

TENUTA CARRETTA ★ ★ ★ $-$$$

Carretta's long-lived wines are made with Old World techniques, and so they have intense aromas and flavors with little wood interference. LOOK FOR Barbaresco Cascina Bordino and Barolo Poderi Cannubi.

OTHER TOP-NOTCH PRODUCERS

Elio Altare *(Barolos Arborina and La Morra)*, Marchese di Barolo, Batasiolo, Giacomo Borgogno & Figli, Lodovico Borgogno, Ca'Bianca *(Barolo)*, Pio Cesare *(Barolo, Barolo Ornato, Barbaresco)*, Corino *(Barolos Vigna Giachini and Rocche)*, Cortese *(Barolo and Barbaresco)*, Luigi Einaudi, Silvio Grasso, Marchese di Gresy, Sorì Paitin, Parusso, Prunotto *(Barolos Bussia, Cannubi, and Ginestra; Barbarescos Montestefano and Rabajà)*, Renato Ratti *(Barolos Marcenasco and Rocche)*, Giuseppe Rinaldi *(Barolo Brunate)*, Roagna *(Barbaresco and Barolo)*, Bruno Rocca *(Barbaresco)*, Sandrone *(Barolo Cannubi Boschis)*, Seghesio *(Barolo La Villa)*, Pianpolvere Soprano, Vietti

TRADITIONAL VS. NEW-STYLE

In Barbaresco over two decades ago, Angelo Gaja, scion of one of Piedmont's most respected winemaking families, shocked the local establishment by using small, new-oak barrels rather than large, old-chestnut casks for aging. Soon, many vintners in Barbaresco and Barolo started catching up with modern methods and tastes, which demanded a fruitier wine that didn't need years of aging. Now there are plenty of new-style wines, made not only using new barrels but also limiting maceration to just a few days instead of up to several months. There are still staunch traditionalists who stick to the tried and true— getting all the tannin from the grape skins by long maceration and then giving the tannin plenty of time in neutral casks to calm down. There's room for both, but in truth, our memories of aged, traditional Barolos and Barbarescos are more bewitching than those of newer-style wines.

Other Nebbiolo-Based Wines A slew of other wines from Piedmont include the Nebbiolo grape. Like Pinot Noir, Nebbiolo is finicky, but it loves the soil in the Langhe hills near Alba. Look for wines labeled Nebbiolo d'Alba (neh-b'YOH-lo-DAHL-bah) and Nebbiolo delle Langhe, both of which are 100 percent Nebbiolo. Farther north, the simpler but still worthy Gattinara is usually about 85 percent Nebbiolo, and Ghemme (GHEM-meh) is usually about 65 to 85 percent Nebbiolo. Carema, in the northwest, produces some good, medium-bodied Nebbiolos.

at the table

Dishes that call for a red but not so full a one as Barolo or Barbaresco will go well with these wines. For instance, rabbit, chicken cooked in red wine, or even fish with a red-wine sauce will be better off for a glass of one of these Nebbiolos at its side.

bottom line Look here for bargain wines that resemble their bigger brothers. Prices are often in the mid-teens. When you see a low-priced Nebbiolo d'Alba or Nebbiolo delle Langhe from one of the excellent Barolo or Barbaresco producers listed on pages 103-105, snap it up.

recommended wines

1996 Parusso Bricco Rovello Rosso, Langhe 🍷 ★★★★ $$$
This is a knockout. It may seem tame at first, but there's wildness just below the surface. The wine blossoms into a very aromatic Rosso, with vivid fruit flavors. There are touches of tar and wet soil here, too, along with a full spicy cough-syrupy quality.

1998 G. Voerzio Serrapiu, Langhe Rosso 🍷 ★★★★ $$$
Barbera and Nebbiolo work well together here in an appealing, new-oaky wine. It's filled with blackberry tea and intense tobacco flavors, and it has a long finish with a bit of toast flavor.

1996 Paolo Scavino, Langhe 🍷 ★★★ $$$
Wow, what a color! This is a very full-bodied blend of Nebbiolo, Barbera, and Syrah. The nose is slow to come around—other than some paint thinner and a touch of carnation—but, once it starts to open up, it has beautiful black-cherry and raspberry flavors, as well as licorice and a dusting of cardamom. The wine is full-bodied.

1998 Bruna Giacosa, Nebbiolo Valmaggiore ★★ $$$
A great big baby Barolo with a remarkably lovely aroma of licorice, flavors of tar and tea, and lots of tannin.

1995 Nervi Vigneto Molsino, Gattinara ★★ $$$
A swell wine with layers of aromatics, a full velvety texture, good tannin, and lots of earthy, bittersweet chocolate and red-fruit flavors.

1996 Coppo Mondaccione, Piedmont ★★ $$
You won't often run into the grape called Freisa, so enjoy the encounter. This is an oak-aged wine with lots of gamey, intense, smoky and meaty aromas and a little peach fuzz on the tongue.

1996 Nino Negri La Tense Sassella, Valtellina Superiore ★★ $$
A wine with good Nebbiolo characteristics—mild leather aromas and fruit flavors that are beautifully balanced by acidity and tannin. The wine has a spicy oak-influenced finish.

Barbera & Dolcetto Once inexpensive entries, Barbera (bar-BEAR-ah) and Dolcetto (dohl-CHET-oh) are now experiencing price zoom. Many of the winemakers who work with the vibrantly acidic Barbera grape are reducing their yields to get more fruit flavor. And, of course, fewer grapes means higher-priced wine. The young Barbera is put into small new-oak barrels that impart both additional flavor and the tannin that is missing from this grape; presto chango, you have wines that are delicious and also ageworthy.

Dolcetto, literally *little sweet one*, has lots of cherry and plum flavor. It's dry with a slightly bitter finish and is generally drunk young and fruity, but some producers are making a more sophisticated style.

at the table
We find Barbera and Dolcetto are almost interchangeable when it comes to matching them with food. Barbera's acidity makes it one red wine that can take on cream sauce. Both shine with roast chicken, veal, pork, pizza, or pasta.

bottom line
Though there are still a few of these wines to be found under $10, there are more at $15, and some Barberas even ring up at $30. Look for both Barbera and Dolcetto on wine lists for around $40; they're excellent restaurant choices, since they go well with so many things.

what to buy BARBERA & DOLCETTO

1991	1992	1993	1994	1995
★★★	★★	★★★	★★	★★★★

1996	1997	1998
★★★★	★★★★	★★★

recommended wines

1997 Podera Rosset, Barbera 🍷   ★★★★ $$
A must for lovers of Barbera, either the new style or the old. Clear blackberry flavor and good acidity in a wonderfully complex wine. Another glass, please.

1997 Coppo Pomorosso, Barbera d'Alba 🍷   ★★★ $$$
In this wine, there's an initial flavor hit of new oak that's followed by lovely tastes of black cherry and black tea.

1998 Elio Altare, Dolcetto d'Alba 🍷   ★★★ $$
Another New World wine, but a lovely one. Raspberry and cherry aromas, a hint of pencil shavings and spice on the tongue, and plenty of tannin.

1998 Corino, Barbera d'Alba 🍷   ★★★ $$
A full-bodied wine with wild-fruit flavors and lots of smoky spice. Yummy.

1998 Bruno Giacosa, Barbera d'Alba 🍷   ★★★ $$
Full-bodied and old-fashioned, this Barbera offers caramel aroma and black-raspberry flavor. There's also black tea and a little heat from alcohol.

1997 Ca'Bianca, Barbera d'Asti 🍷   ★★ $$
Chock-full of currants and cloves, the wine sparkles in the mouth. It's complex for a little Barbera. A bit of mild bitterness.

1998 Cortese, Dolcetto d'Alba Trifolera 🍷   ★★ $$
This is serious stuff—sophisticated with more tar than fruit. We love it.

1998 Rocca Albino Vignalunga, Dolcetto d'Alba 🍷   ★★ $$
A full-bodied, serious Dolcetto with mellow black-cherry and smoky flavors that intensify the more the wine aerates in the glass.

1998 Silvio Grasso, Barbera d'Alba 🍷   ★★ $$
This has an invigorating blueberry flavor, a blueberry-tea finish, and typical Barbera tartness.

1998 Vietti Tre Vigne, Dolcetto d'Alba ♈ ★ ★ $$
A bit of pine on the nose, then moderate smoky-fruit and earth flavors.

1998 R. Voerzio Priavino, Dolcetto ♈ ★ ★ $$
Pure-tasting fruit is nicely concentrated in a wine with great acidity and a little bit of licorice.

1997 Coppo Camp du Rouss, Barbera d'Asti ♈ ★ ★ $
Here's a fine wine for the price. Medium-to-full-bodied with gentle acidity, a hint of tannin, and flavors of black cherry, leather, spicy plum, and a little bit of earthiness.

white wines of piedmont

The rumor that Gavi (from the Cortese grape) is Giorgio Armani's favorite wine pumped up its popularity. The fashionable, lime-like wine, however, actually deserves its fans. Roero Arneis (roh-AIR-oh ahr-NAY'Z) is another Piedmont original: peach-scented and somewhat nutty. New-style, oaky Chardonnays also thrive in the region. Sweet Piedmont Moscatos, with their fresh-blossom perfume, can be just spritzy or fully bubbly (see "Sparkling Wines of Italy," page 267).

at the table

Take a chance and try the citrusy Gavi with a garlicky pesto, or play it safe with seared scallops. Both Gavi and Arneis will complement shellfish, lean finfish, and uncomplicated chicken dishes.

bottom line These can't be considered amazing values for the money. Gavi starts at $13 and runs to $30. Roero Arneis follows a similar pattern.

recommended wines

1998 Almondo Arneis Vigne Sparse, Roero ♈ ★ ★ ★ ★ $$
A gorgeous, refreshing wine with a gentle ocean smell and *fraise du bois* flavor. Comforting.

1998 Almondo Arneis Bricco delle Ciliegie, Roero ★★★ $$
This is Almondo's barrique-aged wine. It seems almost gardenia scented, and it has gorgeous fruit flavors.

1998 Monteriolo Chardonnay, Piedmont ★★ $$$$
A very good California-style Chard, with some toasty oak in a medium-bodied package and a bit of lemon and hazelnut on the finish.

1998 Ca'Bianca, Gavi ★★ $$
Generous mandarin-orange and mineral aromas lead the way to a refreshing, medium-bodied wine. It has good intensity of flavor, and a hint of creaminess on the finish.

1998 Ceretto Arneis Blange, Roero ★★ $$
Interesting wine, with the aromas of nuts and canned fruit. On the palate, it's got a touch of almond, lemon, and licorice.

1998 Pio Cesare Arneis, Roero ★★ $$
Vinified to accent the mineral qualities. The wine has nice lemon and pistachio flavors on the refreshing finish.

1998 Deltetto Arneis, Roero ★★ $$
Pretty honeydew nose with a slight almondy overtone. Full-bodied and full-flavored, with hints of licorice and fennel, this is a wine that can easily take on spicy food.

1999 Bruno Giacosa Arneis, Roero ★★ $$
The amazing nose on this wine reminds us of sunflowers or daisies, with an underlying smell of grappa and lemon. A yummy wine.

1999 Vietti Arneis, Roero ★★ $$
Sure, there's a little vegetal quality on the nose, but the overall impression is of abundant lemon and honeysuckle.

tuscany

Americans find Tuscany enchanting. We vacation there in great numbers, and, at home, we look for Tuscan wines, especially Chianti, the region's most widely known, and Brunello di Montalcino, its most expensive.

grapes & styles

Sangiovese (san-joh-VAY-zeh), literally *blood of Jove*, is planted all over Italy, but the grape is most closely tied to Tuscany, where it has many clones. Brunello, Morellino, Prugnolo Gentile, Sangiovese Grosso, and Sangioveto are all variations of Sangiovese, each just slightly different from the other. The wines made from Sangiovese most typically have medium body, good acidity, and cherry, prune, and herb flavors. However, they can range from simple and pleasant to complex and powerful, with lots of charming stops in between.

chianti

The two most important of the seven wine zones of Chianti are, first and foremost, Chianti Classico, which lies between Florence and Sienna, and secondly Chianti Rufina, northeast of Florence. In the past, Chianti, though primarily Sangiovese, was a blend, including small percentages of traditional red and also white grapes. Today's requirements allow international favorites like Cabernet Sauvignon into the blend and also permit 100 percent Sangiovese Chiantis.

Although most Chianti is still aged in old wood, new-oak barrels are now popular, and the resulting pumped-up wines are tasting more like Brunellos (see page 114) all the time. These oak-aged Chiantis gain body and mellow vanilla flavor, but they also lose that go-with-everything, fresh- and dried-fruit taste that used to be a Chianti hallmark. Bottles that are labeled Riserva have been aged longer before release and are worthy of further cellar aging.

at the table

A simple Chianti with nice, lively tart-cherry flavor is great for red-colored casual food like pizza or pasta and a good choice for a simple snack of paper-thin prosciutto. Aged Chiantis, with their silky texture and complex flavors, can take on sharp cheeses like Pecorino (Tuscany's most important cheese), full-flavored poultry, and steak. Rabbit is another natural with one of these older Chiantis.

bottom line Why are prices going up? "We want more respect," said one Chianti producer whose prices doubled in the past year. Certainly, many of these wines have come a long way from the fiascos-in-straw-bottles of yore. It's hard to find a great Chianti for $15. More likely you'll be coughing up $25 or more.

what to buy CHIANTI

1991	1992	1993	1994	1995
★★★	★★	★★★	★★★	★★★★

1996	1997	1998
★★★	★★★★	★★★

recommended wines

1997 Collelungro Vigna Rovertom, Classico ♈   ★★★★ $$$$
This is one for the cellar. But if you don't have the patience to wait, its full body, relatively light acidity, and cherry and raspberry flavors make it appealing right now.

1997 Frescobaldi Chianti Montesodi, Rufina ♈   ★★★★ $$$$
A potent Chianti with gorgeous tannin, lively acidity, and a primo mix of earthy and fruity aromas and flavors.

1996 Corrina Riserva, Rufina ♈   ★★★★ $$
Here's a new favorite producer that, from the most basic Chianti all the way up, can do no wrong. This Riserva is a tannic big boy with the acidity and the fruit flavor to support it. Full black cherry, leather, a bit of anise, and clove. A killer Chianti.

1995 Fattoria di Petroio Riserva, Classico ♈   ★★★★ $$
We love this complex and tasty Chianti. The flavors of cherry in a tobacco-y, silty wine keep us coming back for another glass.

1998 Antinori Chianti Peppoli, Classico ♈   ★★★ $$
A smoky cherry bouquet finds a home in an especially full-bodied Chianti. The flavors are potent, with a good mix of fruit and woodsiness. Very satisfying.

1995 Carobbio Riserva, Classico ♈   ★★★ $$
No flash, no bells and whistles, just a straightforward, beautifully made Chianti. There's a scent of roses, a taste of tar, and refreshing acidity on its long finish.

1996 Casavecchia di Puiatti Il Sogno, Classico ♥ ★★★ $$

A great example of an unwooded Chianti, and it's a charmer. Aromas are of cherry and raspberry, and there's a touch of licorice flavor. The tannin is smooth and mellow.

1993 Casina di Cornia Chianti Riserva, Classico ♥ ★★★ $$

Tasting this organic wine is like taking a walk in a pine forest. Minty eucalyptus and anise meld with pine-toned fruit aromas. Lots of bitter cherry and chocolate flavors and a bit of mellow tannin.

1995 Melini Massovecchio Riserva, Classico ♥ ★★★ $$

New World Chianti—which means lots of new oak. It's an appealing wine, with aromas of blackberries and blueberries, mild tannin, and a finish that goes on and on.

1996 Castello di Fonterutoli Riserva, Chianti ♥ ★★ $$$

We'll admit, it's slightly over-oaked, but it's still good. This is a medium-to-full-bodied, complex, dry Chianti that offers aromas of black cherry and blackberry, along with a lick of chocolate and licorice.

1997 Monsanto Riserva, Classico ♥ ★★ $$$

At first, the wine is quite light and then, as it aerates, the red-grape aroma deepens into that of dried rose petals. On the palate, there are some herbs, fennel, and blueberry.

1997 Geografico, Classico ♥ ★★ $$

A tasty, silky wine with dried rose petals on the nose, a little bit of licorice flavor, and medium body.

1995 Loborel Riserva, Classico ♥ ★★ $$

A pleasant dried-cherry nose. On the palate, there's a slight pimento bitterness and some black pepper to liven things up.

1995 Messer Pietro di Teuzzo Riserva, Classico ♥ ★★ $$

Here's a big, bold wine with spice-box aromas and lovely flavors from oak. At the moment, it has a rough, tannic texture that needs some time to smooth out. The wine is still a bit too young.

1998 Badia di Coltibuono, Classico ♥ ★ $$

The dried-rose-petal aromas of this wine make it immediately appealing and promise a good, old-fashioned Chianti. In the mouth, though, it's just a simple, friendly wine. Enjoy it for what it is.

1997 Geografico Contessa di Radda, Classico ♥ ★ $$

A Chianti Classico that is piney and entirely pleasant—and as easy to drink as a glass of chocolate milk.

1995 Melini Vigneti La Selvanella Riserva, Classico ♥   ★ $$
A puff of smoke, a touch of spice, and a taste of yummy fruit make this a pleasant, though not terribly complex, wine that's almost too easy to drink.

1998 Cecchi, Classico ♥   ★ $
A satisfying Chianti packed with fennel and cherry, with no wood aging.

montalcino

Brunello, an early clone of Sangiovese going back at least to the 14th century, is the grape variety; and Montalcino is the hometown of Italy's youngest top-notch wine. Brunello di Montalcino (broo-NELL-o dee mon-tahl-t'CHEE-no) was first bottled in the 1880s, late for an Italian wine, a full-bodied, harshly tannic powerhouse that needed 20 years to mellow. In the 1970s, new methods and technology—and an appreciation of the changing international palate—led to fruitier, less tannic versions of Brunello di Montalcino. The new-style wines are ready to drink in half the time. All Brunellos must be aged for a minimum of two years, but many vintners keep their wines for the traditional three before release. Riservas are held longer.

Rosso di Montalcino (aka Baby Brunello) is made from the grapes of lesser or younger Brunello vines. In poor years, the entire crop may be deemed beneath Brunello and go into Rosso. The wines are generally lighter than Brunellos and need be kept only a year before release, which also helps keep their prices down.

at the table
Since Brunello di Montalcino is fuller than Chianti, it goes with food that has plenty of oomph. The wine is great with roasted meats of all kinds, including game such as venison or boar, and it's often savored with aged cheese, perhaps a truffled Pecorino. Try a Rosso with a wild bird like quail, duck, or pheasant.

bottom line Brunellos are expensive. Nothing under $30 is worth drinking, and even at $30 the pickings are slim for a knock-your-socks-off bottle. Riservas often kick off at $70. For a more reasonable alternative, look to the Rossos, which are better than ever and are easy to find at under $20 a bottle.

recommended wines

1995 Cerbaiona, Brunello di Montalcino ▼   ★ ★ ★ ★ $$$$
A very nice, flavorful Brunello. Inviting aroma of red berries, with intense follow-through on the palate, and refreshing acidity.

1995 Lisini, Brunello di Montalcino ▼   ★ ★ ★ ★ $$$
Lisini continues to produce beautiful wines, and this vintage is a fine example of gorgeous Brunello. If you like the sound of intense red and black fruit flavors with a substantial tar-like undercurrent, along with food-worthy acidity, this wine's for you.

1995 Castello Banfi, Brunello di Montalcino ▼   ★ ★ ★ $$$$
Dried cherries and roasted mixed nuts are cloaked with a strong blanket of oak in a medium-to-full-bodied wine of luscious complexity.

1995 Castiglion del Bosco, Brunello di Montalcino ▼   ★ ★ ★ $$$
More intense on the nose than on the palate, this wine is still very alluring. There are strong aromas of licorice and black cherry, with subtle follow-through in the flavor.

1995 La Poderina, Brunello di Montalcino ▼   ★ ★ ★ $$$
More full-bodied and robust than previous vintages, this wine is still beautifully balanced and complex. Intensely flavored dark stone fruits and spicy chocolate are enfolded in an impeccable velvet texture.

1998 Castiglion del Bosco, Rosso di Montalcino ▼   ★ ★ ★ $$
A Rosso that comes on strong, with intense aromas of charred beef and roasted chestnuts. The wine's rustic smells and flavors are mellowed by a light misting of vanilla.

1997 Castello Banfi, Rosso di Montalcino ▼   ★ ★ $$
Here's a Rosso di Montalcino that walks the middle line—an easy-drinking, straightforward wine with moderate black-cherry, tar, and earth flavors.

1995 Col d'Orcia, Brunello di Montalcino ▼   ★ $$$
The nose on this Brunello is very appealing: flowers, vanilla, and cherries. Then there's licorice—definitely more on the nose than on the tongue—and subtle tannin.

1995 Geografico, Brunello di Montalcino ▼   ★ $$$
So earthy is this Brunello di Montalcino, it's like holding a clump of sweet soil to the nose. The flavors here are mellow cherry and a little bit of licorice, in an almost old-fashioned wine that's a little oxidized and doesn't have a lot of oak to get in the way.

AN AMERICAN FAMILY IN TUSCANY

The winery Castello Banfi, considered by many to produce the best Brunello di Montalcino available, is American-owned. In 1978, the Marianis, an American family, bought property in Montalcino. They had already achieved success with their company, Banfi, the largest U.S. importer of Italian wine, and were looking to expand their sphere of influence. The Marianis brought with them a thorough understanding of New World tastes and modern technology and were soon in the forefront of developing contemporary Montalcinos. Cristina Mariani, the current proprietor of Castello Banfi, continues the family tradition, making wines that not only lead the way but outshine most, some say all, Tuscan wines.

other sangiovese-based wines

Chianti and Montalcino aren't the only areas that make satisfying wines from Sangiovese. Other zones often offer better values.

Carmignano The name of both the wine and the area where it's produced, Carmignano is far from a household word; hence good prices abound. The wines are more like Brunello than Chianti; they have lowish acidity and strong tannin. The Sangiovese is almost always blended with a small percentage of Cabernet Sauvignon.

Morellino di Scansano The village of Scansano lies in the up-and-coming area of Maremma, where high-powered producers are rapidly buying land. The local Sangiovese clone Morellino (*little cherry*) can produce gorgeous, fruity wines that are a tad less acidic than a typical Chianti and often represent great bargains.

Rosso and Vino Nobile di Montepulciano Montepulciano (mohn-teh-pool-t'SHA-no) is a grape that grows in Apulia and Abruzzi. In Tuscany, though, Montepulciano is a town that grows the Sangiovese clone Prugnolo. Montepulciano's Rosso requires only one year of aging before release and is relatively inexpensive, while the Vino Nobile gets two or three years and thus costs a bit more.

1993	1994	1995	1996	1997	1998
★★★	★★★	★★★★	★★★	★★★★	★★★

recommended wines

1997 Trerose Simposio, Vino Nobile di Montepulciano ♥ ★★★ $$$$
A full-bodied wine, with strong flavors of new oak, spice, and plum. It tastes good now, but could use a few years for the wood and fruit to meld fully.

1995 Cecchi, Vino Nobile di Montepulciano ♥ ★★★ $$$
Here's an intense nose that leaps out of the glass with aromas of tobacco, cherry, and clove. The wine is full-bodied and the flavor, acidity, and tannin are in beautiful balance.

1995 Dei, Riserva Vino Nobile di Montepulciano ♥ ★★★ $$$
Stick your nose in the glass, and what a whiff of perfume! It's intense aroma-therapy—wildflowers, smoke, and berries, along with some tar and just-ground coffee beans. Underneath all of that opulence is a wine with strong, yet silky tannin.

1997 Ambra Vigna di Santa Cristina, Carmignano ♥ ★★★ $$
A full-bodied wine with good tannin and acidity and sweet fruit flavors—almost too sweet. It needs some time to become balanced, but all the right elements are there.

1997 Erik Banti Aquilaia Rosso, Tuscany ♥ ★★★ $$
Though the wines from the forever-experimenting Mr. Banti have been some-what inconsistent, this one remains a perennial favorite. There's a bit of fresh coconut on the nose and a mix of bitter chocolate and sweet, concentrated cherry on the palate.

1998 Monte Antico Rosso, Vino Nobile di Montepulciano ♥ ★★★ $
After a few years off, this Monte Antico is back to being one of the best Baby Brunellos around. We've had wines eight times the price that we didn't like as much. An all-around lovely wine.

1999 Val delle Rose, Morellino di Scansano ♥ ★★★ $
Here's an organically made newcomer. It's a medium-bodied wine that has subtle scents of vanilla and licorice, a cherry core of flavor, and good acidity.

1995 Castello di Monsanto Fabrizio Bianchi Sangiovese, Tuscany 🍷 ★ ★ $$$

Dark-berry flavors are covered with a layer of wood, giving this tasty wine a velvety texture and lots of tannin.

1998 Villa di Capezzana, Carmignano 🍷 ★ ★ $$

The aromas in this Carmignano are of black currants and plums. There is also sufficient tannin and spice to hold your interest and keep the wine's finish going and going.

1998 Castello di Cacchiano Rosso, Vino Nobile di Montepulciano 🍷 ★ $

A good everyday table wine that has an inviting bouquet of baked blueberries (remember the aroma of Mom's blueberry pie?), subtle bitter-cherry and anise flavors, and especially gentle tannin.

1998 Cecchi Sangiovese, Tuscany 🍷 ★ $

This is a simple, medium-bodied wine, packed with refreshing fruit flavors. Perfect for weekday meals.

1998 Moris, Morellino di Scansano 🍷 ★ $

There's an ocean breeze on the nose—in the mouth, the texture is velvety smooth and the flavors are of tar and tea. This is a nice table wine.

1998 Rocca delle Macie, Morellino di Scansano 🍷 ★ $

Pleasing but simple. The wine is full of fruit, with pepper and allspice and a rough, dry finish.

super tuscans

In the early 1970s, a wine named Sassicaia rocked the wine world. Produced on the Sassicaia estate in the Bolgheri area near the Tuscan coast, this revolutionary wine was made with non-indigenous Cabernet Sauvignon grapes and aged in small oak barrels. Sassicaia broke the floodgates: Many, many wines made with new methods and unsanctioned grapes poured forth. Flouting the rules made these new-wave winemakers rich rather than poor as predicted. Even though their wines had no status in the official Italian wine system and are still labeled simply Vino da Tavola, they made a huge splash that sent what came to be called the Super Tuscans right to the top.

Now, every significant Italian wine house, including those in Chianti and Montalcino, makes its version of a Super Tuscan. It might be a Merlot, Cabernet Sauvignon, or Syrah single varietal or a blend of two or more of these French grapes. It might also be made from the local Sangiovese or Sangiovese blended with a French variety or varieties. The small oak barrels give Super Tuscans a spicy edge and lush velvety texture, along with a fair amount of body.

bottom line The top Tuscans, the Sassicaias of the world, are extremely difficult to find, but you can get much better deals anyway. Prices for the most in-demand wines start at $75, although some wine blends that are made in Super style can be as low as $15.

what to buy SUPER TUSCANS

1994	1995	1996	1997	1998
★★★	★★★	★★★	★★★★	★★★

recommended wines

1997 La Rampa Di Fugnano Bombereto ▼   ★★★★ $$
"Power and Beauty in Sangiovese" could be another name for this wine. There are explosive flavors of blackberry, cherry, and smoke complementing the wine's strong tannin.

1996 Antinori Toscana Solaia ▼   ★★★ $$$$
A full-bodied Cabernet-based wine that's young and potent. Full plum and Bing-cherry flavors are almost overwhelmed by oak at this point. Keep this one in the cellar for at least three more years to increase its charms.

1996 Belnero Pinot Noir ▼   ★★★ $$$
Subtle and delicious black-cherry aromas and flavors emerge from a dusty, foresty wine.

1996 Cabreo il Borgo Ruffino ▼   ★★★ $$$
Blending Sangiovese and Cabernet creates aromas of intense black cherry and blackberry, cloaked here in vanilla-scented new oak. There's a bit of clove on the palate and plenty of tannin to ensure that the wine will age beautifully. The 30 percent of Cabernet in the mix really adds to this wine, but will take a little time to mellow.

1995 Coltassala Castello di Volpaia ♥ ★ ★ ★ $$$
Ah, a straightforward Sangiovese, one that shows off the goodness of the Tuscan grape. A roasted-chestnut aroma followed by dried-cherry flavor.

1996 Frescobaldi Lamaione Merlot ♥ ★ ★ ★ $$$
From the beautiful vineyards at Castle Giacondo in Montalcino, this Merlot explodes with wood and plum aromas, and has a bit of fennel, tobacco, licorice, and cocoa. It's complex now and will be even better in a few years.

1996 Summus ♥ ★ ★ ★ $$$
A combination of Sangiovese, Syrah, and Cabernet. Medium-to-full-bodied, with lots of fruit and spice character and moderate acidity, oak, and tannin.

1996 Tavernelle ♥ ★ ★ ★ $$$
Put this one in the crowd-pleaser category: A nutmeg nose leads to a luscious wine with a core of black cherry.

1997 Corrina Vigna Spartigalla ♥ ★ ★ ★ $$
Straddling the line between the Old and New World, this wine starts with a blast of mineral and pencil shavings, then moves on to a toasty oakiness and a rush of black cherries, currants, and woodland berries. Tangy acidity.

1997 Mandrielle Merlot ♥ ★ ★ $$
There's candied plum on the nose, but the palate gives way to more serious tea, tar, and coffee.

1998 Col di Sasso ♥ ★ $
A successful low-priced Super Tuscan that's quite pleasant, with a subtle and appealing smoky cherry flavor.

TUSCAN SOUND BITE

By now all of Tuscany has more or less had to take the Super Tuscans to its heart. The latest proof comes from Cortona, the region's most recently approved wine area, complete with laws that must be obeyed if a bottle is to be labeled with the area's name. Beginning with the 1999 vintage, released this year, Cortona wines must have at least 85 percent of one of several approved grape varieties: Cabernet Sauvignon, Merlot, Pinot Noir, Sangiovese, and Syrah for reds; Chardonnay and Sauvignon Blanc for whites. Notice that only one of the seven varieties allowed is indigenous to Tuscany. The wines that ignored the laws have now been brought into the institutional fold.

white wines of tuscany

The Tuscans are not known for their whites, but they have rein-
vented the native Vernaccia di San Gimignano, changing it from
oxidized and old-fashioned into a pleasing, light-bodied wine.
Their Chardonnays are mostly clunkers; we haven't figured out a
good reason why they make Chards or why we should buy
them. Their Vin Santo, however, is another story; see "Dessert
Wines of Italy" (page 284) for information on this captivating wine.

recommended wines

1998 Pomino Bianco ♥   ★ ★ ★ $$
Made from a combination of Chardonnay and Pinot Bianco, this is a seductive
medium-weight wine with a lemony, nutty nose, delicious tart acidity, and a
kiwi and almond finish. It's a goodie.

1999 Colli di Lapio, Fiano di Avellino ♥   ★ ★ $$
This is a Fiano that gets right to the point with huge fruit flavors. Then there's a
little volcanic-like dust and a slight green-bean quality.

1999 Cecchi, Vernaccia di San Gimignano ♥   ★ ★ $
Autumn aromas, like falling leaves and ripe pears, combine with subtle flavors
of lemon and fennel pollen to make this a good wine and a great deal.

1998 La Rampa di Fignano, Vernacchia di San Gimignano-Alata ♥   ★ ★ $
Floral, fruity, and refreshing—this wine is everything you want a Vernacchia to
be. It's light-bodied and has strong lemony acidity. This is a great hot-weather
wine, with food or without.

1999 Libaio Chardonnay & Pinot Grigio ♥   ★ ★ $
You'll see more of this sort of blend coming out of Tuscany in the future. This
one has only 10 percent Pinot Grigio, but it's enough to calm down the fruitiness of the Chardonnay and make an earthier wine, one that's medium-bodied
with subtle floral, citrus, and fresh-hay aromas. The wine dances on the palate
and finishes with a dash of pepper. An excellent value.

1999 San Quirico, Vernaccia di San Gimignano ♥   ★ $
A spicy and refreshingly dry charmer that has zippy citrus tones as well as a
bit of almond.

veneto

Though much of Veneto's production goes into jug-quality Bardolino, Valpolicella, and Soave, there are more serious wines to be found here, too. The region's jewel, for instance, is Amarone della Valpolicella, a gorgeously full red. Not only is it Veneto's best wine, it's also one of Italy's greatest gifts to the wine-drinking world.

grapes & styles

Flavorful Corvina, acidic Molinara, and bland Rondinella are much-planted grapes in Veneto and are usually used together in red blends that range from cheap and cheerful to full and fascinating. Garganega is the white-wine grape of choice and the mainstay of Soave, which, again, ranges from thin, sour stuff to a desirable drink.

Winemakers in Veneto now grow the internationally popular Cabernet Sauvignon and Merlot. But the experimental Venetians that make use of these grapes don't begin to match Super Tuscans. The would-be pace-setting wines of Veneto are interesting at best and can be dreadful.

red wines of veneto

Bardolino, Valpolicella, and Amarone della Valpolicella all use Corvina, Molinara, and Rondinella as the primary grapes in their blends. However, this combination is where any similarity between the wines ends.

Bardolino is generally light-bodied and simple. Valpolicellas can be light and lackluster as well. But then there's Amarone della Valpolicella, a world-class wine with a dense texture and a complex aroma and flavor profile, including bitter chocolate, dried fruit, clove, and nutmeg. For this wine, the grapes dry on racks for varying periods of time until they become highly concentrated, sweet raisins. The juice is then made into a slightly off-dry wine. The recent trend is toward a shorter drying period, which means less intense wine and, sometimes, the use of new-oak barrels. Even these less traditional Amarones need at least five years of aging after bottling; drinking them immediately amounts to infanticide. In fact, the longer you can keep that corkscrew away from the bottle the better. We like Amarones best at about fifteen years old. Valpolicella Superiore, another excellent wine from the area, is often strengthened in body and flavor by a process called *ripasso*: Dried skins that are left over from Amarone production are used in making the wine, imparting an Amarone-like fullness.

white wines of veneto

The Garganega grape, along with smaller amounts of Trebbiano, Chardonnay, or Pinot Blanc, goes into Soave (s'WAH-veh), the main white wine of the region. Though they're often uninteresting, Soaves can be food-worthy and terrifically fragrant. Be on the lookout for those that are made entirely from Garganega. In addition to Soave, Veneto also makes quite a bit of the sparkler Prosecco (see "Sparkling Wines of Italy," page 267).

at the table

A simple Valpolicella will complement a vegetable stir-fry or lasagna, while Valpolicella Superiore can take on most beef dishes. Amarone della Valpolicella is an intense wine; choose it for food that can stand up to all that flavor, such as Moroccan-scented lamb. Venison is a good bet for Amarone, too. Then again, one of our favorite partners for both Valpolicella Superiore and Amarone is a strong-flavored, blue-veined cheese. Try Veneto white wines with rice dishes, especially the regional favorite *risi e bisi* (rice and peas).

bottom line Amarone della Valpolicella ranges between $30 and $65. While those wines are aging, drink Valpolicella Superiore—excellent ones can be found for between $15 and $30. Plain Valpolicellas are good weekday wines; you can buy them for around $10. A single-varietal Soave will carry a price tag of about $15.

recommended wines

1995 i Castei Amarone della Valpolicella Campo Casalin ♥ ★★★★ $$$$
Packed with some of the biggest black-cherry, plum, and raspberry flavors we've ever tasted. The oak and tannin ensure the espresso-like finish goes on for miles.

1995 Allegrini Amarone Recioto della Valpolicella ♥ ★★★ $$$$
An almost viscous wine with aromas of cardamom and subtle ginger, meaty flavors, and pronounced oak.

1995 Allegrini La Poja ♥ ★★★ $$$
This is 100 percent Corvina. Full-bodied, with eighteen months in oak, it's velvety and redolent of black cherries. Espresso on the finish.

1994 Le Ragose Amarone della Valpolicella ♥ ★★★ $$$
What good is an Amarone if it isn't intense? This one is, and what makes it interesting is that it's not just all fruit; there's espresso and stony minerals.

1998 Tenuta Sant'Antonio Garganega Monte Ceriani ♥ ★★★ $$
Well-made Garganega is one of our current darlings. An intense citrusy bouquet leads to grapefruit and star fruit with a touch of honey on the palate. Even though it's aged in oak for three months, it still has refreshing, clear flavors.

1997 Secco Bertani Valpolicella Valpantera ♥ ★★★ $
It starts with a jasmine-like floral aroma, but then develops into the perfect simple-food wine—not too complex, but interesting. Try it with a burger.

1995 Bertani Villa Novare Albion Cabernet ♥ ★★ $$$
Not much fruit in this wine. You have to love other aromas and flavors. There's musk, oak, barnyard, and cigar box.

1995 Sartori Amarone Corte Bra ♥ ★★ $$$
Lots of fennel and tar, with a meaty aroma that's almost like that of roast beef. Peppery tannin.

1999 Pieropan La Rocca Soave Classico ♥ ★★ $$
Theoretically, we like our Soave pure and fresh, with no wood contact. Even though it's aged in barriques, this one still manages to be refreshing. It has vanilla, apple-blossom, and mint aromas.

1997 Le Ragose Valpolicella Classico Superiore ♥ ★★ $$
Take a beautiful Amarone and imagine it without the acidity and tannin and you'll get the idea of this wine. It's got a healthy amount of fruit and coffee and intense perfume, but without Amarone's heft. Delicious.

1998 Tamellini Le Bine Soave Classico 🍷   ★ ★ $$
Strong earthy mineral content with an overlay of gentle pineapple and a touch of fennel.

1998 Tamellini Soave Classico Superiore 🍷   ★ ★ $$
Welcome to the revolution in the world of Soave. This one's light, lemony, tingly, and refreshing, with a bone-dry, almond-like finish.

1999 Anselmi Capitel Foscarino 🍷   ★ ★ $
The bananas and tropical fruits kind of bowl you over, but the wine is saved by zippy acidity.

1998 i Castei Valpollicella Classico 🍷   ★ ★ $
A subtle dusty aroma and simple cherry flavors with an appealing bitter finish. An easy quaffer.

1999 Cavalchina Bianco di Custoza 🍷   ★ ★ $
The wine is a blend of mostly Trebbiano and Garganega, and the aromas are powerfully fruity, with tart apple and lemon and touches of banana, hazelnut, and tarragon. The acidity is fierce—perfect for fish or goat cheese.

1995 Montresor Capitel della Crosara Amarone della Valpolicella 🍷   ★ $$$
Aromatic layers of marzipan, cocoa, and dried figs with total follow-through on the palate.

other italian wines

abruzzi

No reason to buy most of the whites from this Central Italian region, but do investigate the red wines, especially if you like lots of fruity flavor. Montepulciano d'Abruzzo is an excellent wine that represents terrific value especially in some of the Riserva versions that ring up at just $15.

recommended wines

1998 Barone Cornacchia, Montepulciano d'Abruzzo ♥   ★ ★ $
Not as glorious as it has been in vintages past, this is nonetheless a lovely wine, with sun-ripened raspberries on the nose and palate, along with a touch of cinnamon, and moderate tannin.

1997 Barone Cornacchia Poggio Varano, Montepulciano d'Abruzzo ♥   ★ ★ $
Whereas Montepulciano usually presents a punch of fruit power, this one is more on the smooth and subtle side. There are also earthy and grape-stem qualities to this wine, along with black raspberry and tar flavors, and just a touch of broiled mushrooms.

1998 Farnese Castello Veccho, Montepulciano d'Abruzzo ♥   ★ ★ $
Cherry flavor makes a big immediate impression in this Montepulciano d'Abruzzo, and the taste of toast is important, too. Then the finish is memorable and lingering.

1998 Maschiarelli, Montepulciano d'Abruzzo ♥   ★ $
This medium-bodied, slightly rustic Montepulciano unfailingly delivers—vintage in and vintage out—with plenty of roasted berries, a slight nutty edge, and fantastic acidity.

basilicata & calabria

Each of these southern Italian regions manages to produce one good wine. Aglianico del Vulture is a tannic red from Basilicata that, with age, mellows to a fine silkiness. Calabria's red Cirò (cheer-OH) comes on strong with a high percentage of alcohol; it has only a single major producer, Librandi.

recommended wines

1995 Librandi Gravello, Calabria ♥   ★ ★ ★ $$$
A full-bodied, tannic wine with black-cherry and smoke flavors and a welcome bitterness on the finish.

1995 Librandi Duca San Felice Riserva, Calabria ♥   ★★★ $$
The aromas are of wild herbs, but the flavor is fruity, with cherry and fig.

1995 D'Angelo Canneto, Basilicata ♥   ★★ $$
Medium-bodied and a little hot from high alcohol content. Spicy, especially with pepper, and licorice-y, with a slight taste of prune.

emilia-romagna

Situated northeast of Tuscany, Emilia-Romagna is Lambrusco country. In case you're not old enough to remember, Lambrusco is the fizzy red wine beloved by young Americans in the early '70s, a dubious honor. Now the region has attracted the attention of famed oenologist Riccard Cotarella, who is involved with the Terre del Cedro winery. Look for its Sangioveses, especially Avi and Zarricante.

latium

Central Italy's Latium (LAH-t'yum) may be considered an up-and-coming wine region, but it's sure not happening in a big way for us anytime soon. The main white wine here is Frascati—light, refreshing, and appealing, but not a big deal. Do look out for Castelli Romani, also a white from Marino.

recommended wines

**1999 Falesco Poggio dei Gelsi Est! Est!! Est!!!
di Montefiascone** ♥   ★★ $
This light-bodied wine smells like pear, honey, honeysuckle, and jasmine. The palate repeats the pear, along with some fennel and licorice. Pleasant.

1999 Campo Fattore di Dino Limiti Marino ♥   ★ $
A cocktail of Malvasia, Müller Thurgau, and Bombino Biano boosts the lackluster Trebbiano to make a powerfully fragrant light wine.

lombardy

Each of Lombardy's three main subregions has its own character. Franciacorta produces Italy's most illustrious sparkling wines. Oltrepò Pavese is becoming better known for its Barbara-based reds. Valtellina produces luscious Nebbiolo wines, which can be great values because they're not so well known as neighboring Piedmont's Nebbiolos, Barolo and Barbaresco (see page 102). Look for Lombardy Nebbiolos labeled with the area names Sassella, Inferno, and Grumello.

recommended wines

1998 Martilde Tilde Bonarda Oltrepò Pavese 🍷 ★★ $$
Martilde has a more expensive, oak-aged Bonarda, but we like this one, aged in stainless-steel and unfiltered. Black-cherry flavors balanced by brisk acidity.

1998 Martilde Tina Barbera 🍷 ★★ $$
A somewhat confusing blue-cheese nose leads to a tart, full-bodied wine with concentrated fruit flavors. It's a real conversation piece.

the marches

In central Italy on the Adriatic coast, the Marches (MAHR-kay) region is best known for its dry white Verdicchio, both fizzy and still. Also worth a try: the reds Rosso Piceno, made from Sangiovese and Montepulciano, and Rosso Conero, based on Montepulciano.

recommended wines

1997 Fattoria le Terrazze Sassi Neri Rosso Conero 🍷 ★★★ $$$
When first opened, this wine has very musky aromas and tastes off-balance due to fierce acidity. Then, after about half an hour, it all balances out and knits together with black-cherry, plum, mineral, cinnamon, and allspice flavors.

1999 Sartarelli Verdicchio dei Castelli di Jesi Classico 🍷   ★ ★ $

With its apple and mint aromas and ultra-ripe fruit flavors, this wine borders on the slightly sweet. It's good on its own as an aperitif, or with Thai food or a fruit soup.

1998 Bucci Verdicchio dei Castelli du Jesi 🍷   ★ $

There's a subtle smell of Golden Delicious apples sprinkled with lemon. Then, on the palate, a fair amount of alcohol and mouth-tingling acidity. This is one to chill really well and serve with seafood.

1998 Fazi-Battaglia Sangiovese 🍷   ★ $

A simple wine that, because of its smokiness and full fruit flavors, should be taken seriously.

1994 Saladini Pilastri Rosso Piceno Superiore 🍷   ★ $

The Sangiovese and Montepulciano combination gives off a nose of red-fruit jam, and allspice on the palate.

molise

A single exceptional producer named Luigi Di Majo has put tiny Molise (MOE-lee-zay), in southeastern Italy, on the wine map. Di Majo's wine-growing area is Biferno, from which come dry whites, fruity rosés, and full reds.

trentino-alto adige

The alpine region of Trentino-Alto Adige (tren-TEE-no AHL-to ah-DEE-jay) in northern Italy provides just the right conditions for Germanic grapes like Riesling and Müller-Thurgau—but the wines made from these, while starting to be good, are more aptly described as promises that have yet to be fulfilled. The wines are nevertheless worth a try, as is the region's top-quality Chardonnay. Lots of very fine sparkling wines come from Trentino-Alto Adige. Teroldego Rotaliano is the region's everyday red wine, smooth due to low tannin, and its best red is from Santa Maddalena.

recommended wines

1997 Maso Cantanghel Rosso di Pila
Cabernet Sauvignon, Trentino 🍷   ★ ★ ★ $ $ $

The first impression is of sweet jammy fruit; the second, complexity. We don't need to go much further, other than to say that this is the best example of Cabernet from Trentino we've ever had.

1998 Pojer Sandri Traminer, Trentino 🍷   ★ ★ ★ $ $

A potent Gewürztraminer nose, full of flowers and spice. Light-bodied with a bit of spritz on the tongue. The flavors are less intense than the aromas, but in this kind of wine, that's just the balance we expect. Honeysuckle finish.

1998 Zeni Teroldego Rotaliano, Trentino-Alto Adige 🍷   ★ ★ ★ $ $

No wood here to interfere with the explosive aromas and fruit flavors. There's plenty of red berry, along with candied violet, deepened with cocoa and enlivened by pepper.

1996 Pojer e Sandri Rosso Faye Atesino,
Trentino-Alto Adige 🍷   ★ ★ $ $ $

The aromas and flavors of this blend of Cabernet, Merlot, and Lagrein are of herbs, raspberries, and smoke, with edgy acidity. The wine blossoms next to food—pair it with pizza, or pasta with tomato sauce and Parmesan.

1998 Pojer e Sandri Müller Thurgau, Trentino 🍷   ★ ★ $ $

Could have fooled us—the nose makes us think this is grassy Sauvignon Blanc, not Müller Thurgau. Once in the mouth, the wine shows its light-bodied, re-freshing floral and citrus-y qualities, which lead to an appealing, mellow finish.

1999 Zemmer Chardonnay, Alto Adige 🍷   ★ ★ $

This beautifully made Chardonnay is laden with gentle notes of pineapple and stony minerals. It's a medium-bodied wine with jolting, seafood-worthy acidity.

umbria

Just east of Tuscany, Umbria is famed for the white wine Orvieto, a blend based on Trebbiano. Torgiano Riserva, made from Sangiovese and Canaiolo, is generally considered the best red wine of Umbria, but it can be hard to find. The red made in the Montefalco area from the local Sagrantino grape is a bit more available and is worth trying; it's one of our current favorites.

recommended wines

1996 Antonelli Sagrantino di Montefalco ★★★★ $$$
Intense aromatics of wild herbs and sweet fruit are balanced by the tannin here. The finish goes on for miles. Thanks to the strong tannin, this wine will improve for a number of years, though we adore it already.

1996 Caprai Montefalco Riserva ★★★ $$$
A new-style wine. The fruit flavors are somewhat hidden under oak at first, but following a swirl or two, the scents of gorgeous berries and cherries come forward in a full, satisfying wine.

1998 Castello della Sala Cervaro Chardonnay ★ $$$
Made in a fruity, oaky California Chardonnay style, this wine is packed with tropical fruit, butter, and toast, but a touch of a grape called Grechetto gives the wine herbs and earth. These characteristics and some zippy acidity make for a pretty fine Chardonnay.

1999 Cecchi Orvieto Classico ★ $
A simple wine with apple aromas and flavors. There's not a lot going on, but sometimes, when you don't want to think too much and want something to go down easy, simplicity is just the thing.

WHAT TO DRINK YOUNG

Many wines taste much more complex after a few years in the cellar, but not everything ages well. Some wines are made for drinking early, while in the bloom of youth:

Virtually all **Rosés**

Unwooded **Sauvignon Blancs**

Simple **Côtes-du-Rhônes**

Montepulciano d'Abruzzo

Inexpensive **Sangiovese-based** wines

Traditional **Barbera** (new styles have a longer life)

Traditional **Dolcetto** (new styles have a longer life)

Nonvintage **Champagne** and other sparkling wines

Beaujolais Nouveau (in the year it's bottled))

spain

For centuries, Spain, the world's third largest producer of wine, has been acclaimed primarily for Sherry—and Sherry is, of course, admirable (see page 144). But now Spain's powerfully flavored red wines have taken their rightful place in the international market. Whites, rosés, and sparkling Spanish wines are catching on as well. The most exciting activity is taking place in the northern half of the country, where Rioja (Spain's most famous wine district), Ribera del Duero, Navarra, Priorato, and Rías Baixas take star billing.

grapes & styles

The Tempranillo grape forms the base of Spain's best red wines, Rioja and Ribera del Duero. Fruity Garnacha is the most widely planted red grape; it ends up in some well-regarded rosés, in many inexpensive high-alcohol reds, and in some better blends. French grapes, such as Merlot and Cabernet Sauvignon, have been in the Ribera del Duero region for 150 years, and have been planted elsewhere as well in the last few decades. Some areas, like Penedès, are making Chardonnays or adding the grape to blends based on the traditional white grape Macabeo. Without a doubt, the most fashionable white wine in the country is the aromatic Albariño, made in the Rías Baixas region of Galicia.

Aging in wood has long been important in Spanish winemaking. For traditional winemakers, cask aging from two to eight years is not uncommon. Occasionally, producers keep reds in wooden casks for as long as twenty years. There are new winemakers, though, who want freedom from the laws that set minimum times for aging in wood; they want to experiment with shorter times without having their wines dumped into the less-desirable Vino Joven category (see "On the Label," right).

Featured Wine-Growing Regions

Rías Baixas · Rioja · Navarra · Somontano · Ribera del Duero · BARCELONA · Penedès · Duero River · Toro · Cariñena · Tarragona · Rueda · Priorato · MADRID · Utiel-Requena · La Mancha · Valencia · Guadiana River · Valencia · Valdepeñas · Montilla-Moriles · Málaga · Jerez

on the label

The most important concept here is the Spanish categorization system, which is applied in all regions, with only slight variations.

Vino Joven, the lowest category, needn't be aged in wood at all. It usually isn't, or has seen wood for only a short time. Literally *young wine*, it's released to the market a year after harvest.

Red **Crianza** wines must be aged for at least two years, and a minimum of six months of that time must be in oak. Rosés and whites must be at least two years old before release and see six months in oak.

The more distinguished red **Reservas**, usually made only in good years, have to age for three years, at least one in oak. White and rosé Reservas are aged at least two years, with a minimum of six months in oak.

The finest Spanish reds, **Gran Reservas**, are made only in exceptional vintages. They receive five years aging before release, at least two of which are in oak. Whites and rosés get four years total, with a minimum of six months in oak.

rioja

Look for complex spiciness more than fruitiness in classic Rioja (ree-oh-ha). The old-style wines have a spice-box beauty with waves of vanilla and cinnamon. Most traditional producers age their wines much longer than the minimum requirement (see "On the Label," page 133), thus earning Rioja its well-deserved reputation as one of the few ageworthy wines that's ready to drink upon release.

In response to critics who have said they don't like Rioja because they like wine, not wood, some avant garde wineries are making wines with less aging, less spiciness, and more fruit flavors. Though the primary grapes, Tempranillo and Garnacha, remain the same, Cabernet and Merlot may take the place of the traditional supporting grapes Graciano and Mazuelo. A few rebellious winemakers release their wines within two years of harvest. The newer wines often have less interesting flavors than the old, but some of them absolutely take your breath away.

The long-wooded white Riojas, with their scant fruitiness, sell poorly in the States, but the new-fashioned ones, with less aging in wood, are making an excellent impression on the American market. Macabeo (called Viura in Rioja) is overwhelmingly the grape of choice.

at the table

The pairing trick to remember is that the cinnamon and vanilla in traditional Riojas play well with exotic spices in food. We're crazy about red Crianza Rioja with mild Indian foods like tandoori dishes. Crianza is also a great everyday wine—with steaks, hamburgers, or bean-filled tortillas, for instance. Try a Reserva or Gran Reserva with paella or brandade, or with fish smothered in garlicky, nutty romesco sauce. A traditional white Rioja will complement shellfish beautifully. Modern-style white or rosé wines work well with poultry or fish.

the bottom line
In the last six years, prices for Riojas have almost doubled. Although there are red Crianzas and Reservas to be found for under $15, other Reservas go for $20 or more, and Gran Reservas run from $25 to $60. With many of the

best wines, the aging has been done for you (uncommon among reds), and so the prices are really quite fair. Rosés continue to come in at best-deal prices. Gorgeous ones exist at under $10, as do a bevy of whites.

what to buy RED RIOJA

Rioja winemakers can release their creations anywhere from right after minimum aging to around ten years later, so the current releases you'll see in stores may be from as far back as the late '80s.

1992	1993	1994	1995
★★	★★	★★★★	★★★★

1996	1997	1998
★★★	★★★	★★★

recommended red wines

1995 Bodegas Bretón Alba de Bretón Reserva ♟ ★★★ $$$$
A powerful wine—made from all Tempranillo grapes from vines about eighty years old and aged in lots of new oak for twenty-eight months. It has a refreshing burst of spiciness on the nose, a velvety texture, and fruitiness and acidity that finish long.

1996 Bodegas Bretón Dominio de Conté ♟ ★★★ $$$
This needs some time, but it's going to be a honey. At this point we can already taste the beginnings of great big raspberry flavor, with some rosemary sprigs tossed in. The wine has a long finish with just a hint of caramel.

1996 Bodegas Roda II Reserva ♟ ★★★ $$$
A delightful blend of New and Old World techniques smoothes this baby into the very-interesting-wine category. It's identifiably Rioja, with tomato-jam and spice-box aromas, but the wine also sports the velvety texture that comes from aging in new oak. Then come the full, seductive flavors of prunes and fresh plums, cedar, cocoa, and spices.

1989 Marqués de Villamagna Gran Reserva ♟ ★★★ $$$
The qualities of this wine provide a treat for both nose and mouth. Along with classic Old World Rioja spice aromas and a faint whiff of tobacco, this mid-weight wine has a load of cedar flavor and a nice taste of delicious stewed cherries.

1995 Barón de Oña Reserva ♥ ★★★ $$
This wine, excellent in its own right, is producer La Rioja Alta's concession to the new style of winemaking. It pleases with a silky texture and a taste of cherry.

1995 Marqués de Murrieta Ygay Reserva ♥ ★★★ $$
A seductive star-anise aroma leads into fig flavor. The wine is rather tannic; you'll find more flavors the longer it breathes.

1991 CUNE Viña Real Gran Reserva ♥ ★★ $$$
Though '91 wasn't the most stellar vintage, this wine succeeds with dark-red fruit flavors (especially plum), a touch of smoke, a good sprinkling of pepper, and medium tannin.

1991 Marqués de Arienzo Gran Reserva ♥ ★★ $$
A gentle Rioja—medium- to full-bodied, with slight oak, some complexity, and low acid and tannin. Hints of anise, caramel, coffee, black cherry, herbs, spices, and smoke in this easy-drinking wine.

1995 Baron de Ley Reserva ♥ ★★ $$
A beautiful, almost old-fashioned wine on the nose, with that classic spicy, oaky aroma. On the palate, however, it's a bit different—baked-plum taste and smooth-as-silk texture.

1996 Bodegas Bretón Loriñon Crianza ♥ ★★ $$
Very ripe sun-baked raspberry and a tad of typical tomato-jam aromas mark this tasty, mid-weight, velvety wine.

1995 La Rioja Alta Viña Alberdi Reserva ♥ ★★ $$
Perfect for lovers of delicious, old-fashioned Rioja. The wine offers a compelling meatiness (think lanolin and lamb) brightened by flavors of black currants and spiced coconut.

recommended white wines

1999 Bodegas Bretón Loriñon Blanco ♥ ★★ $$
This is all Macebeo (called Viura in Rioja), and it has a lovely peachiness with an edgy acidity that makes for a refreshing, palate-cleansing wine.

1994 La Rioja Alta Viña Ardanza Blanco Reserva ♥ ★★ $$
If you want to know what old-fashioned traditional white wines of Rioja taste like, do yourself a favor and check this one out. The color is almost like that of a golden cognac and, in a blind tasting, you might even take it for a Fino Sherry. You'll find the taste of coconut, with touches of cedar and cardamom.

1999 Marqués de Cáceres Blanco ♀ ★★ $

Light and lemony, this is an ideal choice for summer quaffing and also a great party wine.

1998 Conde de Valdemar Blanco Fermentado en Barrica ♀ ★ $$

This generally mid-weight wine is a little lighter-bodied than in years past. However, it still has its touch of Sauvignon Blanc-like grassiness and mouth-watering tropical fruit flavors, with the added value of coconut and vanilla on the nose and palate.

recommended rosé wines

1999 Marqués de Cáceres Rosado, Rioja ♀ ★★★ $

The crowd goes wild for this wine full of rose-petal aroma and strawberry flavor. With great acidity, it's very refreshing—perfect for poolside sipping. It's also ridiculously inexpensive.

1999 Marqués del Puerto Rosado, Rioja ♀ ★★ $

Tempranillo and Garnacha combine to make a full-bodied rosé with medium acidity. Subtle rose and cherry aromas follow through on the palate with the addition of a teensy bit of refreshing bitterness. The wine is great either with food or without.

BY ANY OTHER NAME

Grape varieties change names as they travel. The two most important Spanish red grapes and the single most important white are virtually the same whatever the moniker:

Garnacha	Grenache (France)
	Cannonau (Sardinia)
Tempranillo	Tinto Fino (Ribero del Duero)
	Tinto del Pais (Ribero del Duero)
	Tinto de la Rioja (Rioja)
	Tinto de Toro (Toro)
	Cencibel (La Mancha and Valdepeñas)
	Tinta Roriz (Portugal)
Macabeo	Viura (Rioja)
	Maccabéo (France)
	Maccabeu (France)

ribera del duero

The wines of Ribera del Duero (ree-BAIR-ah del doo-EH-ro) are among the best in Spain—and in some cases, notably those from Vega Sicilia, they're among the most expensive, too. Like Riojas, Ribera del Dueros are based on Tempranillo (called Tinto Fino or Tinto del Pais in this part of Spain), but are generally fuller in taste and body. The inclusion of the French varietals Cabernet Sauvignon, Malbec, and Merlot is commonplace; they've been in the region since the mid-nineteenth century. There's little rosé or white wine of note.

at the table

Roast lamb and whole roasted suckling pig are the traditional matches. The wine is also a no-brainer choice for hearty beef, but the most imaginative pairings are with earthy vegetables, like sautéed eggplant or pasta with olive oil, garlic, and mushrooms. On the other hand, a chunk of blue-veined Cabrales will also tame the tannin in this bold wine effectively.

the bottom line The prices of fashionable wines from areas with limited production, like Vega Sicilia, are inflated at $50 to $150 or more per bottle, but other areas provide quite a bit to choose from in the $15 to $25 range as well as the $30 to $40 range.

what to buy RIBERA DEL DUERO

1994	1995	1996	1997	1998	1999
★★★★	★★★★	★★★★	★★★	★★★	★★★

recommended wines

1996 Condado de Haza Alenza ♟ ★★★ $$$$
At first whiff and taste, this full-bodied wine registers with a "Wow!" It's got a tremendous concentration of black-fruit flavors, followed by hints of smoke, licorice, and coffee. But drinking it now is something of a waste. It's way too young. Better to hold off for at least a couple of years, when it will have become a great wine.

navarra & priorato spain

1997 Bodegas Mauro Tudela del Duero ♟   ★ ★ ★ $$$

Deliciously plummy on the nose. In the mouth, this medium-bodied wine echoes the aroma with lots of plum and adds a touch of blueberry and a tad of tea and tar.

1995 Protos Reserva ♟   ★ ★ ★ $$$

This wine hints at tomato paste both in the aroma and in the flavor. It has a subtle toastiness and an ever-so-slight hit of licorice on the finish, as well as healthy tannin.

1996 Protos Crianza ♟   ★ ★ $$$

The flavor of this wine is still restrained, but it hints at chocolate, mushrooms, allspice, vanilla, blackberry, and black pepper. Give it time.

1998 Briego Tinto Roble ♟   ★ ★ $$

Low on aromatics but high on compelling flavor, this wine becomes better with each taste. At first, there's black cherry, then coffee bean and a little walnut on the lingering finish. Time for another sip.

1995 Viña Mayor Reserva ♟   ★ $$

There's not that much going on here, but what is there is good enough to bring us back for more. At first whiff, there's a bit of meatiness, like braised beef. Once you get past that, it's fruit flavors all the way—mostly blackberry, with a hint of dark plum.

navarra & priorato

After Rioja and Ribera del Duero, the Navarra and Priorato (pree-oh-RAH-toe) areas are arguably the next two most dominant forces on today's Spanish wine scene.

Navarra is Rioja's nearest neighbor. It has traditionally been known for dry Garnacha-based rosés, but is now exporting a number of Tempranillo-based Rioja-style wines that are slightly lighter and are available at more moderate prices. The New World encroaches—older Garnacha vines are rapidly being replaced not only with Tempranillo, but with Cabernet Sauvignon and Merlot. Chardonnay has made the scene as well, but is usually blended with the familiar Spanish Macabeo.

Priorato is located in Catalonia, on the Spanish side of the Pyrenees. Dry, stony soil leads to low yields and, therefore, intense wines. Garnacha rules here, and Priorato is among the few places where truly fine wines are produced from this high-alcohol grape. The excitement of the moment comes from a group of boutique wineries working with blends of Garnacha and the French varieties Cabernet Sauvignon, Merlot, and Syrah.

at the table

A Navarra rosé is just the thing for tapas. The new reds from the area will meet their match in roast chicken or pork dishes. Since the Prioratos are high in alcohol, match their bite with steak au poivre, or anything made with a lot of black pepper.

the bottom line Look to Navarra as an excellent source of well-priced rosé and for stellar new-style wines at bargain prices starting in the vicinity of $10. Many of Priorato's stylish wines sport extravagant prices—$50 to $70—but there are bottles to be found for as little as $15.

recommended wines

1997 Clos Martinet, Priorato ♥   ★ ★ ★ ★ $$$$
Is it worth so much more than the Bru (directly below)? That's up to you. But this wine's undeniably a knockout. Imagine the Priorato Bru with more body, an added taste of darkest plum, and a sprinkling of nutmeg and clove. This is the stuff.

1997 Clos Martinet Bru, Priorato ♥   ★ ★ ★ ★ $$
An excellent blend of traditional grapes, this wine ends up with lots of tannin yet a silky texture. There's a taste of blueberries and a dry finish. Considering the prices usually charged by this extraordinary producer, this wine's a bargain.

1997 Celler Cecilio L'Espill, Priorato ♥   ★ ★ ★ $$$
Classic Spanish spice and pepper, with espresso coffee, sweet sun-baked fruit, and clove. It's a blend of Garnacha and Cabernet.

1998 Pasanau La Morera de Montsant, Priorato ♥   ★ ★ ★ $$$
Though a bit rough around the edges at first, the wine smoothes out with some aeration. Then the baked fruitiness from a large percentage of Garnacha grapes turns into a nice medium-bodied wine, with cherry flavor, some plum, and a touch of cinnamon and vanilla.

1998 Bodegas Guelbenzu Cascante, Navarra ♥ ★ ★ ★ $$

Cabernet Sauvignon characteristics come shining through here. The wine is full-bodied, spicy, and fruity, with a touch of dried rosemary and smoke.

1998 Bodegas Guelbenzu Evo, Navarra ♥ ★ ★ ★ $$

Here's a Navarra for the California wine lover. The aromas and tastes of very ripe blackberries and blueberries, smoke, toast, and tar combine in a full-bodied wine with an allspice-accented, ultra-long finish.

1997 Clos Mogador, Priorato ♥ ★ ★ $$$$

Bitter cherry, black plum, and a certain meatiness are enlivened by some anise and spicy pepper and clove. Powerful and exciting.

1995 Bodegas Piedemonte Cabernet Sauvignon Crianza, Navarra ♥ ★ ★ $$

Fourteen months in American oak and six months more in the bottle puts this wine in the California-style category. There's a little bell pepper and clove on the nose (almost Cabernet Franc-ish), but a sip shows lots of fruit flavor.

1999 Julián Chivite Gran Feudo Rosado, Navarra ♥ ★ $

A rosé that's on the earthy side, with a little Campari-ish bitterness in the finish, which makes it an excellent companion for food.

1999 Bodegas Nekeas Viura-Chardonnay Vega Sindoa, Navarra ♥ ★ $

A great little wine at a great little price. Pear and buttery oak make you think of a fruit tart with a filling that's got a hint of nutmeg and a silky texture.

other red wines of spain

The Penedès (peh-neh-DESS) area in Catalonia is certainly a spot to watch. The great producer Miguel Torres, trained in Burgundy, has had a big influence, and now others, too, blend the Tempranillo grape with French varietals for international success. Somontano, a region high up in the Pyrenees, also produces excellent wines made in this style.

the bottom line There's a range of interesting, fairly priced wines to be found from the Penedès and Somontano. Expect to pay from $12 to $35.

recommended wines

1996 Torres Gran Sangre de Toro, Penedès 🍷 ★ ★ ★ $$
People just love this wine. It's got gobs of bitter cherry, a bit of baked rhubarb, and lots of spicy pepper. Medium-bodied and great from the first to the last sip.

1996 Montesierra Crianza, Somontano 🍷 ★ ★ $$
If plum pudding were made into a wine, it would be this Moristel-Tempranillo blend. It's warm and mouth-filling, full of gaminess, mint, clove, and nutmeg.

1996 Bodegas Pirineos Señorío de Lazán Reserva, Somontano 🍷 ★ ★ $$
Mostly Tempranillo, this wine gets twelve months in French and American oak, plus eighteen months in the bottle before release. It's full-bodied with a tart black-cherry core and a little sage and rosemary. Lots of food-matching possibilities.

1996 Castillo Perelada Crianza, Costa Brava 🍷 ★ ★ $
A hot-weather, Mediterranean kind of wine with Port-like roasted aromas: roasted plums, roasted coffee, roasted wheat. They make for an interesting wine that's mellow in the mouth, but with enough acidity to take on spicy food.

1998 Bodegas Pirineos Moristel, Somontano 🍷 ★ $
Cedar, pine, and mint come together in a tannic and tangy wine that screams to be partnered with spicy food.

ACROSS THE STRAIT

Morocco, which is situated just across the narrow Strait of Gibraltar from Spain, makes what are considered to be the best wines in North Africa today. They're currently trendy—and inexpensive, too. Skip the whites and look for Moroccan reds from the Meknès-Fez district, specifically the two from Les Trois Domaines called Tarik and Chante Bled—and the general category of rosés called Vin Gris. All of the wines in the under-$10 group are great values. Try them with grilled spicy sausages or with tagines, or any exotically spiced stew.

other white wines of spain

The wine from the Rías Baixas (ree-ahs bah-EEX-sahs) area of Galicia shows the world that Spain really knows how to make a great people-pleasing white. Albariño (ahl-bah-REE-n'yoh) is the indigenous grape that makes this tart, aromatic, fairly full-bodied treasure. In the Duero valley, the Rueda zone produces refreshing, fruity, slightly nutty whites from the Verdejo grape. Chardonnays are popping up all over, and you don't have to look too hard to find a bargain Chard or two.

the bottom line Rías Baixas Albariños can be pricey, with top bottles hitting the mid-$20s. Merdejo and Chardonnay, on the other hand, can be quite a bargain, with tasty wines under $10.

recommended wines

1999 Lusco Albariño, Rías Baixas ♀   ★ ★ ★ $$
With all of its grapefruit, star-fruit, and lemon flavors, this wine's acidity is really pretty zippy. Yet the overall effect is not simple but subtle and thoroughly compelling. Sophisticated Albariño drinkers will like it.

1999 Torres Viña Esmeralda, Penedès ♀   ★ ★ ★ $
Mostly Muscat, with a tad of Gewürztraminer. There's fresh hay and gardenia, peach and jasmine, but also a squeeze of lemon that refreshes it all. Delightful.

1999 Bodegas Angel Rodríguez Martínsancho Verdejo, Rueda ♀   ★ ★ $
That big fat aroma of honeysuckle is pretty darn appealing. The fact that it carries through on the palate with a touch of gooseberry makes for an embarrassment of riches.

1999 Huguet de Can Feixes Blanc Seleccio, Penedès ♀   ★ $$
The yeastiness on the nose is reminiscent of beer, but the wine adds a gentle squirt of lemon aroma. On the palate a lovely pear taste comes through. A perfect hot-weather choice.

1999 Morgadío Albariño, Rías Baixas 🍷 ★ $$

A simple, straightforward Albariño with an attractive nose of honeysuckle, a slight taste of banana, and the acidity and fruit flavor in good balance.

1999 Bodegas INVIOSA ar de Barros Macabeo, Tierra de Barros 🍷 ★ $

It's full of peaches and apples, with a hint of banana and terrific acidity. All this wine needs is a piece of broiled fish with a squeeze of lemon as the perfect companion.

1998 Viña Mocen Verdejo Special Selection, Rueda 🍷 ★ $

Here's a tangy wine that has a little mandarin-orange flavor and a splash of pineapple.

SHERRY

When we think of Sherry, the dusty bottle of cooking Sherry languishing in Mom's cupboard may come to mind. Well, forget about that. The popularity of higher quality Sherries is on the rise, and Sherry is in fact one of the best values out there. A good one can go for as little as ten bucks, but even if a bottle's expensive, you're likely to be getting your money's worth.

Sherry is a nonvintage wine fortified with alcohol, and each company has its own formulas for aging and blending the different types so they remain consistent from year to year. There are essentially two main styles of Sherry, Fino and Oloroso, each with its respective sub-styles:

Fino Characteristic yeasty, floral, slightly nutty flavors are due to *flor*, an oxygen-repelling yeast that grows on the surface of the wine while it's maturing. The flor also keeps the Sherry light in both body and color. Fino does not have a long shelf life; drink up. LOOK FOR Pedro Domecq La Ina Very Pale Dry and Osborne Pale Dry.

Manzanilla Finos that were aged in the Sanlúcar de Barrameda area of Spain, where the climate is ideal for the growth of flor. Manzanilla (mahn-thah-NEE-yah) tastes fresh and almost salty. Again, you'll want to drink it soon after bottling. LOOK FOR Hidalgo La Gitana.

Amontillado Extremely complex, since it's aged both with flor and without. The effect of yeast and then oxygen produces an especially nutty flavor. Some Amontillados (ah-mon-tee-YAH-dohs) are sweetened to produce a medium-dry wine. LOOK FOR Pedro Domecq 51-1a Very Rare and Valdespino.

Pale Cream Finos that have been sweetened with grape-juice concentrate. LOOK FOR Croft Original and Garvey Bicentenary.

Oloroso Matured without flor, Olorosos are exposed to oxygen during the aging process and develop nut, smoke, and tobacco flavors along with a dark-amber color. Olorosos are usually sweet to very sweet, though some, considered to be excellent, are dry. LOOK FOR Emilio Lustau Don Nuño Dry .

Cream Oloroso sweetened with Pedro Ximénez and Moscatel wine. LOOK FOR Emilio Lustau Solara Reserva Rare and Osborne.

Palo Cortado The rarest Sherry of all. It's Oloroso that has by chance developed some flor. Dark, complex, intensely flavored, nutty wines with hints of yeast. LOOK FOR anything you can find.

portugal

The wines of Portugal have come a long way since the days of Mateus and Lancers, those soda-like hits of decades past. Now plenty of mighty tasty reds and whites have joined Portugal's always excellent Port and Madeira on wine-shop shelves. We predict Portugal will be the next hot source of well-priced wines. Try them and see what wonders money and modernization (largely a result of membership in the European Union) can perform.

grapes & styles

Portugal claims hundreds of grape varieties, most of them unrecognizable even to the Portuguese. But a few do have a shot at future fame: Touriga Nacional, which Port lovers will recognize as one of that wine's most important grapes; Tinta Roriz, Portugal's name for Tempranillo; and Baga, noted for producing some of the country's most important and full-flavored red wines. Most Portuguese wines are blends. The reds are generally aromatic, medium-bodied, and fruity. The only white grape of note is Alvarinho, which often forms the base of the slightly sparkly Vinho Verde. Winemakers sometimes use Alvarinho as a solo act, turning it, as well as others like Fernão Pires and Arinto, into varietal wines.

on the label

The wine categories in Portugal predate even the important French classification system. Here, however, the categories are almost meaningless in terms of quality. Two words you *will* want to pay attention to are *Reserva*, indicating a vintage wine that's passed the test of a tasting panel, and *Garrafeira* (gah-rah-FAIR-ah), which signifies a Reserva that's been aged two years in cask and one in bottle if red, six months in cask and six in bottle if white.

Map of Portugal showing featured wine-growing regions:

Vinho Verde, **Douro**, **Dão**, **Bairrada**, **Ribatejo**, **Bucelas**, Colares, Carcavelos, Arruda, Setúbal, **Alentejo** (Borba, Redondo, Reguengos, Vidigueira), Algarve

PORTO • — Douro River
• LISBON
Tagus River

Featured Wine-Growing Regions

red wines of portugal

Dão, Douro, Bairrada, Alentejo, and Ribatejo are among the main areas for reds, and they produce wine styles that stretch from light and quaffable to tannic, gamey, and ageworthy. The reds from Bairrada tend to need more age to mellow the tannin than those from other areas.

at the table

Portuguese red wines are great with hearty foods that have lots of flavor. They can be a wonderful complement to chicken cooked with tomatoes and garlic, to spicy sausage, or even to pizza with peppers and onions. Try the Reservas and Garrafeiras with game or lamb.

the bottom line Prices for Portuguese red wines are going up, but there's still a lot of quality at a low price point. Bypass the really cheapo table wines and explore the $8 to $20 range for good, food-friendly wines. There are some worth buying in the $20 to $50 range, too.

recommended wines

1997 Quinta do Mouro, Alentejo ♥ ★★★★ $$$
Here's a wine that's destined to become a cult classic—that is, if anyone ever starts to buy it. The combination of Periquita, Cabernet Sauvignon, and Tinta Roriz (Tempranillo) grapes produces a genuine blockbuster of a wine with a velvety texture.

1997 Evel Grande Escolha, Douro ♥ ★★★ $$$
The aromatics practically jump out of the glass. Lots of ripe cherries and roasted blackberries are blanketed in vanilla, while a hint of green bell pepper lurks beneath. It's almost too easy to drink.

1997 Luís Pato Quinta do Ribeirinho Primeira Escolha, Bairrada ♥ ★★★ $$$
The famed producer Luís Pato makes this excellent Bairrada primarily from the Baga grape. The wine is full-bodied, with charming cherry flavor and silky texture.

1995 J.P. Vinhos Tinto da Anfora, Alentejo ♥ ★★★ $
Delicate and intense at the same time, this Tinto is a lovely blend of traditional grapes, about a third of which are Periquita. It has piercing aromas—mostly of luscious cherry, with some baked raspberries—along with gentle tannin and a long spicy finish.

1997 Quinta dos Aciprestes, Douro ♥ ★★ $$
Wine grapes typically used in Port give this Douro an almost Bordeaux-like quality. The medium-bodied wine has a slight animal muskiness, balanced with lots of deep, dark plum.

1995 Casa Cadaval Trincadeira Preta, Ribatejo 🍷 ★★ $$
There's lots of cherry here that's beautifully balanced with exotic spices and a touch of cedar and sandalwood. A powerful wine.

1997 Porca de Murça Reserva, Douro 🍷 ★★ $$
A mix of traditional grapes comes together here with new oak. Though low in aroma, this is a really tasty wine with rhubarb tartness. It's full-bodied, and the tannin is subtle.

1997 Quinta de la Rosa, Douro 🍷 ★★ $$
Pruney and rosy in both aroma and taste, this wine is a yummy traditional blend of grapes.

1995 Quinta de São João Baptista Reserva, Tomar 🍷 ★★ $$
Mixed berries and apricot jam with a touch of cedar and clove make this wine a stand-out. It's perfect right now but can also be aged.

1997 Sogrape Reserva, Douro 🍷 ★★ $$
Like an Eastern European fruit soup, with a dash of nutmeg and a sueded tannic finish.

1994 Caves Dom Teodósio Cardeal Reserva, Dão 🍷 ★★ $
A medium-bodied wine with an intense Port-like aroma and a nutty taste. The nicely tannic finish has just a touch of caramelized sugar.

1997 Duque de Viseu, Dão 🍷 ★★ $
Old World grapes, New World style. Here's an intense fruit salad of a wine, with strong violet mustiness and a lingering cassis finish.

1996 Quinta de São João Baptista Periquita, Tomar 🍷 ★★ $
Check out this all-Perequita wine. It's medium-bodied, peppery, and smoky, with touches of dried apricot.

1990 J.P. Vinhos Palmela Garrafeira, Palmela 🍷 ★★ $
Love it or leave it, this is a wine that creates debate. It's full-bodied and a bit astringent, with flavors of espresso and cherry and an extreme tarriness. Pair it with a lamb shank and you'll be thrilled.

1996 Herdade de Santa Marta, Alentejo 🍷 ★ $
Perfect for easy drinking. Subtle, Port-like aromas are immediately apparent, and repeat on the palate along with smoke and a drop of cassis for a smooth, medium-weight wine.

1997 Jose Maria da Fonseca Periquita, Terras do Sado 🍷 ★ $
A perennial favorite, this wine only gets better each year. There's a wonderful melding of deep dried cherry with spice, earth, and smoke.

1997 Quinta de Pancas Cabernet Sauvignon, Estremadura 🍷   ★ $
Herbal flavors, an intense taste of green pepper, and a nice lift from acidity make this wine reminiscent of a mid-level Bordeaux.

1997 Vinha do Monte, Alentejo 🍷   ★ $
Mushroomy and tarry on the nose—then, in the mouth, a burst of fruit flavor. The wine may be a bit two-dimensional, but sometimes that's just fine for an inexpensive yet very pleasing table wine.

white wines of portugal

For years, Vinho Verde (VEEN-yoh VAIR-day) has been a favorite summer wine in the States, but we like it any time of year. The literal translation is *green wine*; in other words, it's meant to be drunk young. Usually a blend of various grapes like Alvarinho, Loureiro, and Trajadura (though sometimes it's made with Alvarinho grapes alone), Vinho Verde has a low alcohol content, a mineral edge, racy acidity, and a shot of carbon dioxide. Other aromatic white blends are coming out of the Bairrada and Bucelas areas. Unblended Alvarinhos and other white varietals tend to be fuller and more complex.

at the table
Don't anguish over pairing food with Portuguese white wine; it's really not that complicated. Vinho Verdes are great for aperitifs, picnics, and beachside clambakes. Because these wines are refreshingly acidic, they are especially good with fried shellfish, but they're also a fine match with almost any kind of fish. Try the varietal whites with fish, too, as well as with roast chicken or pork chops.

the bottom line
You can find excellent examples of Vinho Verde for under $10, as well as in the $10 to $20 range. Varietal whites in the $8 to $12 range are a bargain.

recommended wines

1999 Casa de Vila Verde, Vinho Verde ♥   ★ ★ ★ $

Complex aromas and flavors, with enamel-ripping acidity. First, a bit of baby powder on the nose, some green leaf, tangerine; a little rose on the tongue; and peach skin on the finish.

1999 Quintas de Melgaço Alvarinho, Vinho Verde ♥   ★ ★ $$

A peachy, gingery nose and powerful green-almond on the palate. A very snappy little wine.

1999 Portal do Fidalgo Alvarinho, Vinho Verde ♥   ★ ★ $$

Though it seems almost neutral at first, keep sipping. A touch of cedar and honeysuckle, along with a beautiful acidic edge, make it a winner.

Quinta da Aveleda Casal Garcia, Vinho Verde ♥   ★ ★ $

A refreshing wine with a slight spritz. It's bone dry, with a hint of lemon and star anise, which lingers on the finish.

Quinta da Aveleda Grinalda, Vinho Verde ♥   ★ ★ $

An appealing, subtle lemon nose followed by chalky, nutty, and beer-like—almost hoppy—flavors.

1998 Duque de Viseu, Dão ♥   ★ ★ $

Intense flowers and fruit meet in this bottle, most specifically honeysuckle and peaches.

1998 Evel Vinho Branco, Douro ♥   ★ ★ $

At first whiff, it smells like it might be a blend of Chenin Blanc and Sauvignon Blanc, but what you have here is really a combination of traditional Portuguese grapes. The result is a wine with a pear-like aroma and flavor and a bit of honey and licorice added to the taste. It is totally bone dry.

1998 Porca de Murça Reserva, Douro ♥   ★ ★ $

The wine may smell like a barrel-fermented white Bordeaux, but look at the label and you'll find that, lo and behold, it's 50 percent Sémillon and 50 percent traditional Portuguese grapes. The combination is delicious, full and mellow in the mouth, with a hint of cedar and a bit of peach sharpened by the perfect level of acidity.

1998 Quinta da Romeira Arinto, Bucelas ♥   ★ ★ $

The aromas here are of lemon peel and chalk, with a hint of cardamom; the wine is luscious and even creamy but with definite sharpness. Even the hot sun of Portugal can't bake out the acidity in the Arinto grape.

PORT

The most famous wine from Portugal is Port, the brandy-fortified wine that's remained in vogue since its invention in the seventeenth century. It is always a blend of different grape varieties, and usually a mix of vintages, too. Ignore such words as *fine old* and *rare* on the label; they're just window dressing. Pay attention, instead, to the style:

White Port Generally wood-aged for less than two years, these clear Ports made from white wine are usually medium-sweet and simple.

Ruby Port Made from red wine, Rubies are usually sold after three years of aging in wood. Inexpensive and uncomplicated, they taste of huckleberries and pepper.

Reserve or Vintage Character Port This designation indicates a more expensive Ruby Port that has been aged for four to six years and has a subtle flavor of nuts and caramel.

Late-Bottled Vintage Port Ruby Ports from single vintages of lesser quality than those earmarked for Vintage Ports (below). Late-Bottled Vintages are aged four to six years in casks before bottling and are ready to drink when you buy them.

Vintage Port Made from the best red grapes from the best vineyards in the best vintages, these Ports are the crème de la crème. They are rare, and, because they mature only two to three years in wooden casks, they need a lot of bottle aging. Topflight Vintage Ports can continue to improve for half a century.

Tawny Port The least expensive Tawny Ports are sort of a cheat; they're blends of White and Ruby Ports. The real thing is a Ruby that has been matured so long that its purple color has faded to brown. The flavors include prune, fig, roasted pecan, and dark caramel.

Tawny Port with an Indication of Age Excellent and expensive Tawny Ports sometimes bear these words on their labels. Because they are blends from various years, the "indication of age" is an average.

LOOK FOR Cockburn, Noval, and Calem & Filho.

MADEIRA

A bitter, almost burned tang and a yummy, nutty caramel flavor characterize Madeira. It's an alcohol-fortified wine that has spent a minimum of three months in heated casks or tanks so that the sugar in the wine caramelizes and the wine maderizes (oxidizes). The highest quality Madeiras spend longer periods of time at lower temperatures, usually heated by the sun. Lesser quality Madeiras spend shorter periods at hotter temperatures that are artificially created, usually with steam heat.

After maderizing, the aging process may continue for upwards of twenty years. On the label, you will find these indications of age:

Reserve At least five years old.

Special Reserve At least ten years old.

Extra Reserve More than fifteen years old.

The grape variety determines the style of the Madeira:

Sercial is made into the driest Madeira. Very rare and best after at least ten years of aging.

Verdelho makes medium-dry Madeira.

Bual, as rare as Sercial, becomes a medium-sweet Madeira. Despite its sweetness, the finish is dry rather than cloying.

Malmsey makes the sweetest Madeira of all, with luscious toffee and dried-fruit flavor. In Portugal, this grape is called Malvasia.

LOOK FOR Blandy's or Cossart.

greece

Before you dismiss Greece as the place where they add pine resin to wine (to make Retsina), treat yourself to some of the country's good stuff. Greece produces a spectrum of invigorating whites, spicy rosés, and full-bodied reds. Though not a large country, Greece has various climates that range all the way from island heat to mountain cool, and the variety in the types of wine reflects these dramatic differences.

grapes & styles

The island of Santorini, with its crushed volcanic-ash soil, produces a terrific white from the traditional Assyrtiko grape, which retains its apparently indestructible acidity in spite of the island's searing heat. Seek out this wine for its vibrant honeysuckle and citrus flavors.

The Pátras area of the Peloponnese region, southwest of Athens, produces white wines with apple and honey flavors, made from the Roditis grape. In the Mantinia area, pink-skinned Moscophilero is grown to make refreshing, spicy whites. The Neméa area of the Peloponnese makes reds based on the indigenous Agiorgitiko grape. On its own, the grape makes full-bodied, assertive, cherry-flavored wines, and it also takes well to blending with international varieties—especially Cabernet Sauvignon.

In the Macedonia region, the Náoussa area produces a full, heavy red from the Xynomavro grape. The name means *acid black*, which gives a clue to its qualities. The wines can be harsh when young, but age well. Also important in Macedonia is the Côtes de Meliton area now making reds, whites, and rosés that blend traditional and internationally popular grape varieties.

A bit further north is Thrace, another significant region for wine production. Here wines are made from a combination of Greek and French varieties.

Featured Wine-Growing Regions

Goumenissa
Drama
Thrace
Macedonia
Náoussa
Rapsani
Zitsa
Côtes de Meliton
Ankíalos
Aegean Sea
Pátras
ATHENS
Neméa
Mantinia
Ionian Sea
Peloponnese
Santorini
Mediterranean Sea
Archanes
Daphnes
Siteaia
Crete
Peza

on the label

Since the 1980s, the Greeks have followed a strict system of categories that was set up based on the French AOC structure:

VQPRD This stands for *Vin de Qualité Produit dans une Region Determinée*, or quality wine from a specific area. Various factors are controlled, such as the grape varieties allowed, the cultivation techniques, and the production methods. Among these wines, a blue tape strip over the cork means the wine is sweet. A red strip indicates a dry wine. The label on all VQPRD bottlings will proudly include the name of the area from which the wine comes. The term *Réserve* or *Grande Réserve* will be on the label of VQPRD wines that have received extended aging.

155

Vin de Pays Another term borrowed from France, the Vin de Pays designation is indicated on the label by the Greek word *Topikos*, which means "local." This is a good indication of what's inside the bottle—a typical local wine. Though the area is controlled, the grape varieties are not.

Vin de Table The only geographic regulation for Vin de Table is that it be from Greece. And any grape is fair game.

at the table

You don't have to eat Greek food with Greek wine, but it's not a bad idea. Assyrtiko is perfect for grilled fish. Its edgy acidity also lets it stand up to the strong flavors of *meze* like hummus (chickpea and sesame puree), tsatsiki (cucumbers, yogurt, and garlic), and taramasalata (creamy fish roe). Fruity Agiorgitiko is lovely with moussaka or lasagna. Try the earthy Xynomavro with smoked pork chops or roast leg of lamb.

the bottom line
Expect to pay $12 or less for excellent whites, and in the mid-teens for a nice spicy rosé. Good red table wines abound in the $16 to $23 range, while lovely, quality reds aren't much more.

recommended wines

1998 Koutsogiannis Melanas, Peloponnese ♥   ★★★ $$
Lots of fruit—plums and blueberries. The whole wine is anchored with a bit of tartness and tar and spicy black pepper. This organic wine is a crowd pleaser, and a super example of Agiorgitiko.

1994 Boutari Grande Reserva, Macedonia ♥   ★★ $$
It's nutty, mushroomy, and woodsy at first. Give this one some time in the glass and it will start to offer some red fruits, as if they were buried under a forest bed of pine needles.

1997 Domaine Mercouri Refosco, Peloponnese ♥   ★★ $$
Refosco is usually associated with Italy, which makes this version a bit of an oddity. It's of medium weight and has a definite aroma and taste of pine resin, though not nearly so pronounced as in Retsina. Suspend judgement and take another sip. The wine becomes very tasty—bursting with plums and berries, with a dash of pepper.

1998 Vassiliou Vineyards, Peloponnese ♚   ★★ $$

Here's a rosé that is serious enough to match with food. It has strawberry and raspberry notes, but it's no soda pop. This wine is a beauty matched with herbed lamb.

1999 Amethystos, Drama ♚   ★★ $

Made from sturdy Cabernet Sauvignon, this is a full-flavored, tannic wine with sun-baked raspberry and cherry flavors and a touch of gooseberry. Its tiny bit of mineral on the tongue makes it eminently food-worthy.

1999 Amethystos, Macedonia ♚   ★★ $

Assertive, grassy Sauvignon Blanc is tempered with a touch of flowery Sémillon and is bolstered by the acidic Assyrtiko grape. The result is a perky, flavorful wine.

1999 Antoniou, Santorini ♚   ★★ $

The wine's subtle aromas don't prepare you for its big, bold flavor. Lemon and mandarin orange come together with laser-beam acidity and a few intriguing hits of fennel.

1998 Boutari, Santorini ♚   ★★ $

A gorgeous, chalky, peach-scented wine, bone dry and searingly acidic. Perfect for a plate of garlicky Greek *meze*.

1999 Gaia Estate Thalassitis Assyrtiko, Santorini ♚   ★★ $

Along with the subtle aromas typical of the Assyrtiko grape, there are aromatics here of lemon and guava. The flavor is anything but subtle, with powerful lemon and orange as well as star fruit, and hopping acidity.

1998 Kouros, Peloponnese ♚   ★★ $

The Roditis grape gives this wine its apple-blossom flavor and a teensy suggestion of honey. On the finish, there's a touch of refreshing pine, along with vegetable and herb flavors, particularly fennel and tarragon. A lot of interest for a little money.

1999 Domaine Spiropoulos Mantinia, Peloponnese ♚   ★★ $

The finish is slightly metallic, but this organic wine, made from Moscophilero, is still a fascinating one. Full and spicy, it's packed with apple, peach, and pear, both on the nose and on the palate.

1998 G. Tsibidis & Co Monemvasvias Laloudis, Peloponnese ♚   ★★ $

A tremendously earthy Moschophilero-based wine with a lovely acidic edge and gooseberry flavor.

germany

Once internationally admired, German wines lost their stellar reputation, beginning in the 1960s, through a series of miscues that unleashed a rush of unsophisticated wines onto the world market. Still, the good houses continued to make some of the finest wines produced anywhere. Through the decades, until rather recently, Germans retained a taste for excellent off-dry to sweet wines; they just kept most of the good stuff in the country. Now, responding to new preferences at home for serious dry whites, German winemakers are providing a range of wines, from bone-dry to exquisitely lush and honeyed.

grapes & styles

There's little argument: If you're looking for the highest quality in German white wines, you need look no further than Riesling (reez-ling). Five other varieties make up most of the balance of German production: Silvaner, Müller-Thurgau (a hardy hybrid of Riesling and Silvaner), Kerner, Grauburgunder (Pinot Gris), and Weissburgunder (Pinot Blanc). German wines, which are generally low in alcohol and almost never aged in oak, have the happy facility of reflecting powerfully both the flavor of the grape and the particular characteristics of the region's growing conditions. The most exciting whites stand out for their aromatic abundance and their food-friendly balance between fruit flavors and tongue-tingling acidity.

German red wines account for little more than 20 percent of the country's production, and they can be difficult to find in the U.S. Interest in reds is growing in Germany, though, and exports may follow. The best are made from Spätburgunder (Pinot Noir) and range from fairly light to full-bodied.

Featured Wine-Growing Regions

- Mittelrhein
- Rheingau
- Rheinhessen
- Ahr
- Mosel-Saar-Ruwer
- FRANKFURT
- Nahe
- Franken
- Hessische Bergstrasse
- Pfalz
- Württemberg
- Baden
- HAMBURG
- BERLIN
- MUNICH

on the label

One glance at a German wine label can chill the heart of a novice, but all those pieces of information are important and are there to help the buyer choose knowledgeably—honest. Included are the producer's name, the vintage, the grape variety, the region, and usually the town and vineyard where the grapes were grown. (See label, next page.) Two words sometimes included are *trocken* (dry) and *halbtrocken* (literally, half dry).

In addition, the important German categorization is always on the label. German wine law establishes two broad types: Tafelwein and Qualitätswein. Tafelwein—*table wine*—is rarely found in the U.S., and that's no loss. Qualitätswein is subdivided into two categories: *Qualitätswein bestimmter Anbaugebiete* (usually called just Qualitätswein or QbA), which means quality wine from a particular

germany

region, and *Qualitätswein mit Prädikat* (QmP), quality wine with distinction. Producers of wines with the higher designation of QmP must meet the standards for QbA wines and, in addition, are forbidden to add sugar as an aid in the fermentation process.

Qualitätswein mit Prädikat is further subdivided into six Prädikat categories, based on the ripeness of the grapes, which is determined by their sugar level at harvest. The three sweetest—Beerenauslese, Trockenbeerenauslese, and Eiswein—are usually dessert wines (see "Dessert Wines of Germany," page 280).

Kabinett Wine made from grapes allowed to ripen to standard levels. These wines are the lightest-bodied; they're dry to medium dry, delicate in flavor, and low in alcohol.

Spätlese (sh'PAY't-lay-zuh) Wine made from grapes that have ripened fully ("spät" means *late*, "lese" means *harvest*) and therefore have full flavor. Spätleses can be dry to medium-dry but are usually sweeter than Kabinetts, as well as fuller-bodied.

Auslese (OUSE-lay-zuh) Wine made from selected clusters of overripe grapes chosen from the late harvest ("aus" means *from the*, "lese" means *harvest*). Ausleses are usually sweet but can be dry or off-dry.

Beerenauslese (BEAR-en-OUSE-lay-zuh) Literally, *selected grapes from the harvest*. The fruit for these wines is individually selected from late-harvested bunches. The carefully culled grapes are often affected by botrytis, the desirable mold called "noble rot." The wines' sweetness is beautifully balanced by high acidity.

160

Trockenbeerenauslese (TRAH-ken-BEAR-en-OUSE-lay-zuh) Not a dry (*trocken*) wine, but rather, wine made from dried grapes, in this case those that have been shriveled to raisins by botrytis. Heavenly nectar indeed.

Eiswein (ice-vine) Made from grapes that have been allowed to freeze on the vine. Very rare, very dear.

at the table

Originally intended to be enjoyed on their own (Germans traditionally drink beer with their food), these wines are perfection as aperitifs. You'll nearly always want to stick to dry or off-dry versions both before and during dinner—until dessert, that is. Fiery foods demand wines that deliver fruit flavor and palate-refreshing acidity, and German whites have loads of both. And, as they tend to be low in alcohol, they can be quaffed as often as spicy dishes require without leaving you face down in the chicken vindaloo. Their residual sweetness and sharp citric flavors are ideal with hard-to-match Asian and fusion cuisines, and even with vinegar-imbued dishes like salads dressed with vinaigrette. In fact, we turn to German wines whenever a dish presents pairing problems: smoked fish, foie gras (the exception when you might go for a sweet version), duck with fruit sauce, or the wild melee of sweet and savory flavors that makes up our traditional Thanksgiving meal. These wines are also dynamite with cream soups and with crab cakes.

mosel-saar-ruwer

The steep slate-soil slopes of the Mosel River hold the key to the incredible white wines produced in the region. Along the Mosel and its tributaries, the Saar and Ruwer, impossibly angled vineyards enhance what sun is available in these northern climes, and the mineral flavor from the soil adds a flinty dimension to the heady fruit and flower aromas and flavors. The best estates in the region are dedicated to Riesling and produce wine of great distinction, held in the traditional tall, slim, green bottle called the Mosel flute.

the bottom line Since you will find no better Rieslings anywhere on earth, the fact that good Qualitätswein, Kabinett, and Spätlese can be had for $10 to $25 is remarkable. You may have to pay more, of course, but the wine will most likely be worth it. Auslese will set you back at least $25 a bottle.

what to buy MOSEL-SAAR-RUWER

1995	1996	1997	1998	1999
★★★★	★★★★	★★★	★★★	★★★★

recommended producers & their wines

FRITZ HAAG, MIDDLE MOSEL ★★★★ $$-$$$$
Concentrated flavors of ripe peaches and apples with citrusy acid mark owner Wilhelm Haag's work. The wines are considered best with at least ten years of age. LOOK FOR wines from the Brauneberger Juffer and Brauneberger Juffer-Sonnenuhr vineyards.

EGON MÜLLER, SAAR ★★★★ $$-$$$$
The Beerenauslese, Trockenbeerenauslese, and Eiswein here are unparalleled and set the standard for powerful German sweet wines. Müller still vinifies his wines in wood, which is rather old-fashioned, but you can't argue with these results. LOOK FOR anything you can find.

C. VON SCHUBERT MAXIMIN-GRÜNHÄUS, RUWER ★★★★ $$-$$$$
The estate with the longest reputation for excellence in the Ruwer brings intense flavors to dry Rieslings, along with strong acidity and aromatics, especially in spicy late-harvest wines. LOOK FOR anything you can find.

DR. LOOSEN, MIDDLE MOSEL ★★★★ $-$$$$
Complex wines with peach, apricot, and grapefruit flavors, good acidity, and sometimes spicy minerality. The Rieslings are some of the best in the world. LOOK FOR anything you can find.

JOH. JOS. CHRISTOFFEL, MIDDLE MOSEL ★★★ $$-$$$$
Christoffel produces wines with apple and floral aromatics and adds minerality to the list when it comes to flavors. The balance of sweetness and acidity is perfect in these wines. LOOK FOR Treppchen of Erden and the more aromatic Würzgarten of Ürzig.

GRANS-FASSIAN, MIDDLE MOSEL ★ ★ ★ $$-$$$$

An underrated producer of wines with lush fragrance, intense pineapple and orange notes, and startling acidity. Grans-Fassian uses barriques for certain wines, which is not at all typical in Germany. LOOK FOR Trittenheimer Apotheke and Leiwener Laurentiuslay.

VON HÖVEL, SAAR ★ ★ ★ $$-$$$$

The Saar is known for its zingy wines, and von Hövel's are no exception. They're light-bodied, consistently high-quality wines with green-apple notes. The Beerenausleses and Eisweins are particularly luscious. LOOK FOR wines from the Oberemmel vineyard of Hütte.

KARTHÄUSERHOF, RUWER ★ ★ ★ $$-$$$$

Exceptional late-harvest powerhouses as well as bracing Kabinetts and Spätleses. The wines are minerally, steely, and full of fruit. LOOK FOR anything you can find, especially Eitelsbacher Karthäuserhofberg.

SCHLOSS LIESER, MIDDLE MOSEL ★ ★ ★ $$-$$$$

Revived by Wilhelm Haag's son Thomas, this house is known for crisply acidic wines with refined flavors as well as full-bodied creaminess. LOOK FOR the Niederberg-Helden and the excellent dry Auslese.

J.J. PRÜM, MIDDLE MOSEL ★ ★ ★ $$-$$$$

Wonderful wines, including Ausleses redolent of apricot, honey, and lime peel that last for years. The wines do need aging, though—they're not as good young. LOOK FOR Wehlener Sonnenuhr and Graacher Himmelreich.

S.A. PRÜM, MIDDLE MOSEL ★ ★ ★ $$-$$$$

Using grapes from some of the same vineyard areas as J.J. Prüm (above), S.A. Prüm shows promise with carefully made, long-cask-aged wines. LOOK FOR Kabinetts and anything from the Wehlener Sonnenuhr and Graacher Himmelreich vineyards.

ST. URBANSHOF, SAAR ★ ★ ★ $$-$$$$

Wines with elderflower and gravel aromas and flavors of wild yeast and mountain herbs, with some spiciness. LOOK FOR Ockfener Bockstein.

WILLI SCHAEFER, MIDDLE MOSEL ★ ★ ★ $$-$$$$

Lively, lovely wines, with a lime zip and slate interest. They're long-lived wines, too, good for more than twenty years. LOOK FOR Wehlener Sonnenuhr and Graacher Domprobst.

SELBACH-OSTER, MIDDLE MOSEL ★ ★ ★ $$-$$$$

Explosive peach and pear nose, with honeysuckle, slight petrol, and slate notes characteristic of evolved Rieslings. Most of the wines are aged in old-oak casks. LOOK FOR wines from the Bernkastel Badstube and Zeltinger Sonnenuhr.

ZILLIKEN, SAAR   ★ ★ ★ $$-$$$$
A quiet producer of penetrating dry wines, with some concentrated and richly rewarding sweeter wines. LOOK FOR Saarburger Rausch.

OTHER TOP-NOTCH PRODUCERS
MOSEL Wegeler Erben *(Bernkasteler Doctor)*, Reinhold Haart *(Piesporter Goldtröpfchen)*, Heribert Kerpen *(Wehlener Sonnenuhr)*, von Kesselstatt *(Scharzhofberger, Piesporter Goldtröpfchen)*, Merkelbach *(Ürziger Würz-garten)*, Dr. Pauly-Bergweiler *(Bernkasteler Lay and Bernkasteler Badstube)*, Dr. H. Thanisch *(Bernkasteler Doctor and Bernkasteler Lay)*, Dr. F. Weins-Prüm *(Wehlener Sonnenuhr and Graacher Himmelreich)*
SAAR von Othegraven *(Kanzemer Altenberg)*, Schloss Saarstein *(Serriger Schloss Saarsteiner)*
RUWER Karlsmühle *(Lorenzhöfer, Kaseler Nies'chen)*, von Kesselstatt *(Kaseler Nies'chen)*

THE RIESLING TREND

Wine trends tend to start in restaurants and work their way into the mainstream. For six years now, sommeliers have been promoting food-friendly Riesling as the new Chardonnay, an imminently sensible idea since oaky, high-alcohol Chardonnay has ruined many a dish. It's been slow going, but the restaurant experts are having an effect: Sales are up. Luscious German Rieslings are increasingly available, and we can also expect to see more of this varietal from Alsace, Austria, New York State, the Pacific Northwest, Canada, Australia, and New Zealand.

pfalz

Warmth, sufficient rain, and a diversity of soil—sandstone, chalky loam, limestone, clay, and slate—result in a plentiful harvest and a variety of Pfalz wines. They range from the tropical-fruit flavors and lively acidity of the northern Pfalz Rieslings to the spicy, full-bodied wines from the southern part of the region. Pfalz producers have had good success with Scheurebe (SHOY-reh-buh), a Silvaner and Riesling cross, and with Gewürztraminer, making assertive whites worth watching. Spätburgunder makes up only a tiny fraction of the Pfalz production but is the best red in the region.

the bottom line As with most German regions, bargains abound. Shoppers should have no difficulty finding good $12 to $25 bottles.

what to buy PFALZ

1995	1996	1997	1998	1999
★	★★★★	★★★	★★★	★★★★

recommended producers & their wines

BASSERMANN-JORDAN ★★★★ $$-$$$$
Spicy and long-finishing Rieslings with lots of grapefruit, lime, and apricot notes and electric acidity. LOOK FOR a variety of vineyard wines from the villages of Deidesheim and Forst.

BÜRKLIN-WOLF ★★★★ $$-$$$$
Wines with vibrant citrus flavors and great individuality in all price ranges. Bürklin-Wolf is a leading light in modern dry Rieslings. LOOK FOR anything you can find, especially Forster Kirchenstück and Ruppertsberger Gaisböhl.

MÜLLER-CATOIR ★★★★ $$-$$$$
Intense and sought-after wines with concentrated apricot and peach flavors and zingy acidity. LOOK FOR anything you can find.

KURT DARTING ★★★★ $-$$$$
Pretty floral aromas and luscious peach and citrus flavors, along with the requisite excellent acidity. LOOK FOR anything you can find from Dürkheimer and Ungsteiner Herrenberg.

REICHSRAT VON BUHL ★★★ $$-$$$$
Fruit and flower aromas matched with refined sweetness. LOOK FOR anything from Forster, especially sweet wines.

LINGENFELDER ★★★ $-$$$$
Well-balanced Rieslings redolent of spice and citrus peel, and unusually winning Scheurebes. LOOK FOR anything you can find.

rheingau

Eighty percent of the Rheingau's vineyards are planted with the noble Riesling grape, and while the region's wines may not be so thrilling as the Mosel's, many consider this area to be the historical home of Germany's international wine reputation. In terms of geography, it's especially well-situated for yielding superior Rieslings: The vineyard slopes all face the southern sunshine, which enhances ripening, and the Taunus Mountains are on hand to protect the grapes from winds from the north. Spicy aromas, full body, racy acidity, and ripe flavors typify Rheingau's best wines, and while many old estates rest on their 19th century laurels, aggressive winemakers are pushing to rebuild this famous region's slightly tattered image.

the bottom line The excellent, long-held reputation of Rheingau wines dies hard, meaning there are fewer bargains than from other German regions. Traditional houses keep their prices high, and the wines from the best producers are much sought after. Expect to pay $15 to $25 for Kabinetts and $30 and up for Spätleses.

what to buy RHEINGAU

1995	1996	1997	1998	1999
★★	★★★	★★★	★★★	★★★★

recommended producers & their wines

GEORG BREUER ★★★★ $$-$$$$
Intense and full-bodied with an enticing mineral/petrol quality, the wines of Georg Breuer could seemingly last forever. LOOK FOR anything you can find.

ROBERT WEIL ★★★★ $$-$$$$
A true Rheingau star, estate director Wilhelm Weil produces extraordinarily full-flavored and complex wines from the Kiedricher Gräfenberg. LOOK FOR anything you can find, especially sweet wines.

JOHANNISHOF
★ ★ ★ $$-$$$$

Earthy, spicy, and sophisticated Rieslings from one of the best Rheingauers. LOOK FOR Johannisbergers and Rüdesheimers.

FRANZ KÜNSTLER
★ ★ ★ $$-$$$$

Full-flavored, spice-laden wines with smoky, slatey nuances. LOOK FOR anything from Hochheimer.

SCHLOSS REINHARTSHAUSEN
★ ★ ★ $$-$$$$

A major financial investment is yielding great results for this resurgent producer. The sweet wines show special promise. LOOK FOR Hattenheimer Wisselbrunnen, especially Ausleses.

SCHLOSS SCHÖNBORN
★ ★ ★ $$-$$$$

A producer of Rieslings from a variety of vineyards, Schönborn is having particular success with smooth and delicious Kabinetts and Spätleses. LOOK FOR anything you can find.

rheinhessen

The flat plains of Rheinhessen are home to the original Liebfraumilch (a blend containing 70 percent or more of Kerner, Riesling, Silvaner, and Müller-Thurgau) plus a hodgepodge of other varietals. Most wines produced here are considered mild in flavor compared to those from other German regions, and simple rather than complex. However, the best winemakers frequently manage to make world-class wines, and some of the young producers are diligently developing new, often dry, Rheinhessens. The Rieslings from the Rheinterrasse, right along the river from just north of Worms to Mainz, can be as good as those of the Rheingau. The wines from this stretch of the Rhine have their own unique combination of peach and grapefruit flavor, stirring acidity, and great aging capability.

the bottom line Even the better winemakers turn out Kabinetts at less than $15 and Spätleses at $20 and under. Rheinhessens don't generally command much shelf space in the U.S., but if you can find them, they're great values.

what to buy RHEINHESSEN

1995	1996	1997	1998	1999
★★	★★★★	★★★★	★★★	★★★★

recommended producers & their wines

GUNDERLOCH ★★★★ $$-$$$
Wines bursting with floral aromas and concentrated peach and grapefruit flavors, as well as the mineral taste from one of the region's best sites, the red slate Nackenheimer Rothenberg. LOOK FOR anything you can find.

FREIHERR HEYL ZU HERRNSHEIM ★★★ $$-$$$$
Another red-slate producer, Herrnsheim delivers earthy and subtle wines with a pungent spiciness and a creamy texture. LOOK FOR any Niersteiners.

J. U. H. A. STRUB ★★ $-$$$$
The wines of this producer are underrated. They have good acidity and steely minerality. Zesty when young, they mellow with age. LOOK FOR Niersteiner Hipping and Niersteiner Paterberg.

ST. ANTONY ★★ $$$
A respected producer of dry Rieslings with berry and pear flavors. LOOK FOR Niersteiner Oelberg and Niersteiner Pettenthal.

other regions

The vast and sunny Baden region at the Black Forest's edge is the warmest growing zone in Germany and produces some of the better Spätburgunders as well as aromatic, spicy whites. The steep, terraced vineyards of the chilly Mittelrhein bring forth great bargain Rieslings of startlingly crisp acidity. A range of soil types in the Nahe (NAH-huh) valley produces Rieslings with a delicate spiciness, while the earthy and full-bodied Franken wines are considered by many to be Germany's best Silvaner-based whites.

recommended producers & their wines

BADEN

Dr. Heger *(Ihringer Winklerberg vineyard)*; Andreas Laible *(Durbacher Plauel-rain vineyard)*

MITTELRHEIN

Toni Jost *(Bacharacher Hahn vineyard)*; J. Ratzenberger *(Steeger St. Jost and Bacharacher Wolfshölle vineyards)*; Weingart *(Bopparder Hamm Feuerlay)*

NAHE

Crusius *(Traiser Bastei and Schlossböckelheimer Felsenberg)*; Diel *(Dorsheimer Pittermännchen and Goldloch)*; Dönnhoff *(Giederhäuser Herrmannshöhle and Oberhäuser Brücke vineyards)*; Kruger-Rumpf *(Münsterer Dautenpflänzer)*; Prinz zu Salm *(Schloss Wallhausen Kabinett)*; Schonleber *(Monziger Frühling-splätzchen)*

FRANKEN

Burgerspital *(Würzburger Stein)*; Fürstlich Castell'sches Domänenamt *(Casteller Bausch and Kugelspiel)*; Juliusspital *(Würzburger Stein and Würzburger Innere Leiste vineyards)*

austria & switzerland

Austria may share a border with Switzerland, as well as a similar climate and an emphasis on white wines, but their wine trades have diverged significantly. Austria has been basking in the glow of international praise for most of the last decade, while Switzerland, though it produces some excellent wines, has only just begun exporting them to other countries. Swiss wines may be hard to come by, but they're worth seeking out.

Schaffhausen

Thurgau

ZURICH

St. Gallen

Neuchâtel

Switzerland

Lake Geneva

Vaud

Rhône River

GENEVA

Valais

Ticino

austria

A phenomenal wine renaissance has taken place in Austria since the additive scandal of the mid-1980s (see "Recovery from Scandal," page 175). With young winemakers pushing for ever-higher quality standards, Austrian wines have never been better. And, judging by the increasingly loud buzz among the cognoscenti, these wines are poised to emerge as international favorites.

Kremstal
Wachau
Kamptal
Donauland
Niederösterich
Weinviertel
Traisental
Vienna
• VIENNA
Carnuntum
Neusiedlersee
Neusiedlersee-Hügelland
Burgenland
Thermenregion
Austria
Mittelburgenland
Südburgenland
Weststeiermark
Styria
Süd Osteiermark
Südsteiermark

Featured
Wine-Growing
Regions

grapes & styles

Austrian winemakers are blessed with soil and climate conditions that allow them to grow many kinds of grapes successfully. About 80 percent of their varieties are white, and plantings of the zippy, peppery, sometimes smoky Grüner Veltliner account for more than 35 percent of vineyard space. Müller-Thurgau, Riesling, Welsch-riesling (vel'sh-REEZ-ling,) and Weissburgunder (VICE-boor-gun-der), which is the same as Pinot Blanc, are all important white grapes here as well. Of the reds, Zweigelt is the most widely planted, and the full-bodied, spicy wines that are made from this grape give producers hope for its future as the nation's red standard-bearer. Other top red grapes include Blaufränkisch, Blauer Portugieser, and Blauburgunder (Pinot Noir). Austrian wines are not always aged in oak, and—excluding dessert wines, of course—all but a few of them are completely dry. They are as refreshing and aromatic as German wines but generally more full-bodied. Although these wines are usually drunk young, they age well for five or more years.

on the label

Like those in Germany, Austrian labels include the name of the producer, the place of origin, the vintage, the grape variety, and the all-important category that's based on the ripeness level of the grapes at the time of harvest—Kabinett, Spätlese, Auslese, Beerenauslese, or Trockenbeerenauslese (see Germany's "On the Label," page 159). However, Austria's wine laws require a higher level of ripeness than the German regulations demand for the same categories. There are other differences between the countries, too. Austria's Wachau region, for instance, has its own categories for dry wines; the light Steinfeder, the medium Federspiel, and the powerful Smaragd (named for a local lizard) are close counterparts to Kabinett, Spätlese, and Auslese. The wines of Wachau, along with those of Kremstal and Kamptal, are among the best from Niederösterich, Austria's largest wine region. The other great region of Austria is Burgenland, which lies south of Vienna.

at the table

The spicy, herbal qualities of Grüner Veltliner position the wine perfectly to match with pork, including sausages, as well as other Austrian favorites like tangy sauerkraut, root vegetables, and salads. Try the Grüner Veltliners, too, with fish and poultry. Austrian Rieslings, just like Rieslings all around the world, can stand up to spice and heat, and, in fact, they do well with virtually anything but red meat. Austrian red wines tend to be fruity with light tannin. They're good with roast chicken or casual fare such as hamburgers.

the bottom line
Due to relatively low levels of production and export to the United States, Austrian wines can be difficult to find outside of restaurants that feature the country's cuisine. The wines won't be bargains, either. You're unlikely to find many Grüner Veltliners or Rieslings below $20, and most of them cost more. Still, wines from the better producers will be well worth the price.

what to buy WHITE WINES

1995	1996	1997	1998	1999
★★★	★★★	★★★★	★★★	★★★★

GRÜNER WHO?

If you want to know something about Austrian wines, acquainting yourself with the Grüner Veltliner (GROO-ner felt-LEE-ner) grape is the place to start. More than a third of Austria's grapes are of this variety, far more than any other. The grape, a late ripener, is particularly well-suited to Austria's mild climate, and does best in the Niederösterich region, especially the Wachau subregion. Grüner Veltliner produces refreshingly acidic whites that can be herbal or spicy. With some similarity to Alace wines in aroma and body, Grüner Veltliners are typically dry, but they're sometimes barely off-dry. While the wines can be plain, in the right hands they are sublime, and only Rieslings (which account for under 3 percent of production) top them in Austria.

niederösterich

Literally *lower Austria*, Niederösterich has eight subregions: Wachau, Kamptal, Kremstal, Carnuntum, Donauland, Weinviertel, Traisental, and Thermenregion. Together they form Austria's largest wine region. The three areas responsible for the best wines of Niederösterich—Wachau, Kamptal, and Kremstal—offer superior Rieslings and Grüner Veltliners.

recommended producers & their wines

BRÜNDLMAYER ★ ★ ★ ★ $$$-$$$$
Known for classic dry Rieslings and creamy Grüner Veltliners of great subtlety and complexity. Bründlmayer also makes great barrique-aged Chardonnays. LOOK FOR anything you can find, especially Riesling Alte Reben from Heiligenstein and Grüner Veltliners from Ried Lamm.

FX PICHLER ★★★★ $$$-$$$$

Gorgeous, intensely flavored, and expensive, Pichler's wines blossom after a few years aging in the bottle. Grüner Veltliners taste smoky and floral, Rieslings are sharp and concentrated. LOOK FOR anything you can find; his wines are in short supply.

FRANZ PRAGER ★★★★ $$-$$$$

This Austrian dry-wine pioneer's range includes intense, fruity Grüner Veltliner and apricot-and-lime Riesling with a strong mineral character. LOOK FOR Rieslings; anything from Achleiten and Steinriegl.

FREIE WEINGARTNER ★★★ $$$-$$$$

Dry Rieslings with touches of plum and exotic spices teamed with lime, petrol, and slate. LOOK FOR all Rieslings.

LOIMER ★★★ $$-$$$$

Touches of lentil flavor in Grüner Veltliners, Rieslings redolent of tree fruits and nuts—these are wines to be drunk young. LOOK FOR Grüner Veltliner Langenloiser and Spiegel, and Riesling Langenloiser and Silberbuhel.

FRANZ HIRTZBERGER ★★★ $$-$$$

One of the Wachau's wine leaders, Hirtzberger makes zingy, citrusy Rieslings and spicy, smoky Grüner Veltliners. The wines are normally higher in alcohol than most Austrian wines. LOOK FOR Riesling Singerriedel Smaragd, Riesling Hochrain Smaragd, and Grüner Veltliner Honivogl Smaragd.

FAMILIE NIGL ★★★ $$-$$$

Sophisticated wines with floral grace notes, especially honeysuckle. The steely Grüner Veltliner is long on the finish, and the Riesling balances fruitiness and acidity beautifully. LOOK FOR Riesling Höchacker and Grüner Veltliner Senftenberger.

E & M BERGER ★★ $-$$$$

Great values compared to most Austrian wines. The Grüner Veltliners have a distinct slate and acid punch, with typical pepper and lentil aromas. LOOK FOR Grüner Veltliners, especially in bargain liter bottles.

HIEDLER ★★ $$-$$$

Producer of mellow Rieslings with subtle honeysuckle and lime-leaf flavor and just enough acidity. Underrated for Grüner Veltliners. LOOK FOR the Riesling called Maximum as well as Rieslings from Gaisberg.

RUDI PICHLER ★★ $$-$$$

Creamy, lush Grüner Veltliners with a floral explosion in the mouth and peach-tasting, easy-drinking Rieslings—both off-dry. LOOK FOR Riesling Achleiten ʼkirchen and Grüner Veltliner Wösendorfer.

RECOVERY FROM SCANDAL

In 1985, the tumult over wine additives effectively ended the commercially successful enterprise of pushing syrupy whites. Some unscrupulous producers, most of whom were eventually punished, were adding diethylene glycol to their wines to give them more body. There were no reports of consumer injuries, but the wine industry's reputation was devastated. Now, due to laws passed in the wake of the scandal, Austrian wines are produced under arguably the most stringent controls in the world.

burgenland

Beginning just southeast of Vienna and extending south along the Hungarian border, Burgenland houses four subregions—Neusiedlersee, Neusiedlersee-Hügelland, Mittelburgenland, and Südburgenland. They produce full-bodied whites, promising reds, and intense dessert wines (see "Dessert Wines of Austria," page 282).

recommended producers
& their wines

ALOIS KRACHER ★ ★ ★ ★ $$$-$$$$

Noted for opulent sweet wines with good acidity, this producer also makes excellent dry wines. LOOK FOR anything you can find, though the dry Chardonnay-Welschriesling is particularly worth a try.

WILLI OPITZ ★ ★ ★ $$-$$$$

A sweet-wine specialist with great ideas—like Schilfwein, made from grapes that are dried on reeds to concentrate their flavor and sugar. Opitz makes Auslese and Beerenauslese Grüner Veltliners, too, as well as respectable Blauburgunders and Weissburgunders. LOOK FOR anything you can find.

175

HEIDI SCHRÖCK ★ ★ ★ $$-$$$$

Features an array of unusual (to American palates) varietals: Furmint, Muscat, Vogelsang, Grauburgunder, and Zweigelt, as well as Weissburgunders. LOOK FOR anything you can find.

HEINRICH ★ ★ $$-$$$

Maker of easy-to-drink and appealing Austrian red varietals with blackberry and cherry flavors, Heinrich specializes in fruity wines made from Zweigelt, but there are some steely, zesty whites here, too. LOOK FOR Zweigelts, Blaufränkisch, Weissburgunders.

HOPLER ★ ★ $$-$$$

Lively Grüner Veltliners, brisk and fruity Weissburgunders, gentle Blauburgunders, excellent sweet Ausbruch, and delicious Trockenbeerenauslese. LOOK FOR Elisio Ausbruch and Weissburgunder.

styria & vienna

Styria is the most popular region among Austrians looking for light-bodied wines with good acidity, and Vienna boasts more vineyards than any other major city in the world. Most Viennese wines are enjoyed on the spot—as soon as they're made, while they're still frothy and fun—in the wine cafés of the city.

recommended producers & their wines

E&M TEMENT, STYRIA ★ ★ $$-$$$$

Known for excellent Sauvignon Blancs, aromatic Muscats, oaky Chardonnays, and refreshing Welschrieslings. LOOK FOR wines from the Zierreg vineyard.

POLZ, STYRIA ★ ★ $$-$$$

The Polz brothers use a combo of stainless steel and large new-wood casks to produce interesting, modern-style whites—pungent Sauvignon Blanc and Weissburgunder with an oaky finish. LOOK FOR Hochgrassnitzberg Sauvignon Blancs and any Weissburgunder.

WIENINGER, VIENNA ★ ★ $$-$$$
As with most Vienna producers, Fritz Wieninger's wines are mostly destined for quaffing in wine bars, but he also produces good Chardonnays and Pinot Noirs that are exported. LOOK FOR Chardonnays and Pinot Noirs.

OTHER TOP-NOTCH PRODUCERS FROM THROUGHOUT AUSTRIA
Emmerich Knoll *(Riesling Smaraøor Schütt)*, Kollwentz *(red and sweet wines from Burgenland)*, Weingut Ernst Lang *(Grüner Veltliner, Riesling)*, Dinstlgut Loiben *(Riesling Kremser Pfaffenberg and Riesling Loibner Loibenberg)*, Mantlerhof *(Roter Veltliner)*, Nikolaihof *(Rieslings and Grüner Veltliners from the Steiner Hund and Vom Stein vineyards)*, Pockl *(Burgenland Zweigelts)*, Erich Salomon *(Kremser Rieslings)*, Ernst Triebaumer *(Blaufränkisch Ried Gmark)*, Umathum *(Blauburgunder and Zweigelt)*, Familie Zull *(Grüner Veltliners)*

switzerland

Though bordered by four great wine-producing countries (Italy, Germany, France, and Austria), Switzerland produces wines that retain their own identity. Until recently, few have been exported, but slowly the number of Swiss wines crossing the Atlantic is increasing. Despite the country's white-wine tradition, some excellent reds are being produced, and its rosés are also of interest. Like a Swiss watch, the wines are finely wrought and delicate, even the reds.

grapes & styles
German and French varieties like Müller-Thurgau, Pinot Noir, Syrah, Merlot, and Riesling are grown, but it is the white Chasselas that is most prolific. The Valais and Vaud in the western part of the country are the top two wine-producing regions, and Chasselas reigns in both, though under a different name—Fendant—in the Valais. The Valais also produces a medium-bodied red from Pinot Noir and Gamay, often labeled Dôle. Gamay is the most important red in the Vaud.

North of the Vaud is Neuchâtel. Chasselas once again dominates, though Pinot Noir is made into interesting reds and rosés, especially the light rosé called Oeil-de-Perdrix *(partridge eye)*. Ticino, in the Italian-speaking part of Switzerland, is the most important area for reds; Merlot accounts for 85 percent of the yield.

switzerland

on the label

Most Swiss wines are labeled by grape variety, though as mentioned in "Grapes & Styles" (page 177), the names do change.
The word VITI on a Ticino Merlot label guarantees a regulated
level of quality.

at the table

Chasselas works well with hard-to-match asparagus and artichokes. Swiss whites and rosés are shoo-ins for lean fish, such
as the local favorite lake perch. The Pinot Noirs and Gamays
work whenever you're in doubt between white and red—think
salmon, turkey, and pork. The fruity Merlots are wonderful with
dishes that have a slight sweet element, such as pasta in a red-
pepper sauce or duck with fruit sauce.

the bottom line You'll pay between $20 and $40 for
these hard-to-find but worth-the-search wines. The Swiss drink
about twice as much wine as they make, so there's not much
incentive to export at bargain rates.

recommended wines

1998 Luc Massy Dézaley Chemin de Fer, Vaud � ★★★ $$$
An impressive, medium-weight wine with appealing and intense aromas and a
flavor of mellow apples sprinkled with lemon. There's a slight licorice tang and
plenty of mineral content, like licking a slab of slate (one of those wine-taste
descriptions that sounds horrible but is really positive).

**1997 Bon Père Germanier Balavaud Cayas Syrah,
Valais** ♟ ★★ $$$
There's something Côte-Rôtie-like here with blackberry, smoke, and meat aro-
mas, flavors that suggest new oak, subtle acidity, and gentle, velvet-like tannin.

1997 Rouvinez Château Lichten, Valais ♟ ★★ $$$
A medium-bodied wine with cherry and plum aromas and flavors that are ac-
cented by a sprinkling of rosemary and sage.

**1997 Bon Père Germanier Dôle Balavaud Grand Cru,
Valais** ♟ ★★ $$
This is a medium-bodied wine with full cherry and raspberry aromas, along
with hints of orange.

178

1998 Jean Louis Bovard Calamin Cuvée Speciale, Vaud ♀ ★★ $$
Pass the seafood, please—that's just what's called for with this sort of dry, lemony, mineral-rich wine with flinty stoniness.

1998 Jean Louis Bovard St. Saphorin Chasselas, Vaud ♀ ★★ $$
Of all Swiss wines, Bovard's are the easiest to find in the United States right now—and that's a good thing because they're excellent. The wine is lychee scented and lemon flavored, with a touch of pine and fennel on the finish.

1998 Fendant de Sion Les Murettes Gilliard, Valais ♀ ★★ $$
Like a good Muscadet, this Valais is made *sur lie* (the residue of yeast and grape pulp, seeds, and skins is left in the wine for a while before bottling, intensifying the flavor). Medium-bodied, with pleasant lemon and tangerine aromas and flavors and an old-fashioned spritziness on the tongue.

1998 Badoux Aigle Les Murailles, Switzerland ♀ ★ $$$
Can't believe we're saying this, but if you buy this wine just for the stunning lizard graphic on the label, we'll understand. Pop the cork and inside is a musky little wine, low on fruit and high on stony mineral content.

1997 Rouvinez Dôle de Sierre, Valais ♀ ★ $$
There are subtle aromas of cherry and raspberry here, along with a hint of smoke. Flavors of black currant and violet meld together as the tannin softens and fades.

1995 Rouvinez Le Tourmentin, Valais ♀ ★ $$
A lovely blend of grapes—including Pinot Noir and Syrah—results in a flavorful wine with a rich aroma of vanilla, candied cherry, and prune, accented by a touch of clove.

1997 Rubro Merlot del Ticino Valsangiacomo, Ticino ♀ ★ $$
An interestingly earthy Merlot, with more lanolin than fruit flavor, and a nice smooth texture.

california

A couple of statistics give the picture of California's success. Though wine is made in forty-eight of the fifty states, 95 percent of the country's total wine production takes place in California. Three of every four bottles sold in the U.S. are from the Golden State. California turns out bold warm-weather wines, and its winemakers rev up the taste even more with their generous use of wood. Americans love the jolt of flavor, and the California oak-enhanced style, for better or worse, has had a powerful impact on winemaking throughout the world.

grapes & styles

If Henry James's *Portrait of a Lady* heroine, Isabel Archer, were a wine she'd be a Californian: appealingly straightforward and out-spoken, a bit lacking in sophistication and experience but learning all the time. In an effort to coax sweet, sun-ripened fruit into a more complex beverage than it normally would become, most California vintners use new oak rambunctiously, which gives the wine even more potent flavor and fuller body. Whether from one of the starring varieties (Chardonnay, Sauvignon Blanc, Cabernet Sauvignon, Merlot, Pinot Noir, and Zinfandel) or an up-and-comer (Marsanne, Viognier, Syrah, Cabernet Franc, and Sangiovese), California wine is generally neither shy nor mysterious, and therein lies its tremendous popularity. Subtlety can be lacking, but, on the whole, what the wine may lack in finesse it more than makes up in the Bam! factor.

on the label

California wines are mostly varietals. By law, the label Chardonnay or Cabernet Sauvignon means that there's at least 75 percent of the advertised grape in the bottle; the other 25 percent could be

Mendocino

Lake

SACRAMENTO •

Sonoma **Napa**

SAN •
FRANCISCO ○ —— Livermore

—— *Santa Cruz Mountains*

San Benito

Monterey

San Luis Obispo

Santa Barbara

Santa Ynez

• **LOS ANGELES**
—— Temecula

SAN DIEGO •

■ **Featured
Wine-Growing
Regions**

anything. When the label designates only California, the grapes can be purchased from all over the state. A further regional designation, like Napa Valley, means 85 percent of the grapes come from within the region. Meritage is a blend of Bordeaux grape varieties (see "Grapes & Styles," page 32). Reserve and Special Reserve usually mean that better grapes were chosen, and the wine often has had more contact with oak than the house's other wines—usually new oak, which imparts more flavor than old—during fermentation and aging. These terms, however, are not governed by law. Another California-ism is Fumé Blanc. Robert Mondavi melded two names from the Loire—the grape Sauvignon Blanc and the wine Pouilly Fumé—and came up with this appealing substitute name for Sauvignon Blanc. Other firms now use his moniker, generally to refer to an oaky Sauvignon.

chardonnay

All of the fuss started in 1976 when a Parisian wine store staged a blind tasting that pitted white Burgundies (traditional Chardonnays) against California Chards. Three of the four winning wines were from California. American producers were quick to seize the marketing opportunity, and the wine gained worldwide recognition. Today's typical California Chard has loads of tropical-fruit taste as well as a tremendous amount of vanilla-butter flavor. These come from both the ripe Chardonnay grapes and the wood fermentation. On top of that are the spicy, toasty flavors from barrel aging.

Though oaky Chardonnay is still California's big commercial success, a backlash has begun. Slowly, more Chardonnays are entering the market that never see wood or are barrel-fermented for shorter periods. Wine mavens often prefer these wines that show off the pure Chardonnay fruit flavors.

at the table

California Chardonnays in their oaky incarnations are notoriously difficult to pair with food. It's better to match characteristics than to contrast: Repeat the wine's full body and buttery flavor with something like corn and lobster chowder, or let the toastiness echo that of something grilled, like fish steaks or chicken. Lighter-style Chardonnays work well with lean fish or roasted chicken.

the bottom line
Chardonnay prices span a broad range, from $6 for a supermarket special to $80 for a boutique beauty. Lots of good drinking can be found between $15 and $25.

what to buy CHARDONNAY

1997	1998	1999
★ ★ ★	★ ★ ★	★ ★

recommended wines

1998 Far Niente, Napa Valley 🍷 ★ ★ ★ ★ $ $ $
At first, this wine is restrained—then layers of apricots, lemons, and toast unfold.

1998 Flora Springs Lavender Hill Vineyard, Napa Valley ♥ ★★★ $$$
One look at the wine's sunny, buttery color and you know you're in for something full in both flavor and body. And what you see is what you get. It starts with lime blossom on the nose and key lime on the palate. The long finish has a blast of yeasty buttered toast and a touch of cedar. A classic.

1997 Robert Sinskey, Carneros ♥ ★★★ $$$
Hard to take your nose out of the glass, so seductive are the aromas here. Lemon, pear, nuts, and buttered toast sprinkled with vanilla sugar—these just keep on coming. The wine is kept lively by a nice tangy lemony flavor and finishes with more toast.

1998 Sonoma-Cutrer The Cutrer Vineyard, Russian River Valley ♥ ★★★ $$$
After specializing in Chardonnay for nearly twenty years, this winery certainly knows what it's doing. The wine has a good dose of apples and honey on the palate; the oak is there, but it has a supporting, not a starring, role.

1997 ZD Wines Reserve, Napa Valley ♥ ★★★ $$$
Eighteen months of barrel-aging tell you it's going to be a powerful wine. In fact, it smells and tastes like a more mature Chardonnay, with aromas that come on full throttle. The wood adds vanilla, coconut, and spice elements. The wine finishes with a touch of honey and a great deal of toast. Strong but sophisticated.

1998 Au Bon Climat Le Bouge D'à Côté, Santa Maria Valley ♥ ★★★ $$
This is a light and brisk wine—think buttery lemon tart with an underlying taste of mouthwatering guava. But there is also lanolin, stony minerals, and a touch of chalk. The experience ends with the yummy taste of malt.

1998 Cakebread Cellars, Napa Valley ♥ ★★★ $$
Refreshing, with a slight piney aroma. The wine has pure, tropical Chardonnay fruit flavors; a dollop of oak on the finish only deepens and strengthens the experience. An excellent summer wine and a versatile food choice.

1998 Chalone Vineyard, Chalone ♥ ★★★ $$
Acidity, alcohol content, and flavor are perfectly balanced here, and there's a lovely taste of pear.

1998 Paul Hobbs, Russian River Valley ♥ ★★ $$$
This is a big boy with potent mouthwatering flavors of smoke and oak. Fruit flavors are here, too, but they're not of the tropical-fruit salad you'd expect. Rather this wine tastes of snappy grapefruit and tart Granny Smith apples. It's a riveting Chardonnay.

california chardonnay

1998 Cuvaison, Carneros ♥ ★ ★ $$
The big flavors here will make California Chardonnay lovers smile. There's a mélange of intense fruit—mango, apricot, and pineapple—in the center, followed by a deep taste of caramel.

1998 Hanna, Russian River Valley ♥ ★ ★ $$
Sure, vanilla-scented oak is the first thing you notice on the nose and tongue, but lovely aromas and flavors of grapefruit and lime follow right on its tail.

1998 Clos LaChance, Santa Cruz Mountains ♥ ★ ★ $$
Here's the rare California Chardonnay that's more focused on earthy elements than fruit. Think Village Chablis and you're on the right road. It marries some fruit with smokiness and complex minerality beautifully.

1998 Edna Valley Vineyards, San Luis Obispo ♥ ★ $$
The first impression is of lemon and orange aromas, and a touch of green bean. On the tongue, the wine is full-bodied, and then the tastes come on strong with a mouthful of lemon and star fruit. A touch of canned asparagus sneaks up right behind these, and then the wine finishes with a little almond-crunch flavor. If this sounds out of kilter, it is a bit—but the wine is still very enjoyable, especially with food, which evens out the oddities.

1997 Raymond Napa Valley Reserve, Napa Valley ♥ ★ $$
A medium-bodied wine with a nice amount of oak, and subtle lemony orange aromas. A good summertime selection.

1998 M. Trinchero Founder's Estate, Napa Valley ♥ ★ $$
Think of this as a Chardonnay that tries to be a beer—and the experiment works. The nose is a bit hoppy and lemony; in the mouth, the wine is full-bodied, with a touch of mango and guava and a spicy oak finish.

1998 Clos du Bois, Sonoma ♥ ★ $
The winery's workhorse, and for good reason: It's a straightforward, reliable Chardonnay. Broil a fish with some rosemary, pour a glass, and enjoy.

1998 Farallon Cellars, North Coast ♥ ★ $
Lots of concentrated flavors crop up in this simple wine—vanilla, butter, pear, mango, and coconut.

1999 Hawk Crest, California ♥ ★ $
A great little bargain Chardonnay, packed with pineapple that's tempered by some fresh-cut hay.

1998 Heron, California ♥ ★ $
With a center of pears and apples dressed up with a little vanilla and zesty touches of lemon peel, this is a wine with good acidity at a good price.

sauvignon blanc

From briskly acidic and assertive to oaky and coconut-y, California Sauvignon Blanc gets a wide variety of treatments. In the worst-case scenario, it masquerades as a lusty, over-oaked Chardonnay. In the best, it reveals its tingling acidity and strong herbal flavors.

at the table

One of the brisker California Sauvignon Blancs will perk up rich fish like bluefish, tuna, salmon, sardines, or mackerel. The acidic style also works well with special-ingredient salads like shaved fennel with Pecorino, in addition to dishes that are enlivened with cilantro, which can be difficult to match. The oakier style of Sauvignon Blanc—the so-called Fumé Blanc—is an interesting choice with broiled chicken or fish, and also serves well as an aperitif wine with some rich hors d'oeuvres, such as nuts or cheese pastries.

the bottom line Since most of the attention goes to Chardonnay, good Sauvignon Blanc can be overlooked and therefore underpriced. Delicious examples can be found in the $8 to $16 range.

recommended wines

1999 Cakebread Cellars, Napa Valley ♥   ★ ★ ★ ★ $$
Is it the soil of their vineyards or what? Cakebread Cellars can do no wrong, and their Sauvignon Blancs are consistently among the finest California can offer. The aroma here has subtle hints of grapefruit and lemon that come through on the palate as well. There's a tad of fennel, a tad of pepper, a tad of honeysuckle, and a finish that is really beautifully balanced between acidity and its other flavors.

1998 Duckhorn Vineyards, Napa Valley ♥   ★ ★ ★ $$
Clearly defined fruit flavors face off with a creamy texture, and the combination really works. The wine is medium-bodied. It has floral and grapefruit aromas and citrus and nectarine flavors, along with a bit of vanilla evened out with some sobering slate.

1999 Frog's Leap, Napa Valley 🍷 · ★ ★ ★ $$

The subtle nose doesn't prepare you for the joyride ahead. There's an intense streak of lovely lime and chalk, along with quite a bit of mineral content, almost like stainless steel. The wine finishes nice and tart, with a slight reference to licorice.

1999 St. Supéry Vineyards & Winery, Napa Valley 🍷 ★ ★ ★ $$

Grapefruit, grass, and kiwi give a one-two-three punch out of the glass, and follow through vibrantly on the palate—this time with a little nectarine thrown in as well.

1999 Baron Herzog, California 🍷 ★ ★ $

What a deal! And with so much going on here, it's hardly a one-trick pony. There's lemon and orange on the nose. The wine's flavor is powerful and includes hints of cedar and gooseberry. The little bit of spritzy effervescence on the tongue is fun. All for under $10.

1999 Preston of Dry Creek Estate, Dry Creek Valley 🍷 ★ ★ $

The nose is not strong here. There's a teensy bit of vanilla and some subtle green-bean aroma. The main flavors follow through on the grassy side. The wine finishes on a note of grapefruit, making it moderately complex and also quite food-friendly.

1998 Chateau St. Jean Fumé Blanc, Sonoma County 🍷 ★ ★ $

A medium-bodied wine with an intense freesia and peach perfume. There's a bit of vanilla on the palate and some taste of toast.

1999 Amberhill Vineyards, California 🍷 ★ $

Not a terribly sophisticated bottle of wine, but there's absolutely nothing wrong with it—certainly not for the price. Subtle and pleasant flavor.

1999 Clos du Bois, Sonoma County 🍷 ★ $

Thanks to the addition of some Semillon grapes, this Sauvignon Blanc-based wine is more full-bodied than most. The flavors please with mellow melon set off by some baked lemon.

1999 Montevina Fumé Blanc, California 🍷 ★ $

It's hard to argue with a wine this good at a price this low. Tropical-fruit flavors are complemented with some noticeable lemon balm, grass, orange, and peach. Somehow it all comes out uncomplicated and enjoyable. The wine is medium in body.

1998 Villa Mt. Eden Coastal, Mendocino 🍷 ★ $

A subtle Sauvignon Blanc with a typically herbaceous character and perhaps a touch of tropical fruit (but just a touch). Nice and simple. This is a perfect, refreshing wine for summer quaffing.

rhône whites in california

Finicky in the field as well as in the winery, the Viognier (vee-oh-n'yay) grape is the current Rhône-white-variety darling, capable of turning out a pretty, melony, citrusy wine. Marsanne and Roussanne also turn up as varietals, but the most exciting Rhône-style wines are blends. Some of these are blockbusters with lush, caramel flavors and have become cult classics.

at the table

The Rhône grape varieties grown in California tend to become exotic, full-bodied, perfumed wines that are high in alcohol. You might want to pair their voluptuousness with crab or lobster. Also, there's no better way to make basic roast chicken or plain broiled fish into a compelling meal than by putting one of these wines on the table.

the bottom line Since Viognier is difficult to grow and has tiny yields, it's pretty pricey. Figure on $20 as a starting point. You can find some Marsannes and Roussannes on the shelves for about $15. The cult blends, which usually end up in restaurants rather than stores, weigh in at over a hundred dollars on wine lists.

recommended wines

1998 Callaway Vineyard & Winery Viognier, Temecula 🍷 ★ ★ $$
At first there's a little green bean on the nose, typical of New Zealand Sauvignon Blancs, but then there are also pineapple aromas, and so we took a sip. Flavors of spices, lots of pepper, and honeysuckle give this Viognier many food-pairing possibilities. It's not for mindless sipping.

1999 Miner Family Vineyards Viognier, California 🍷 ★ ★ $$
Seductive aromas of honey, peaches, and peonies. On the palate, the wine is delicious and straightforward.

**1999 Preston of Dry Creek Estate Viognier,
Dry Creek Valley** 🍷 ★ ★ $$
A nice Viognier with honeyed pineapples and peaches, as well as a complex mineral note.

**1997 Rabbit Ridge Viognier Heartbreak Hill,
Sonoma County** 🍷 ★ ★ $$
What a beautifully clear-flavored Viognier—nice and tart. On the nose, there's a touch of cedar, and on the tongue, lots of grapefruit tanginess mixed with honeysuckle.

1998 Preston Vineyards Marsanne, Dry Creek Valley 🍷 ★ $$
Slightly muted nose but nice and spicy on the palate, with subtle floral notes and ripe-pear accents. Good acidity.

1998 Sobon Estate Roussanne, Shenandoah Valley 🍷 ★ $
Roussanne is often a full-bodied wine, and this one fills the bill with an almost oily feeling in the mouth. Flavors of tropical fruit and ripe peaches.

other white wines & rosés of california

There's little chance of a Californian Chenin Blanc being mistaken for one from the Loire, but there are some refreshing, simple lemony and orangey versions around. Gewürztraminer is another varietal to look for; it's usually in the off-dry style and is great with Asian food or as an aperitif. Pinot Blanc, Chardonnay's genetic cousin, seems to do well on California soil. Pinot Gris, the same as the Italian Pinot Grigio, is fuller in both flavor and body here. California rosés, made from the grapes Pinot Noir, Grenache, and/or Cinsault, among many others, are finally gaining the popularity they deserve. Fruity and fun, they match perfectly with the ever-popular cuisines of the Mediterranean.

the bottom line Chenin Blancs and white blends will tend to be inexpensive entries coming in at under $10, while Pinot Blancs and Rieslings will range between $12 and $20. Most California rosés go for between $10 and $20.

A WORD ABOUT ROSÉS

Due to the American mistrust of rosés, many vintners produce only small quantities, and those few bottles are often available only at the winery. Perhaps a rosé by any other name would smell as sweet, but sometimes names do count. Cakebread Winery in the Napa Valley cleverly dubbed their pink wine Vin de Porch—and it sold out immediately. Although rosés are not as widely available as other California wines, we did sample a few yummy ones that are available in stores now.

recommended wines

1999 Robert Sinskey Vineyards Vin Gris of Pinot Noir, Carneros ♀ ★★★ $$

This wine starts with an especially fragrant orange-blossom nose. The flavor is strong and perfectly delicious—peach, apple-blossom, rosewater, with just a touch of licorice and not much sweetness. A light mineral, almost coppery taste as well.

1998 Swanson Vineyards Rosato, Napa Valley ♀ ★★★ $

Even though the wine has lovely strawberry and vanilla flavors, its spicy undertones make it a sophisticated rosé. You can count on this one. It's always a crowd pleaser.

1998 Etude Pinot Blanc, Napa Valley ♀ ★★ $$

A tasty Pinot Blanc with a whole lot of flavor going on. There's white chocolate and the taste of tropical fruit, with an emphasis on pineapple. A buttery lemon-tart angle comes through on the palate, too, as well as a bit of fresh-cut grass.

1998 Handley Cellars Gewürztraminer, Anderson Valley ♀ ★★ $$

A dry wine that's floral and pear-like, with a bit of lovely peachiness. Gewürztraminers are typically very fragrant, and this one is piercingly so. It's well worth seeking out.

1998 Flora Springs Pinot Grigio, Napa Valley ♆   ★ ★ $
A full-bodied wine with an almost oily mouth-feel, and quite tasty, with mellow fruit flavors of peach and nectarine, a touch of anise, and lots of pepper. An excellent Chardonnay alternative.

1999 Baron Herzog Chenin Blanc, California ♆   ★ ★ $
This one goes down easy. With its fruit-bowl lemon and orange acidity and a touch of honey, it's simple and delicious.

1999 Miner Family, Mendocino ♆   ★ ★ $
A powerful rosé that will convince the guys that pink wines aren't just for girls. It's got some strong flavors— anise and peach, and a bit of cranberry acidity.

1999 Preston of Dry Creek Vin Gris, Dry Creek Estate ♆   ★ ★ $
Cinsault, Mourvèdre, Grenache—this is a Rhône-grape-based rosé with a strong fragrance of roses. It's full-bodied, and there are slight hints of melon and orange blossom on the finish.

Rosenblum Cellars Vintners Cuvée Blanc, California ♆   ★ ★ $
The Palomino, Chardonnay, and Viognier really swoop out of this wine. It's peachy and very perfumed, with excellent tangy acidity. A wine like this really calls for food; with the right dish, featuring a fair amount of exotic spice, it would be sensational.

1998 Vigil Vineyard Desperada, North Coast ♆   ★ ★ $
What a whacked-out wine! Made from aromatic grapes like Palomino (of Sherry fame), with some French Colombard, White Muscat, Chenin, and Sauvignon Blanc thrown in, it's a regular roller-coaster ride. The nose is subtle with some grassiness, some honeysuckle, and some Muscat perfume; on the palate, the wine is light-bodied, acidic, and refreshing. Finishes with the same aromas still lingering. Perfect with goat cheese.

1999 Beaulieu Vineyards Pinot Noir Vin Gris Winemaker's Collection, Napa Valley ♆   ★ $
The pale salmon color appropriately indicates the light, refreshing quality of this wine. There's a touch of clove and some watermelon.

Ca'del Solo Il Pescatore, California ♆   ★ $
Sauvignon Blanc, Pinot Meunier, Marsanne, Roussanne, and Riesling—yup, it's another wild California combo. The wine has an earthy fragrance and lots of body; a little bit of anise, fennel, and minerality and a touch of honey. It all adds up to a great everyday wine.

1999 Shooting Star Pacini Zin Gris, Mendocino ♆   ★ $
Never thought we'd like a buttery rosé, but this one makes the cut. It's full-bodied and full-flavored, with a touch of tannin, pine, and caramelized strawberries.

cabernet sauvignon & cabernet franc

For the past three decades, the Napa Valley has produced the preeminent California Cabernet Sauvignons, though the grape is grown all over the state. With their aromas and flavors of mint, eucalyptus, black olive, cherry, and rosemary, and their substantial tannin, Napa Valley Cabernet Sauvignons make lovers of the grape turn somersaults. Like their Bordeaux counterparts, the ordinary Cabernet Sauvignons are drinkable on release and improve with age, though they may not last as long. The elite wines, however, should be set aside for years. Sonoma, just next door to Napa, also makes fine Cabernet Sauvignons, usually in a simpler, fruitier style.

Cabernet Franc—another important Bordeaux variety, though used there mainly in a supporting role—is still something of a novelty in California but is growing well on Napa mountains and in Santa Barbara County. The California Cabernet Franc varietals are full-bodied, with a nice black-pepper tingle.

at the table

No mystery here: These wines go with meat. Make it a sizzling steak, maybe even a buffalo steak. Vegetarians can throw red peppers on the grill and toss pasta with a bit of smoked mozzarella and have equal enjoyment. With Cabernet Sauvignons, especially those from the Napa Valley, stay away from hot spices and cilantro. Cabernet Franc is more flexible. It works with meat, of course, with anything grilled, naturally, but it can also handle a little spicy heat and a bit more complexity in a dish.

the bottom line Are Napa Cabernet Sauvignons really worth $80 and up? At a certain point, you're buying status more than taste. But there's plenty of good stuff in the $18 to $30 category. Cabernet Francs start at around $20.

REVOLUTION AT PLUMPJACK WINERY

Hang around with winemakers, and you'll frequently hear discussion of tainted corks (see "How to Handle a Wine List," page 21), often ending with a what-can-you-do-about-it shrug. Gordon Getty, one of the owners of Plumpjack, a small, wildly successful winery in the Oakville district, is not one to stand by helplessly. After getting angry about the frequency of cork-spoiled bottles, he decided he wouldn't take it anymore. He moved boldly into territory where others fear to tread—metal screw tops. The Plumpjack 1997 Cabernet Sauvignon Reserve, released this year, will be available with a screw top or with a cork. The screw-top bottle will cost $135, $10 more than the same wine with a traditional cork. Industry folks generally agree that a screw-top wine delivers the purest flavors. The problem is image, of course, and an unanswered question: Will this closure allow proper aging?

what to buy CABERNET SAUVIGNON

1995	1996	1997	1998	1999
★★★	★★★	★★★	★★★	★★

recommended wines

1997 Diamond Creek Volcanic Hill Cabernet Sauvignon, Napa Valley ♀ ★★★★ $$$$

Lots of complexity in a medium-bodied wine. The aromas and flavors are of earth, violet, black cherry, strawberry, plum, spice, and tobacco. The wine is still pretty tannic, which makes it all the better.

1997 Carmenet Moon Mountain Reserve Cabernet Sauvignon, Sonoma ♀ ★★★ $$$$

A powerful wine. Mint and eucalyptus on the nose follows through on the palate with mint tea, along with chalk, cherry, blackberry, and a dusting of cocoa.

1996 Robert Mondavi Cabernet Sauvignon Reserve, Napa Valley ♀ ★★★ $$$$

What's not to like? This is Mondavi's classic Cabernet Sauvignon, reliably delicious year after year.

1997 Nickel & Nickel Carpenter Vineyard Cabernet Sauvignon, Napa Valley ★ ★ ★ $$$$

An elegant Bordeaux-like Cabernet with blackberry aromas. It's full-bodied and has currant, tobacco, and chalk flavors, plus a kiss of oak.

1997 Nickel & Nickel Rock Cairn Vineyard Cabernet Sauvignon, Napa Valley ★ ★ ★ $$$$

Full California fruit is apparent in this vineyard's wines. Here the taste is high on cherry and strawberry, with a good deal of cocoa and chalk in the aroma as well.

1997 Bedford Thompson Cabernet Franc, Santa Barbara County ★ ★ ★ $$$

Very dusty, silty, and chalky, more like a Bordeaux Cabernet Franc than one from the Loire. Underneath is green pepper and blueberry, with a touch of hazelnut.

1997 Cakebread Cellars Cabernet Sauvignon, Napa Valley ★ ★ ★ $$$

A great choice if you're looking for an utterly excellent Cabernet. There's a little cheddar cheese on the nose and then a burst of wild strawberries. The fruit follows through on the palate with a hint of black tea followed by a long toasty finish. Tasty now, but we'd definitely like to try this one again in a few years.

1997 Frog's Leap Cabernet Sauvignon, Napa Valley ★ ★ ★ $$$

Lovers of old-style Bordeaux and monster New World Cabernet Sauvignons alike will cozy up to this wine. There's a smack of fruit flavor in the middle of this wine that at first seems a little dried out but then comes through nicely. With a tiny bit of aeration, hints of coffee and refreshing eucalyptus come rising up on the nose and palate.

1997 Hendry Block 8 Cabernet Sauvignon, Napa Valley ★ ★ ★ $$$

Wow, what a deep and murky color—and then the aromas start to seduce. The first smell is of fresh fruit and spearmint, then cocoa. A sip, and you think, who opened up the spice box? There's a pinch of cinnamon and a dash of clove and also some sweet red pepper. A delicious wine.

1997 Herzog Special Reserve Cabernet Sauvignon, Alexander Valley ★ ★ ★ $$$

A great Cabernet Sauvignon for those who favor strong bell pepper on the nose, giving way to a lot of cherry on the palate. Very full-bodied, the wine is super-satisfying, with lots of lingering vanilla and espresso. In short, it's pretty yummy.

1996 Reverie on Diamond Mountain Cabernet Sauvignon, Napa ★ ★ ★ $$$

Lots of fruit in this full-bodied wine. Though intense, it's easy to drink now. Cedar, black olive, and rosemary notes.

california cabernet

1997 Freestone Cabernet Sauvignon, Napa Valley 🍷   ★★★ $$
Very delicate, with red berries and stone fruits and a little bit of oaky flavor. The last impression is of a touch of spice on the finish—as well as apparent, but gentle, tannin.

1996 Conn Creek Winery Limited Release
Cabernet Sauvignon, Napa Valley 🍷   ★★ $$$
Here's a happy little wine with a lot going on—blueberry flavors with a touch of cedar and a hint of lanolin.

1997 Cosentino Winery Cabernet Sauvignon,
Napa Valley 🍷   ★★ $$$
There's a fair amount of new oak and tannin here, but the flavors of tobacco-flecked blackberries with a touch of cranberry tartness bear both deliciously.

1997 Joseph Phelps Cabernet Sauvignon,
Napa Valley 🍷   ★★ $$$
Full-bodied and yummy, this wine has a raisiny quality, with a walnutty finish and an appealing silky texture.

1997 Sequoia Grove Cabernet Sauvignon, Napa Valley 🍷   ★★ $$$
A subtle wine that benefits from the winemaker's choice not to overwhelm its beautiful flavor with oak. The wine is medium-weight, with flashes of blueberries and blackberries, leather, and a touch of black olive.

1996 Fetzer Reserve Cabernet Sauvignon, Napa Valley 🍷   ★★ $$
A nicely subtle wine, with a little tea, a bit of tobacco, and a good strong finish.

1997 Ravenswood Cabernet Franc, Sonoma County 🍷   ★★ $$
Though Ravenswood is known primarily for Zinfandel, their Cabernet Franc is pretty great, too. This one has strong, smoky plum and silky cassis components. It's full-bodied and easy to drink right now.

1997 Raymond Reserve Cabernet Sauvignon, Napa Valley 🍷 ★★ $$
A full and fragrant Cabernet Sauvignon with seductive aromas. There's a gentle hint of vanilla from the oak and intense black cherry on the nose and palate.

1997 Louis M. Martini Winery Monte Rosso Vineyard
Cabernet Sauvignon, Napa Valley 🍷   ★ $$
Here's a wine that tastes like intensely flavored wild fruits, especially berries. It leaves the mouth with a touch of mocha and a pucker from the serious tannin.

1997 Amberhill Vineyards Cabernet Sauvignon, California 🍷   ★ $
It's somewhat rustic, but then look what you're getting for the price. There's some sweet fresh fruit on the nose and on the palate as well as some strawberry jam and vanilla. The wine has a pleasant finish, marked by hints of coffee and toast.

CULT WINES

California has fine-tuned the concept of cult wines. They're made in microbatches, often under a thousand cases at a time, which means that even moderate demand can never be met. They take the American taste for extremely flavorful wines to the *nth* degree. And they're impossible to get unless you're at the right auction with plenty of money to burn or you have one of the coveted spots on a customer list or go to a store or restaurant that has. Even then, the wine will be allocated; no one gets much. If a store is allowed a couple of cases, it in turn parcels out the bottles in ones and twos. Naturally, all this makes the wines wildly desirable, with cult-like followings and prices that can reach into the thousands of dollars. Here are nine current cult wines:

1. Araujo Estate Eisele Cabernet Sauvignon
2. Bryant Family Vineyard Cabernet Sauvignon
3. Colgin Cabernet Sauvignon
4. Dalla Valley Maya Cabernet Sauvignon
5. Grace Family Vineyard Cabernet Sauvignon
6. Harlan Estate Cabernet Sauvignon
7. Marcassin Chardonnay
8. Screaming Eagle Cabernet Sauvignon
9. Shafer Hillside Select Cabernet Sauvignon

merlot

In California, the red varietal Merlot plays Chocolate to Chardonnay's Vanilla. It's easy to pronounce and easy to drink, with little of the mouth-puckering tannin that's found in Cabernet Sauvignon. The best of the California Merlots offer aromas of plum, chocolate, and coffee. Napa Valley and the Russian River Valley produce the top bottles.

california **merlot**

at the table

As California Merlot is generally not terribly complex, keep the food on the simple side. Yes to herbs; no to strong spices. Yes to roasted vegetables; no to garlic. Meat is a natural, including light meats like pork. Poultry is fine, too. Merlot even works well with many grilled finfish, including mild ones such as red snapper, grouper, or sea bass.

the bottom line The Merlot that turns up in the inexpensive category often tastes like soda pop. But there are some entirely pleasant California Merlots in the $15-and-up category. Be prepared to spend $30 or more, though, for a wine of greater distinction.

what to buy MERLOT

1996	1997	1998	1999
★★★	★★★	★★★	★★★

recommended wines

1997 Nickel & Nickel Suscol Ranch, Napa Valley ☻   ★★★★ $$$$

Nicely tannic and filled with fresh-fruit flavors. Still, it's subtle. In fact, this is a great Merlot, with evolving strawberry flavors and aromas and a crème-caramel finish.

1997 Frog's Leap, Napa Valley ☻   ★★★★ $$$

Would that all Merlots were this well made. The aromas are berry and cassis, with a touch of ever-so-subtle fresh pine. On the palate, the wine is medium-bodied and extremely tangy, with a touch of tar and leather to hold your interest.

1997 Sterling Vineyard Three Palms, Napa Valley ☻   ★★★ $$$

If you're tired of cellaring Merlots instead of drinking them, pick this one up for tonight's dinner. It's a grand-scale Merlot—full-bodied and packed with plummy and blackberry flavors that go on and on.

1997 Pellegrini Family Vineyards Cloverdale Ranch, Alexander Valley ☻   ★★★ $$

The velvet texture here is paramount. But the wine also has aromas of cherry and cedar, and full flavors of chocolate and raspberries.

1997 Whitehall Lane, Napa Valley ♥   ★ ★ ★ $$

A wine that does not disappoint. It's medium-bodied, with oak, subtle tannin, and lots of aromas—like toffee, mint, and raspberry—all competing for attention. Add to that tastes of black currant, licorice, toast, and vanilla, and you've got this wine's number.

1997 Flora Springs Windfall Vineyard, Napa Valley ♥   ★ ★ $$$

A full-bodied wine with gentle acidity, ultra-mellow berry flavors, and plenty of complexity. There's some tea, touches of cranberry and milk chocolate, and a caramel-toffee finish.

1997 Bocage, Monterey ♥   ★ ★ $

A delectable mix of aromas—tarragon, green pepper, and vibrant raspberry—in a medium-bodied wine with a strong coffee finish.

1997 Joseph Phelps, California ♥   ★ $$$

A full-bodied wine with a very pleasant aroma and flavor of prunes cooked with vanilla; there's a little fresh-cut tobacco, too.

1997 Amberhill Vineyards, California ♥   ★ $

For very little money, you get a nice toasty flavor in an easy-drinkin' wine. It works with or without food.

pinot noir

The weather can be so warm in many parts of California that it's easy for growers to raise fully ripe fruit in abundance—but, unfortunately, it's when the vines struggle that they develop character. Burgundy, of course, is the benchmark for Pinot Noir, and though California Pinot Noir will never be the same as red Burgundy, that doesn't mean that there aren't some lovely California Pinots out there. They're just different. A few years ago, California Pinot Noir suggested cherry Coke. Now flavors are becoming less obvious, more sophisticated, especially from the cooler microclimates in Sonoma's Russian River Valley, Carneros, and parts of Santa Barbara County. Styles range from light, almost a deep blush wine, to fairly full, with good body and delicious berry flavor touched by an intriguing note of tar.

at the table

Since Pinot Noir is lighter than most American reds, it's the red wine of choice for fish (salmon is the classic). Fruit-glazed duck makes a great match, as does pasta with a light, creamy tomato sauce. Avoid flavors and spices that will overpower the wine, but feel pretty free to experiment. Pinot Noir is forgiving.

the bottom line Pinot Noirs around the world are expensive, and California's no exception. There's the occasional bargain at $12, but more likely you'll see bottles from $18 to $35.

what to buy PINOT NOIR

1995	1996	1997	1998	1999
★★★	★★	★★★	★★★	★★

recommended wines

1998 Iron Horse Vineyards, Sonoma County ♥   ★★★★ $$$
A medium- to full-bodied wine with lots of smoky cherry and strawberry flavors and dashes of herbs and pepper that accent the fruits' vibrancy.

1996 Calera Mt. Harlan, California ♥   ★★★ $$$$
Give this full-bodied wine some time to open up; in fact, if you're drinking it this year, you might want to decant it. As the wine develops in the glass, a real Burgundian black-cherry core becomes apparent, as well as subtle tannin.

1997 Acacia Beckstoffer Las Amigas Vineyard, Carneros ♥   ★★★ $$$
Intense blackberry aromas in a medium-bodied wine that offers hints of orange and nutmeg flavors.

1998 Flora Springs Lavender Hill Vineyard, Napa Valley ♥   ★★★ $$$
A wine that blends luscious fruit with some earthy underpinnings. On the palate, there's boysenberry, wild strawberries, a bit of flinty pencil shavings, some smoky bacon, sage, and a slight touch of vanilla.

1998 Flowers Vineyard & Winery, Sonoma Coast ♥   ★★★ $$$
This is not your blushing-violet, coax-me-onto-the-dance-floor Pinot. The aromas and flavors are full, fruity, and inviting. The wine is saturated with blackberry and black-cherry flavors and has some come-hither smokiness.

1998 Williams Selyem, Central Coast 🍷 ★★★ $$

Here's a Pinot to sink your teeth into. It's complex, with substantial oak aromas that, frankly, need to settle down and mellow out a bit. Give it a little time. There's a lot of smoky, chocolate-covered raspberry, a touch of mushroom, and plenty of vibrant acidity which, in combination, make this a delicious and appealing wine.

1998 Au Bon Climat La Bauge Au-dessus, Santa Maria Valley 🍷 ★★ $$

Though the wine needs another year, the evidence indicates that it will become very good indeed. Right now, there's a battle for dominance between the almost orange-like acidity and the other flavors. But underneath the conflict is an earthy Pinot Noir just screaming to get out. Already discernible are a few roses, a little bit of tar, and then a faint touch of toasted, yeasty bread on the finish.

1997 Fetzer Reserve Bien Nacido Vineyard, Santa Barbara County 🍷 ★★ $$

Here's a fruit bomb for you. A black-cherry nose follows through on the palate, along with gentle vanilla, a little pepper, and good acidity.

1997 Hendry Ranch, Napa Valley 🍷 ★★ $$

This is a Pinot in the Corton style—a bit mouth-puckering and rough due to the tannin, but that's what promises excellence in a few years.

1997 Domaine Carneros, Carneros 🍷 ★ $$$

A pleasing wine with some caramelized-sugar aromas, and a little bit of strawberry-vanilla ice cream on the finish.

zinfandel

In the '70s, a lot of the Zinfandel produced was lousy. Then California winemakers discovered what it could be: an herbal, earthy, gravelly wine with gobs of brambly fruit. Elegant it ain't. Delicious it is. In the early '90s, when all red wine was aspiring to be smooth, mellow Merlot, Zinfandel went through an identity crisis and transmogrified into a full-bodied, highly alcoholic monster that was nevertheless praised in many quarters. Now both styles are on the market.

california **zinfandel**

at the table

Fruity, versatile Zinfandel is the patriotic favorite for Thanksgiving. Zinfandel is also terrific with many flavorful Indian dishes, like tandoori chicken or lamb biriyani. It works well, too, with simple, cheesy, tomato-based Mexican or Italian food.

the bottom line   You might find a good entry-level California Zinfandel for $10, but $18 to $30 will get you something spectacular.

what to buy ZINFANDEL

1995	1996	1997	1998	1999
★★★	★★★	★★★	★★★	★★

recommended wines

1997 Gustavo Thrace, Napa Valley ▼   ★★★ $$$
A high-class Zin, and one that takes itself seriously. There's a little oxidized taste, but the wine makes up for that by gushing all over the palate with plummy flavor and just the right amount of tannin.

1998 Frog's Leap, Napa Valley ▼   ★★★ $$
At first, the low aroma makes you brace for a tannic, high-alcohol Zin, but a quick sip changes all that; the wine reveals itself as gently berried with nice blackberry tea and vanilla. The flavors, alcohol, and tannin all balance each other nicely.

1998 Rabbit Ridge, Sonoma County ▼   ★★★ $$
An interesting year for Rabbit Ridge. The wine is less lush than those of previous vintages, but alluring in its own way. The aroma is subdued. On the palate, a Zinfandel almost like the old-fashioned, rough-and-ready style of the '70s, but with the addition of vibrant raspberries and other bramble fruits—coupled with lots of wild herbs, especially rosemary—and there's a touch of coffee on the long finish.

1998 Rosenblum Richard Sauret Vineyard, Paso Robles ▼   ★★★ $$
A wine this good makes you wonder why people are complaining about the '98 vintage. It's packed with flavor, perhaps too much; the effect is over-opulent and signals the need for a year or two to calm down. If you must open the bottle now, serve the wine with a potent cheese.

1997 Vigil Vineyards Tres Condados, Napa Valley ♥   ★ ★ ★ $$

An unusual, not to say entirely wild and wacky, Zinfandel. There's cool menthol on the nose, almost as if this were a Shiraz—what's going on here? Nevertheless, the wine turns out to be delicious, even subtle on the palate, with a gentleness that does seem a bit odd after the strong aroma but is much appreciated all the same.

1998 Montevina, Amador County ♥   ★ ★ ★ $

We're stunned by the incredible value here. There's power and vibrancy—a bit of that old-fashioned Zinfandel rusticity. The aromas are spicy, especially peppery, with a little roasted-red-pepper sweetness, and then bright berry jam dances on the palate, brought out by the zingy acidity that also makes it all very food friendly.

1998 Hendry Block 7, Napa Valley ♥   ★ ★ $$

An edgy little number than can easily use another year in the bottle to develop and smooth out. Good things are happening in this wine already, though. The slight touch of oak on the finish softens the blackberry and pepper on the nose and the earth on the palate.

1996 Topolos at Russian River Vineyards Bella Lisa, Russian River Valley ♥   ★ ★ $$

This wine smells a little like tomato sauce—and that's generally considered a good characteristic, certainly not bad. It's just unexpected here. Then on the palate, the wine positively hops with mint, eucalyptus, and basil, and has a delicate but definite finish. Interesting!

1997 Fetzer Home Ranch, Mendocino ♥   ★ $$

This is decent, regular Zinfandel. It's not terribly exciting but comes at a fair price. It's a good and safe bet—and sometimes that's what's important. The wine delivers a nice bit of vanilla and blackberry on the nose, and then is gentle on the palate, with a small taste of herbs and spices. This is a wine that's easy to drink all by itself.

1997 Clos du Bois, Sonoma County ♥   ★ $

This little Sonoma County baby is on the rough, tannic side, but we often like our Zinfandels that way; we just call them old-fashioned and honest. The wine has some typical Zin characteristics: lots of black pepper and some brambly fruit, also a nice bit of vanilla.

Rosenblum Cellars Vintner's Cuvée XVIII, California ♥   ★ $

If you could cross a red wine with raspberry sorbet, this is what it would taste like. Here's a fairly light-bodied, vibrantly raspberry-toned wine that is consistent from aroma through flavor. Tiny bits of Mourvèdre and Cabernet add just the right amount of tobacco character so that the wine can be taken seriously, but not too seriously.

italian varietals & rhône reds in california

California wine culture has strong roots in Italy, with many of the pioneer Golden State vintners having Italian backgrounds, yet the grape varieties from that country took a long while to catch on. Now, there are plenty of Sangioveses, a sampling of Barberas, and the occasional Nebbiolo. These grapes all have lots of flavor when grown in the California climate, but critics note a lack of acidity—and it's the acidity that makes the varietals produced in Italy so food friendly.

Rhône grapes, such as Syrah, Carignan, Mourvèdre, and Grenache, are ideally suited to California's sultriness, where they become plummy and yummy. Syrah, especially, is successful and, in fact, makes some of California's finest red wines.

at the table

Cal-Itals are great with a hunk of youngish Parmesan or thin slices of prosciutto. Since they lack the flexibility of their Italian brethren, pair them with simple food. They'll make fine companions to pizza, burgers, spaghetti with meat sauce, or grilled vegetables.

Rhône-style wines, full-bodied and fruity, are fine choices for rustic dishes—like roast chicken with lots of garlic, and meat or vegetable stews. They also complement, and are flattered by, a bit of spicy heat.

the bottom line
Sangiovese will run between $10 and $30, while the oddball Barbera and Nebbiolo tend to all hover around $20. Syrah-based wine is next in line for California greatness; expect to spend $15 to $30.

what to buy SYRAH

1995	1996	1997	1998	1999
★★★	★★★★	★★★	★★★	★★

recommended wines

1997 Tablas Creek Tablas Rouge, Paso Robles ♥   ★ ★ ★ ★ $$$
The best of France and California combined. Oak is in the aromas here, and it complements the flavors as well. Slightly rough tannin keeps this wine from being a pushover. It's serious stuff.

1998 Beckmen Syrah, Santa Barbara County ♥   ★ ★ ★ ★ $$
Like the turtle that won the race, this wine starts off dull and unpromising and then sweeps your palate off its feet. It may take some work to get at the aromas and flavors now, but the wine is young yet. You will already find a touch of licorice, rosemary, and cinnamon, and though there's no obvious cherry flavor, there is some cherry buried deep within—sort of a dusty, very bittersweet-cocoa-covered cherry at the moment. Importantly, the wine will be tremendously food-worthy.

1998 Vigil Vineyard Tradicion Petite Sirah
Davies Vineyard, Napa Valley ♥   ★ ★ ★ $$$
Intense aroma of sage, with some eucalyptus notes, both of which follow through on the palate. This is a nice full-bodied wine with a bit of sophisticated stony flavor. On the finish, there's a little gravelly earthiness and just the slightest hint of tasty toffee.

1997 Bedford Thompson Syrah,
Santa Barbara County ♥   ★ ★ ★ $$
Intense, intense, intense. That's the word for this wine, with its strong nose of mouthwatering Bing cherry, total follow-through on the palate, and a finish that lingers on and on. Although the wine's a tad one-note, it's undeniably appealing. However, all that powerful flavor does make it difficult to pair with food, though it would be good with a cheese course.

1998 Edmunds St. John Rocks and Gravel, California ♥   ★ ★ ★ $$
There's something special about this blend of Syrah, Mourvèdre, and Grenache. Maybe it's the smell and taste of crushed rose petals, unusual for this kind of blend. A complex, tannic wine with a touch of allspice and tons of character.

1997 Long Vineyards Sangiovese, Napa Valley ♥   ★ ★ ★ $$
A yummy, medium-bodied wine. The velvety texture is most noticeable at first and then the flavors of spices parade through, keeping your interest through the whole glass.

1997 Rabbit Ridge Sangiovese, Sonoma County ♥   ★ ★ ★ $$
This wine is New World and explosive. It's powerful and full-bodied, with intense, black-cherry aromas, and full flavors on the palate that finish with vanilla and star anise.

1997 Atlas Peak Vineyards Sangiovese, Napa Valley ♥ ★ ★ $$

The reserve version of this wine has more oak and costs more money. We like this one much better. It's medium- to full-bodied and moderately complex, with gentle acidity and tannin. The wine smells of cherries and tastes a little of herbs and rose petals.

1998 Chameleon Cellars Barbera, Amador County ♥ ★ ★ $$

Mellow at first—and then along comes a burst of cassis, smoky cherry, a touch of amaretto, and pomegranate-like tartness.

1996 Concannon Vineyard Petite Sirah Reserve, Livermore Valley ♥ ★ ★ $$

The wine's vanilla aroma gives way to full baked plum and licorice flavors on the palate.

PETITE SIRAH

Contrary to popular belief, Petite Sirah is not simply "little Sirah," some kind of Syrah hybrid. However, just what it is remains uncertain. Some think it's a grape called Durif that originated in southeast France, some don't. For the time being, don't worry about what it is. Just drink it. It makes somewhat less aromatic wine than Syrah, but it's a good straightforward red with hints of molasses. The tannin is sturdy, and so the wine goes particularly well with grilled meats. Prices run from $18 to $40.

1997 Foppiano Vineyards Russian River Valley Petite Sirah, Sonoma County ♥ ★ ★ $$

A wine with a subtle nose of dark fruit. On the palate, there's a flavorful fruitiness, and licorice on the finish.

1998 Montevina Syrah, Amador County ♥ ★ ★ $$

The aromas of this Syrah are very appealing: vanilla, black raspberry, purple plum, even a little smoked meat. On the palate, the fruit flavors come across in a mellow wine that has the added flavors of crème brûlée and licorice. Sound like an odd mix? Well, it is, but somehow it works—in perfect harmony.

1997 Joseph Phelps Le Mistral, California ♥ ★ ★ $$

It aspires to be a spicy Rhône-style blend, but it's a fruity Californian through and through—and really tasty. There's lovely roasted fruit and plenty of vanilla and strawberry, all of them yummy. This is delicious with food or all by itself.

1997 Ridge Petite Sirah York Creek, Napa Valley 🍷 ★ ★ $$

A bit of toasty toffee on the nose and powerful tannin in the mouth along with flavors of raspberry, blackberry, and plum. The toffee repeats on the finish.

1996 Topolos at Russian River Vineyards
Alicante Bouschet, Sonoma 🍷 ★ ★ $$

We have to say that this fruit-meets-game-and-herb mixture makes for an interesting wine. First there's cherry and blueberry, then a gaminess that seems to take over, then an alluring touch of eucalyptus and rosemary. We like this wine with a little chill on it in the summer, room temperature in the winter.

1997 Villa Mt. Eden Syrah Grand Reserve,
Santa Maria Valley 🍷 ★ ★ $$

A wine with an aroma that has lots of spice and a little salty sea air. Moderate black-cherry flavor made sophisticated by a nice earthiness.

1997 Noceto Sangiovese, Shenandoah Valley 🍷 ★ ★ $

Delicious wine that swells with dark fruits and has walnut and cocoa notes on the palate. Perfect on its own or with food.

1997 La Famiglia di Robert Mondavi Barbera, California 🍷 ★ $$

The Mondavis have clearly learned a thing or two about making Italian varietals; the wines are getting better and better. Not that this is so typical that we could confidently guess in a blind tasting that it is indeed a Barbera, but the crisp acidity and spicy flavor are there.

1998 Preston of Dry Creek Faux, Dry Creek Valley 🍷 ★ $$

A blend of Mourvèdre, Syrah, Cinsault, Carignan, and Grenache, this wine offers lots of crushed peppercorns on the nose, as well as concentrated aromas of cherry and blackberry. On the palate, it's full-bodied and flavorful with toasted spices.

california blends

Many argue that the art of a great wine is in blending, not in vinifying a single grape. After all, look at the wines of Bordeaux, reckoned by many to be the greatest in the world. Bordeaux are the inspiration for the makers of Meritage (MARE-eh-tij) wines. These blends are made with Bordeaux grapes—Cabernet

Sauvignon, Merlot, Cabernet Franc, Malbec, and Petit Verdot—
and generally no single variety stars, so by law they can't be labeled with a varietal name. (Note: There are also white Meritages,
just as there are white Bordeaux.) Meritages can be counted upon
to be among a winery's most expensive bottles.

On the other hand, we have the blends made from whatever
looks good to the winemaker at a particular time, thrown into
one vat to ferment. The resultant wine often sports an evocative
but generic name, like Big House Red. These can be interesting,
full-bodied wines, and they can be very good deals.

at the table

For Meritages, follow the classic Bordeaux matches of simply
cooked beef or lamb. The wines can also go with stews or braised
meats. The free-form blends tend toward abundance in taste and
body, so don't be afraid to pair them with loads-o'-flavor food.
Provençal dishes, with their garlic, onions, olives, and herbs, will
always work.

the bottom line Meritage wines start at $30 and
zoom up to over $100. The simpler blends can be found be-
tween $8 and $15.

recommended wines

1997 Dominus Estate Dominus, Napa Valley ▼ ★★★★ $$$$
Full-bodied and plummy, the wine is this estate's best in years. It'll need about
a decade to lose its in-your-face oakiness, but if you go ahead and drink it
tonight you'll enjoy it nonetheless. To get down to specifics, the wine is medium-
bodied, with relatively mild tannin. Aromas of black currant, cedar, leather,
licorice, and pencil lead open the door to plum, black-cherry, blackberry,
chocolate, and cinnamon flavors.

1996 Conn Creek Winery Anthology, Napa Valley ▼ ★★★ $$$
A beautifully intense wine with vibrant flavors and aromas of wild berries. It
falls just short of earning that fourth star, but everything just might come together with a few more months of cellaring.

1997 Justin Justification, Paso Robles ▼ ★★★ $$$
Gently kissed by new oak, the aromas in this Merlot and Cabernet Franc blend
are of cola and earth. On the palate, it's pure plum and cherry.

1997 Treana, Central Coast 🍷 ★ ★ ★ $$$

A perfect reflection of the pastiche that is California winemaking: Bordeaux represented by Cabernet and Merlot, the Rhône by Syrah and Petite Sirah, and Italy by Sangiovese. The oak here is fairly light, and there are flavors of cherries, anise, and herbs.

1997 Vigil Terra Vin, Napa Valley 🍷 ★ ★ ★ $

There's a field of grapes in this one—the Vigil people won't say which varieties—and the result is an extra-silky wine that has just the right amount of tannin. Potent notes of tangy strawberry preserves along with some sun-baked apricot are on the finish, with the comforting tastes of café au lait.

1996 Murrieta's Well Red Vendimia, Livermore Valley 🍷 ★ ★ $$

This one's a Cabernet Sauvignon, Merlot, Zinfandel, and Cabernet Franc blend with a cherry-fruit-drop explosion on the nose and palate emphasized by touches of clove and cedar. It's a medium-bodied, constantly evolving wine with a delicate, velvety finish.

1998 Laurel Glen Vineyard REDS, California 🍷 ★ ★ $

Old-vine Zinfandel, Petite Sirah, Mourvèdre, and Grenache go into this blend that is smooth and delicious. A great price makes it go down even easier.

1997 Najiola-Spencer Favorito, California 🍷 ★ $

We love the idea of this Syrah/Mourvèdre/Grenache/Zinfandel/Petite Sirah blend. The wine's a little weak on the finish, but some black pepper and other spices, tar and licorice, and a little bit of currant make it entirely easy to reach for that second glass.

VINEYARD-DESIGNATED WINES

California winemakers have a new toy, and they're calling it Vineyard-Designated Wine. The label proudly announces that the wine comes from a particular vineyard. This is not a new concept. In Europe, when a vineyard has proved itself to be special over generations, bottlings from that single vineyard might eventually be produced. In California, it seems that this idea could well be a marketing ploy to capitalize on the romantic French concept of vineyard *terroir*—the combination of soil, topography, and climate that gives a wine its particular taste of place.

pacific northwest

The wine production of Oregon and Washington put together will never exceed that of California, but it's possible that the Northwest will challenge California's sovereignty as far as quality is concerned. The region is quickly gaining a solid reputation for world-class wines produced from French grape varieties. That the two states have such different climates means that each has the most success with different grapes— Pinot Gris and Pinot Noir in Oregon and Chardonnay, Sauvignon Blanc, Merlot, and Cabernet Sauvignon in Washington.

oregon

Small but strong, Oregon has a wine culture all its own—despite the impact of California, its Brobdingnagian neighbor. Ever since the modern Oregon wine industry began to flourish in the mid-1970s, it has been characterized by a plethora of individualistic boutique wineries (as opposed to Washington State, where one large corporation dominates). Most of Oregon's vintners are located in the Willamette (wil-LAM-et) Valley, where they frequently struggle against difficult, rainy harvests. More often than not, they succeed in their contest against the climate and produce excellent wines.

Featured Wine-Growing Regions

Puget Sound

• SEATTLE

Washington

Columbia Valley

Yakima Valley

Columbia River

• PORTLAND

Walla Walla Valley

Willamette Valley

Oregon

Umpqua Valley

Rogue Valley

grapes & styles

Oregon is renowned for its Pinot Noir above all other varietals. Due to the state's unpredictable weather, however, many vintages produce wines that are lacking in fullness. Nevertheless, the wines generally make up for that with a complex delicacy. Wherever Americans grow wine, there's almost sure to be Chardonnay, and Oregon is no exception. But the best white wines here are made from Pinot Gris, and Riesling, Gewürztraminer, and Pinot Blanc also shine.

on the label

Varietal labeling is the norm in Oregon. Occasionally, you'll find a blend—like Sokol Blosser Evolution, which is a tasty combination of Pinot Gris, Müller-Thurgau, Gewürztraminer, Semillon, Pinot Blanc, Chardonnay, Sylvaner, and Muscat.

pinot gris

More like Pinot Gris from Alsace than the Italian wines from the same grape (Pinot Grigio), Oregon versions can be bone dry or off-dry and are usually medium-bodied with nutty, fruity flavors.

at the table

Just like Alsace's Pinot Gris, Oregon's is a delightful aperitif wine. Its acidity also makes it a zippy food wine, especially good for cutting through rich dishes that have cream or butter sauces. The same quality complements shellfish and chicken or fish dishes made Caribbean-style with spice rubs and fruit salsas.

the bottom line
This is the white varietal that is presently king in Oregon. You'll spend between $10 and $18 for a good one.

recommended wines

1998 Chehalem Reserve, Willamette Valley 🍷 ★★★ $$
A seductive smell, then a full-bodied, fruity wine with a touch of pineapple and subtle tastes of other tropical fruits. It's slightly oaked and is packed with good, snappy acidity.

1998 Willamette Valley Vineyards Vintage Selection, Willamette Valley 🍷 ★★★ $$
Delightfully in-your-face with loads of lemons and oranges, peaches and apricots, and the extra bonus of yeasty, nutty, and spicy flavors.

1998 King Estate, Willamette Valley 🍷 ★★ $$
Subtle vanilla and pineapple aromas, along with that of fresh earth, lead to a full-bodied wine with apricot flavor and a touch of cedar.

1999 Ponzi, Willamette Valley 🍷 ★★ $$
A spicy wine that is light-bodied and has just a touch of apricot on the nose. The finish has a slight tingly-in-the-mouth feeling.

1998 Bethel Heights Vineyard, Willamette Valley 🍷 ★★ $
The wine teases with aromas of melon and mandarin orange, and then delivers with citrusy acidity and a hint of Brazil nut.

1998 St. Innocent Winery Vitae Springs Vineyard, Willamette Valley ♀   ★ ★ $

Here's a wine that has something to say and says it in a straightforward way. It's full-bodied, with gentle acidity, light lemon, and a wash of mineral flavors.

1999 Foris, Rogue Valley ♀   ★ $

Strong mango and honeydew on the nose. Full and spicy in the mouth, with a dose of saltwater taffy in the finish.

other white wines of oregon

Oregon Chardonnays are generally light-bodied, and quality is spotty. The state's versions of Alsatian varietals are the wines that are really worth seeking out. Gewürztraminers and Pinot Blancs are often vinified in a dry style and have compelling aromas.

the bottom line You can find Oregon Chardonnays under $12, some of them good values. The Alsatian varietals often come in under $15, a great price for excellent wines.

recommended wines

Sokol Blosser Winery Evolution, Oregon ♀   ★ ★ ★ $ $

This wine is like a spicy fruit salad, with flavors of lychee and pineapple. It's light-bodied with crackling acidity. The current release is the best yet.

1998 WillaKenzie Estate Pinot Blanc, Willamette Valley ♀ ★ ★ ★ $ $

A medium-bodied wine with few aromatics, but a slew of complex flavors: smoky pear and lemon, peach, and tart apple, to name a few.

1998 Amity Vineyards Pinot Blanc, Willamette Valley ♀   ★ ★ ★ $

Be prepared: The color may be almost neutral, but the wine is anything but. It's full-bodied, full-flavored with orange and lemon—and good.

1996 Foris Chardonnay Reserve, Rogue Valley 🍷   ★ ★ **$ $**

Age this a few more years. Right now, there's strong oak, powerful aromas and flavors of key lime and roasted chestnut, and a mineral finish.

1999 Sokol Blosser Winery Müller-Thurgau, Yamhill County 🍷   ★ ★ **$ $**

Deliciously peppery, lime-splashed, peachy, and apricot-y, this fruity wine also has dreamy floral aromas: jasmine, honeysuckle, and orange blossom.

1999 Foris Gewürztraminer, Rogue Valley 🍷   ★ ★ **$**

A lot of wine for the money. Opulent aromas bust out of the glass—lychees, mango, assertive lime, a touch of lemongrass. The wine is packed with ripe fruit flavor, but it's dry and has a subtle finish.

pinot noir

The typical Oregon Pinot Noir is spicy, with deep raspberry and black-cherry fruitiness and often a little bacon-like smokiness. The tannin is gentle. The best of these Pinot Noirs come close in quality to those of Burgundy, but, different from red Burgundies, they keep well only up to about five years from the vintage date.

at the table

The fruity, smoky quality of many Oregon Pinot Noirs makes them grand choices for foods that include sweet or earthy ingredients, or both, such as beets, sweet potatoes, peas, pancetta, celery root, dried beans, or mushrooms. Think along the lines of beet carpaccio, sweet-pea risotto, wild-mushroom ragout, or salmon with pancetta.

the bottom line
The $12 Oregon Pinot Noirs are getting harder and harder to find. Look for wines in the $15 to $35 range.

what to buy PINOT NOIR

1995	1996	1997	1998	1999
★ ★	★ ★ ★	★ ★	★ ★ ★	★ ★ ★ ★

recommended wines

1998 Belles Soeurs Shea Vineyard, Yamhill County ❦ ★★★ $$$
Delicate aromas of black cherry, blackberry, smoky rose petals, and clove. In the mouth, the smoke comes through, with cranberries, plums, vanilla, and toast.

1997 Chehalem Rion Reserve, Willamette Valley ❦ ★★★ $$$
This is certainly the star of Chehalem's lovely Pinot Noir line-up. Black-cherry fruitiness and a little tar for interest in a luscious wine.

1998 Foris Maple Ranch, Rogue Valley ❦ ★★★ $$$
Foris only makes Maple Ranch single-vineyard Pinot in great years; this wine is still young and hard to judge. It could easily rate four stars by the end of the year. Smoke, plums, and raspberries are on the palate, and the finish is long.

1998 Medici Vineyards, Willamette Valley ❦ ★★★ $$$
Full-bodied; packed with plum and currant flavors, and a touch of strawberry.

1998 WillaKenzie Dijon Clone 777, Willamette Valley ❦ ★★★ $$$
Powerful on the nose and subtle on the palate, this wine attacks with a flood of cherry and plum aromas. Lengthy, satisfying finish.

1998 Foris, Rogue Valley ❦ ★★★ $$
This has been one of the best values in Pinot Noir for several vintages, and that's even more true for 1998 than in past years. A terrific, medium-bodied wine. We tasted it before release and expect it to be even more exquisite by the summer of 2001.

1997 Sokol Blosser Redlands Winemaker Reserve, Yamhill County ❦ ★★ $$$
Subtle and delicately flavored, with hints of bacon fat and currants, and a touch of roses on the finish.

1998 Panther Creek Shea Vineyard, Willamette Valley ❦ ★★ $$
Appealing roses-and-tar Pinot Noir nose. The wine is full-bodied and a bit rough. Needs a few months to relax.

1998 Ponzi, Willamette Valley ❦ ★★ $$
Bitter strawberry on the nose. A medium-bodied wine with some bacon-like flavors, a touch of nutmeg, and good acidity.

1998 Bridgeview Vineyards and Winery Blue Moon, Rogue Valley ❦ ★ $$
A simple Pinot, it's rather light-bodied but should flesh out with a little time. Attractive spicy aromas and flavors that carry through to the finish.

washington state

Oregon and Washington may be neighbors, but don't think their wines are similar. In fact, they're dramatically different, and climate has a lot to do with it. Oregon is cool and damp with little seasonal variation; Washington's grape-growing areas have hot, dry summers and cold winters. Some spectacular wines have been coming out of the state for a while now, many of them still undervalued.

grapes & styles

Whereas Oregon is Pinot Noir territory, Washington has staked out Merlot. Increasingly, Cabernet Sauvignon and Syrah also bring in kudos. Due to the Chardonnay mania in this country, Washington makes its share, and it's quite good—fruity with an earthy twist. Look also for Sauvignon Blancs. Many have the toasty oak so loved in California wines, but here it rarely dominates varietal flavor.

on the label

Labeling stresses the grape variety. Of the regions, the Columbia and Yakima Valleys have the most wine acreage. Though the Walla Walla Valley is tiny, it has many top-quality wineries.

chardonnay

Earth and minerals meet apple and pear in the Washington Chardonnay flavor profile. The addition of buttery, toasty, vanilla-y oak is apparent, too, but it's gentle by California standards.

at the table

With its stony, mineral quality and good acidity, Washington State Chardonnay is more versatile than the California version. Pair one of these Chards with grilled fish, chicken, or quail. Or try one out with a full-flavored pasta dish, such as pumpkin ravioli.

the bottom line Stay under $18 for terrific values in Chardonnays. Wines at this price are good, and, since few expensive Chardonnays seem worth the money, why pay more?

recommended wines

1997 Columbia Crest Winery Reserve, Columbia Valley ★★ $$
Full-bodied and powerful, with pineapple and apricot in addition to the oak-induced spice, vanilla, and toast.

1999 Gordon Brothers Cellars, Columbia Valley ★★ $$
A refreshing Chardonnay that tingles the tongue with a tiny bit of effervescence, has slight oak flavors, and leaves a caramel-like taste in the finish.

1998 Chateau Ste. Michelle, Columbia Valley ★★ $$
Just one sip gives you a mouthful of lime and pear with an overlay of spicy oak.

1998 Hedges Fumé-Chardonnay, Columbia Valley ★★ $
Sauvignon Blanc adds a bit of herbaceousness to fruity, buttery Chardonnay. There's also a touch of honey on the palate in this medium-bodied wine.

1998 Columbia Crest Winery, Columbia Valley ★ $
A refreshing Chardonnay with lots of tropical fruit going on, as well as spice and pineapple notes—all at a gentle, under-$10 price.

1998 Hogue Cellars, Columbia Valley ★ $
A simple everyday wine, with pear on the palate, and a touch of minerals.

1998 Paul Thomas Winery, Washington State ★ $
A subtle Chardonnay, with clear lemon and star-fruit flavor and zesty acidity.

sauvignon blanc

One of the state's first wine success stories was Hogue Cellars' Fumé Blanc (aka Sauvignon Blanc), a zesty wine at a low price. The world is now well aware of Washington Sauvignon Blanc. It's light and herbal with bracing acidity—but not always easy to find.

at the table

Washington State Sauvignons are versatile. They go well with almost anything light—like simple broiled fish or roast chicken—all the better if it's sprinkled copiously with fresh green herbs.

the bottom line There is tremendous value here, and Sauvignons are a great alternative to the ever-present Chardonnay. Look for Sauvignon Blanc under $10.

recommended wines

1998 Columbia Crest Winery Sauvignon Blanc, Columbia Valley 🍷   ★ $
Lots of citrusy aromas and flavors here sprinkled with fennel seed and fresh herbs. A refreshing, enjoyable wine.

1998 Covey Run Fumé Blanc, Yakima Valley 🍷   ★ $
Vanilla and grass are the first things that come to mind. Then this medium-bodied wine mellows out with fruity flavors and an oak-enhanced finish.

1998 Hogue Cellars Fumé Blanc, Columbia Valley 🍷   ★ $
Once again, Hogue puts out a tasty Sauvignon Blanc. Light citrus, grass, and melon aromas come together with grapefruit flavor.

other white wines of washington state

Washington Rieslings can be terrific, frequently in an off-dry style with peach-apricot aromas and zingy acidity. Semillon can also be a hit. It's often blended with Sauvignon Blanc. Gewürztraminer and Chenin Blanc are interesting buys as well, in either dry or off-dry versions. You can expect light body, good acidity, and appealing delicacy from all the Washington State dry whites.

the bottom line Since the Washington varietals aren't among the most popular, many of the wines are available at excellent prices. Look for them at less than $10 and experiment. Some boutique Semillons will run higher.

recommended wines

1998 L'Ecole No. 41 Semillon Fries Vineyard, Columbia Valley 🍷 ★ ★ ★ $$
Beautiful pineapple and kiwi aromas and flavors with a slight vanilla background and good acidity. A lingering, tart finish.

1998 DeLille Cellars Chaleur Estate Blanc, Columbia Valley 🍷 ★ ★ $$
A medium-bodied wine made with a combo of Semillon and Sauvignon Blanc. It's been done up in grand style, meaning lots of new oak. Vanilla-scented, with a touch of honey on the tongue.

1999 Hogue Cellars Chenin Blanc, Columbia Valley 🍷 ★ ★ $
A smidgen of nectarine and honey in this wine balances the snappy acidity. The wine would be wonderful next to a fruit salad.

1999 Hogue Cellars Gewürztraminer, Columbia Valley 🍷 ★ ★ $
Beautifully fragrant without overbearing perfume. This wine has gobs of peaches and gooseberries, and a lovely kiss of lime in the finish.

1999 Columbia Winery Cellarmaster's Reserve Riesling, Columbia Valley 🍷 ★ $
Peach aromas, a lemony peachy taste, and a little bit of sparkle from effervescence on the tongue.

1999 Covey Run Riesling, Washington State 🍷 ★ $
A terrific casual, everyday wine with fruit fragrance, good acidity, and a lovely stony taste to balance it out.

1999 Hogue Cellars Pinot Gris, Columbia Valley 🍷 ★ $
Nice apple and pear aromas in a dry wine. Earthy and a little bit lees-y, with some puckery acid to make it refreshing.

1998 Chateau Ste. Michelle Semillon, Columbia Valley 🍷 ★ $
Aggressively oaked, yet the typical nuttiness of the Semillon grape comes through to create a delicious fruit-and-nut wine.

merlot & cabernet sauvignon

Merlot is the big boy of Washington State red grapes. Unlike so many of California's Merlots, Washington's generally have spunk. Both the Merlots and Cabernet Sauvignons are richly fruity and full-bodied. The style, with a moderate use of oak, falls somewhere between that of Bordeaux and California.

at the table

Whether you get a bargain or a piggybank breaker, Merlots and Cabernets are most often big in both flavor and body. The usual red meats are great companions, as are any sweet-red-pepper-based dishes. And you'll love these wines with a bit of blue cheese at the end of a meal.

the bottom line You'll find inexpensive $12 winners, lots of very good wines between $15 and $30, and superstars that weigh in at $50.

what to buy MERLOT AND CABERNET SAUVIGNON

1995	1996	1997	1998	1999
★★★	★★★	★★★	★★★	★★★

recommended wines

1997 L'Ecole No. 41 Cabernet Sauvignon, Columbia Valley 🍷 ★★★ $$$

A powerful Cabernet with lovely, intense aromas of black cherries and vanilla. It's luscious and full-bodied, with a lingering, toasty caramel finish.

1998 L'Ecole No. 41 Merlot Seven Hills Vineyard, Walla Walla Valley 🍷 ★★★ $$$

It caresses the nose with subtle strawberry, then washes the mouth with a whole mess of jammy berry flavor, with a touch of herbs. The experience ends with a long finish of espresso and toast. Good tannin.

1995 Foris Klipsun Vineyard Cabernet Sauvignon, Washington ♟ ★ ★ ★ $$$

Foris is actually an Oregon winery, but the winemaker, Sarah Powell, is in love with the Klipsun Vineyard of Washington. It's easy to see why: It produces terrific fruit. This wine, made of grapes shipped in from Washington, packs a wallop with cherry and plum, and is further deepened by excellent tannin.

1997 Leonetti Cellar Merlot, Columbia Valley ♟ ★ ★ ★ $$$

There's a lot of complexity packed into this medium-bodied, purple-colored wine. The lush blackberry, cherry, and violet aromas catch your attention, which is then kept with lovely flavors of wild blueberries, red raspberries, toast, and tobacco.

1998 Andrew Will Klipsun Vineyard Merlot, Yakima Valley ♟ ★ ★ ★ $$$

This guy makes gorgeous Merlot. The one from Klipsun Vineyard is spicy on the nose (unexpected for a Merlot), and then brings on fruit and flower flavors. Imagine raspberries and strawberries sprinkled with rosewater. A long, long finish.

1997 Seven Hills Klipsun Vineyard Cabernet Sauvignon, Walla Walla Valley ♟ ★ ★ $$$

This wine needs a few years to come into its own. Underneath the considerable woodiness, cedar, and tongue-coating tannin is a touch of black cherries and blackberries just waiting to explode. Buy now, drink later.

1997 Canoe Ridge Vineyard Merlot, Columbia Valley ♟ ★ ★ $$

This wine has delicate purple plum, accented with black tea and tobacco.

1997 Hedges Cellars Three Vineyards, Columbia Valley ♟ ★ ★ $$

Deeply-flavored blend of Cabernet Sauvignon, Merlot, and Cabernet Franc. A pleasing combination of oak, smoky leather, spice, and raspberry jam.

1997 Chateau Ste. Michelle Canoe Ridge Estate Vineyard Merlot, Columbia Valley ♟ ★ ★ $$

Concentrated but not too assertive; in fact, the wine is mellow. There's a nice taste of black plum, the bite of clove, and a dusting of black pepper.

1997 Bookwalter Winery Merlot, Columbia Valley ♟ ★ $$$

At first this wine smells pretty high-alcohol; then it calms down to a plummy aroma with a substantial bit of mint. There's a fair amount of tart and tarry berry flavor, with good acid and tannin.

1995 Chateau Ste. Michelle Cold Creek Vineyard Cabernet Sauvignon, Columbia Valley ♟ ★ $$

A medium-bodied wine that's not overwhelmed by new oak. With a little time in the glass, it reveals a bunch of blackberries and a nice dose of tobacco and tea.

1998 Paul Thomas Winery Merlot, Washington State ♥   ★ $

If you like mellow Merlot, this is the one to get. It's totally gentle in the mouth—an easy wine to like. Not terribly complicated, but it has some nice café au lait aromas going on, plus flavors of wild berries. The wine is good with food or without.

1997 Paul Thomas Winery Reserve
Cabernet Sauvignon, Columbia ♥   ★ $

A full-bodied wine with a nice big batch of rosemary and chocolate flavors.

other red wines of washington state

Syrah is being planted like crazy in Washington. Flavor comes on strong with exuberant black fruit. Stylistically, these are more in-tune with the Rhône Valley than California. We're hearing great things about Cabernet Francs from the area, but they sure are difficult to find on the shelves. Look for the beautifully tannic Bordeaux-style blends, which often include Merlot, Cabernet Sauvignon, and Cabernet Franc.

the bottom line You'll see more Syrah under $15, though the $15 to $35 range does exist. There are a few Bordeaux blends that hit the $60 mark, but most, as well as the state's Cabernet Francs, will fall between $20 and $30.

recommended wines

1997 Columbia Winery Red Willow Vineyard
Cabernet Franc, Yakima Valley ♥   ★ ★ ★ $ $

A full-bodied and complex wine that has a glorious velvety texture. Perhaps the oak is overdone, but in this wine, it works. The aroma reminds us of a breeze coming through a cherry orchard, and the flavors are of almond, chocolate, coffee bean, cherry, and plum.

1997 Columbia Winery Red Willow Vineyard Syrah, Yakima Valley ♟ ★ ★ $$$

A gentle Syrah with a berry flavor—it goes into the pleasant, easy-drinking category and would marry well with food.

1998 Seven Hills Winery Syrah, Walla Walla Valley ♟ ★ ★ $$$

This is a lovely wine, offering taste sensation after taste sensation. Medium-weight, with touches of black-cherry jam, licorice, plum, coffee, and cardamom, and a subtle flavor of toast in the finish.

1997 Hogue Cellars Genesis Cabernet Franc, Columbia Valley ♟ ★ ★ $$

Cedary, red and green peppery, with a touch of cayenne balanced out by lots of full jammy fruit and a toasty finish.

1996 Hogue Cellars Genesis Blue Franc Lemberger, Columbia Valley ♟ ★ ★ $

A paradoxical wine: It's smooth but also has invigorating acidity. There's plenty of intriguing strawberry and blueberry-like sweetness for balance, along with a hint of vanilla.

1997 Shooting Star Wines Blue Franc Lemberger, Washington State ♟ ★ ★ $

We like these funky, little-known varietals when they're done well—and this one goes down the hatch pretty darn easy. It's got great aromas of vanilla, berries, and herbs and a fruit-packed, pepper-sprinkled flavor.

1997 DeLille Cellars Doyenne Syrah, Yakima Valley ♟ ★ $$$

With vigorous swirling, spices, smoke, pepper, strawberries, and blueberries come out. A slightly mushroomy wine, with tea-like bitterness. Pair it with something grilled.

new york state

When settlers planted grapevines in what was to become New York City, they expected to produce some great wine. The vines failed there, but they did thrive farther north in the Hudson River Valley. Today, a healthy wine industry flourishes in New York State. The historic Hudson River Valley, the Finger Lakes region, and, most prominently, Long Island are the areas that are producing excellent wine.

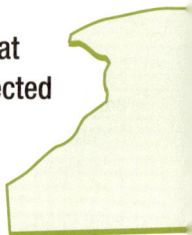

grapes & styles

New York is still figuring out what grows best in its climate and soil. Riesling, especially in the Finger Lakes, is one of its winning experiments. Chardonnay has also been successful in the region, and there is a tradition of sparkling wines made by the *méthode champenoise*.

The Hudson River Valley has yet to make its best wine. It concentrates on French-American varieties, like the white Seyval Blanc, and also dabbles in Chardonnay and Pinot Noir.

Long Island has positioned itself as the Bordeaux of the East Coast. It makes some good Bordeaux-style blends, and has hung its hat on the Bordeaux variety Merlot. Cabernet Franc may have a rosy future as a red varietal here, too. Though Pinot Noir doesn't usually do well here, at least one producer, Lenz Winery, has put out a very tasty one. Among whites, Chardonnay, Sauvignon Blanc, Riesling, and Gewürztraminer thrive in New York, and Pinot Blanc just might become more successful than Chardonnay. Rosés made from Merlot, Chardonnay, or Cabernet Franc are quite tasty.

Finger Lakes

Hudson River

ALBANY •

Hudson River Valley

Featured Wine-Growing Regions

North Fork

Long Island

South Fork

on the label

Bottles are usually labeled by grape variety. Blends sometimes sport imaginative proprietary names, like Fox Run Vineyards' Ruby Vixen and Arctic Fox.

white & rosé wines of new york state

Due to the cool climate, New York's Chardonnays tend to be lighter and more acidic than California's, and thus easier to pair with food. The Alsace whites are winners: Look for Rieslings, Pinot Blancs, Gewürztraminers, and some of the state's refreshing oddball blends. Long Island rosés are charming company on the beach.

new york **whites & rosés**

at the table
Light New York whites go well with shellfish, lean finfish, and chicken. An off-dry blend or rosé makes a good summer aperitif.

the bottom line
Look for whites between $8 and $20. The blends and rosés are similarly priced.

what to buy WHITE WINES

1997	1998	1999
★ ★ ★	★ ★ ★	★ ★ ★

recommended wines

1999 Channing Perrine Mudd Vineyard Fleur de la Terre, North Fork ♀   ★ ★ ★ $$
All the fancy wine lists in New York City have a Channing Perrine wine, and this one is a favorite. Made from Merlot, it's low on aromatics, high on flavor.

1999 Dr. Konstantin Frank Vinifera Wine Cellars Rkatsiteli, Finger Lakes ♀   ★ ★ ★ $
Rkatsiteli is a grape that's widely grown in the former Soviet Union, but it seems to do just great in upstate New York, too. There's lots going on in the glass—peach-blossom nectar, pear, apple, and a positively zingy acidity.

1999 Silver Thread Vineyard Dry Riesling, Finger Lakes ♀   ★ ★ ★ $
Though the label says *dry*, there's a subtle dollop of honey-like nectar here. It's a yummy wine, with a bit of Brazil nut in the finish.

1998 Corey Creek Vineyards Chardonnay, North Fork ♀   ★ ★ $$
Check out this unoaked estate Chardonnay; it's uncomplicated and light-bodied, with green-apple acidity. Perfect with roast chicken or simple boiled lobster.

1998 Fox Run Vineyards Gewürztraminer Penn Yan, Finger Lakes ♀   ★ ★ $$
A full and spicy wine with a bit of petrol on the nose and on the palate, quite a lot of peach and apricot, and a dose of cracked pepper.

1999 Dr. Konstantin Frank Vinifera Wine Cellars Gewürztraminer, Finger Lakes ♀   ★ ★ $$
A mineral-laden Gewürztraminer. It's dry, with lots and lots of peppery spice and a nutty finish.

1998 Lieb Family Cellars Pinot Blanc, North Fork ★★ $$
Citrus fruits, apples, pears, and melons in the bouquet. The grapes for this complex wine were hand-picked and lightly pressed.

1999 Salmon Run Chardonnay, Finger Lakes ★★ $
We love this totally delightful Chard because of its clear flavors of nectarine and peach. It's medium-bodied and delicious.

1999 Standing Stone Estate White, Finger Lakes ★★ $
A snappy, fruity wine made from Vidal grapes with a floral honeysuckle aroma and subtle grapefruit flavor.

1999 Wolffer Estates Dry Rosé, The Hamptons ★★ $
The barest coppery blush colors this crazy combo of Chardonnay, Merlot, and Pinot Noir. Lemon, grapefruit, and lime flavors come together on the nose and follow through on the palate.

1999 Casa Larga Vineyards Viognier, Finger Lakes ★ $$
Light-bodied and very, very peachy, with good acidity. This wine wouldn't be mistaken for a Rhône Viognier—it's not that complex—but it is lovely.

1998 Palmer Pinot Blanc Estate, North Fork ★ $$
Not much aroma here, but the wine is nonetheless refreshing going down, with a clear drop of honeydew flavor. Perfect for a hot day.

1998 Wolffer Estates La Ferme Martin Chardonnay, The Hamptons ★ $$
Lemon, vanilla, and toast aromas in a medium-bodied wine. Finishes with an appealingly dry lemon-and-lime acidity.

red wines of new york state

We find an occasional exciting Pinot Noir, but the best New York State reds are Merlots, with Cabernet Francs a close second, and they're from Long Island. From the same source, look for Cabernet Sauvignons and Bordeaux-style blends.

at the table

Fruity Merlots and herbal Cabernet Francs complement medium-weight foods, like salmon or tuna among fish, quail or duck for birds, and pork among meatier fare. Cabernet Sauvignon and Bordeaux-style blends tend to be tannic and beg for full-flavored protein, so a steak or lamb chop would go well.

the bottom line New York reds run between $12 and $25, with the occasional bottle over $25.

what to buy RED WINES

1995	1996	1997	1998	1999
★★★★	★★★	★★★	★★★★	★★

recommended wines

1998 Standing Stone Pinnacle, Finger Lakes ♥   ★★★ $$
Who says you can't make good Bordeaux-style wines in the Finger Lakes? This one from Standing Stone Vineyards is delicious. There are earth and spice elements, and also fruitiness, with loads of plum.

1998 Wagner Vineyards Meritage, Finger Lakes ♥   ★★★ $
Cigar, tobacco, and green and sweet red peppers on the nose, then lots of fruit and vanilla flavor.

1998 Corey Creek Vineyards Cabernet Franc, North Fork ♥ ★★ $$
Full-flavored and fruity, with berries predominating. Wonderful with grilled sausage or steak.

1998 Osprey's Dominion Vineyard Pinot Noir, North Fork ♥ ★★ $$
A bit of candied strawberry, tar, and earth on the nose. This is a delicate but very flavorful Pinot Noir. In hot weather, put salmon on the grill, chill the wine a little, and have a feast.

1998 Hargrave Vineyard Cabernet Franc, North Fork ♥   ★ $$$
Smokiness defines this light-bodied Cabernet Franc, but there's also subtle blackberry flavor, an earthy, mushroomy quality, and puckering acidity.

1998 Fox Run Vineyards Lemberger, Finger Lakes ♥   ★ $$
Spicy vanilla with appealing hints of violet on the nose. There are tar flavors at first and then blueberry. Gentle tannin.

1997 Fox Run Vineyards Meritage, Finger Lakes 🍷 ★ $$
Slight tarry aromas waft from the glass. There's more wood than fruit in this wine; it's got powerful espresso-like flavor. A large dose of chocolate is also evident, along with plum. More gentle than it sounds, the wine's flavors, acidity, alcohol, and tannin are in beautiful balance. The finish carries a taste of cherries.

1998 Fox Run Vineyards Pinot Noir Reserve, Finger Lakes 🍷 ★ $$
A wine that smells like a grilled steak. Yet it has subtle fruit flavors, with a mild strawberry tang and a dusting of ground pepper on the finish.

SOMMELIERS SOUND OFF

We asked top sommeliers from around the country what wine drinkers are ordering—and what they wish their customers would choose to drink instead.

"They're clamoring for those damned California Cabernets, and I'm trying to get them turned on to Piedmontese reds. It's not working. I console myself with the fact that they're starting to wean off of California Chardonnays and be a little more adventurous."

—KAREN KING, WINE DIRECTOR
UNION SQUARE CAFÉ, NEW YORK CITY

"They're still asking for California Chardonnays, and I'm trying to suggest the white Rhônes: the Viogniers, Marsannes, and Roussanes. If they'd try them, they'd love them."

—CURT BURNS, HUDSON CLUB, CHICAGO

"People are always looking for those star-vintage Burgundies, even though I might have a spectacular '92 on the list that not only is drinking fabulously but is a deal."

—CAT SIRILIE, #9 PARK, BOSTON

"Most people are looking for the current releases of California Cabernets—recently reviewed and got a gazillion points. I'd much rather they chose some of the older Cabernets that have evolved and are more complete wines. For white wines, the Chardonnays are still popular, but I'd love to see people drink more Loire Valley Chenin Blancs. They're great food wines."

—LARRY STONE, RUBICON, SAN FRANCISCO

south
africa

When apartheid ended in the early 1990s, South Africa was being touted as the world's next wine hot spot: great wines for great prices. At that time, there were plenty of wines to choose from, but, in fact, most were inferior. Now the situation is reversed. Many of the wines—scintillating whites, robust reds—are terrific, and the problem is availability. Maybe increased demand will change that. African-cuisine restaurants serving wines of the region are popping up across the country, and even Disney is getting into the act, serving South African wines almost exclusively at its new resort at Disney World's Animal Kingdom.

grapes & styles

South African vintners pride themselves on producing the most European of the New World wines, and rightfully so. In the New World category (primarily the U.S., Australia, New Zealand, South America, and South Africa), theirs are the most subtle and sophisticated. Infrequent use of oak aging and extremely varied soil contribute to the elegance and complexity of South African wines.

Grapes for white wines dominate, taking up about 85 percent of vineyard space. A lot of Chenin Blanc, which has been the primary variety, is now being pulled up to make way for the more popular Chardonnay and Sauvignon Blanc. Among reds are Cabernet Sauvignon, Merlot, and Syrah. The wines are invariably full-bodied with strong tannin, and often have notes of chocolate, dark berries, and even a bit of mint and smoke. The hybrid Pinotage grape shows great potential.

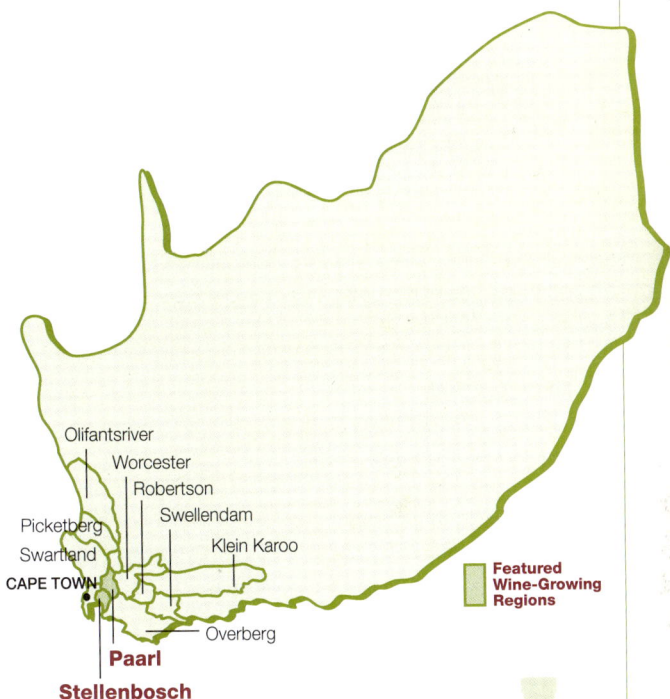

Olifantsriver
Worcester
Robertson
Pickerberg
Swellendam
Swartland
Klein Karoo
CAPE TOWN

**Featured
Wine-Growing
Regions**

Overberg

Paarl

Stellenbosch

STEEN BECOMES CHENIN BLANC

Steen is the South African name for the grape that used to carpet the country, ending its days in lousy jug wine. There are winemakers who can't quite give up on the variety, but they are giving up on its local moniker, which they feel carries a terrible stigma. Chenin Blanc is the same grape, but that name conjures up the great, ageworthy wines of the Loire Valley. In the future, "Steen" will probably make a comeback due to some retro-chic movement, but for the time being, South African vintners are referring to the grape as Chenin Blanc.

on the label

Most of South Africa's wines are varietals and stress the grape name on the label. *Wine of Origin*, or WO, is the South African equivalent of the French AOC (see "On the Label," page 23). The most celebrated areas are Stellenbosch and Paarl.

white wines of south africa

Stop at the South Africa aisle for European-style Chablis-like Chardonnays, intensely grassy Sauvignon Blancs, and easy-drinkin' Chenin Blancs.

at the table

South African Chardonnays, with their high acidity and mineral edge, work beautifully with oysters, making the wine a bargain fill-in for Chablis. The country's brisk Sauvignon Blanc is fantastic with any rich fish, while the melony, appley nature of South African Chenin Blanc makes it a good aperitif and an excellent accompaniment to the flavors of fusion cuisine, such as lemongrass and coconut.

the bottom line
Lovely Sauvignon Blancs and Chardonnays can be found in the vicinity of $18. If you're looking for everyday wines, shop wisely and pick up some tasty, under-$10 Chenin Blancs.

recommended wines

1999 Rustenberg Sauvignon Blanc, Stellenbosch ♟ ★★★★ $$
An extremely limey, blossomy, beautifully seductive and mouthwatering nose highlights an acidic wine that has a touch of nuttiness in addition to clear Sauvignon Blanc herb, citrus, and melon flavors.

1999 Brampton Sauvignon Blanc, Stellenbosch ♟ ★★★ $$
Fruity on the nose, with peach, nectarine, and apricot and just a touch of fresh-cut grass. On the palate, the wine is delicious, with stinging acidity that balances the full-bodied mouth-feel.

1999 Buitenverwachting Estate Sauvignon Blanc, Constantin ♟ ★★★ $$
Aromas of mineral and slate rise in waves from the glass. Then there's the assertive flavor of sage and quite a bit of fig in this full-bodied wine.

1999 Delaire Chardonnay, Stellenbosch ♀️   ★ ★ ★ $$

It grabs attention with complex aromas of flowers, pears, and apples. On the palate it's full, almost oily, but with a beautiful beam of acidity that makes the overall effect refreshing.

2000 Thelema Sauvignon Blanc, Stellenbosch ♀️   ★ ★ $$

Lime and grass aromas lead to a vibrantly acidic wine with some peach-skin, almond, and apple flavors.

1999 Simonsig Chenin Blanc, Stellenbosch ♀️   ★ ★ $

A traditional-style Chenin Blanc with a tiny bit of spritz to set off the clear lemon and floral tastes.

1998 Mulderbosch Chardonnay, Stellenbosch ♀️   ★ $$

A full-bodied, oaky Chardonnay, with pear, citrus, and apple flavors and a mellow toasted-almond and vanilla finish.

1999 Simunye Sauvignon Blanc, Coastal Region ♀️   ★ $$

This is a joint venture between a Californian and a South African company (Simunye means *we are one* in Zulu), so be prepared for some New World influence. The aromas are of melon and lime. The acidity is harsh, but it can, and should, be muted by serving the wine with food: A soft goat cheese would be the perfect antidote.

1999 Swartland Steen, Swartland ♀️   ★ $

Good qualities here are refreshing lemon and melon flavors and fierce acidity. The wine peters out on the finish—which is forgivable for an under-$10 wine.

red wines of south africa

Serious pleasure is yours with a good bottle of Cabernet or Merlot, and, if you can find one of the terrific Shirazes—Syrah in France—you'll be in luck. Pinotage (pee-no-tahj), a South African original, is a cross between Cinsault, which is spelled *Cinsaut* here, and Pinot Noir. Though the Pinotage style is still a bit unsettled, this velvety, fruity-meets-earthy union may become great.

at the table

Cabernet Sauvignon and Merlot thrive with red meat. Peppery and boldly flavored Shiraz is great with meat that's been barbecued or grilled. Pinotage varies in fullness; the lighter ones can be just the thing for a simple dinner of broiled salmon or chicken, while fuller Pinotage will go best with the same big meat flavors as the other South African reds.

the bottom line Values abound because quality has improved faster than the prices have gone up. You'll find a big price range for these reds, from $7 to $30.

recommended wines

1998 Haute-Cabrière Estate Pinot Noir, Franschhoek ♈   ★★★ $$$

Hello, is this Australian? It almost tastes that way. There's a wave of allspice, clove, mint, and menthol, giving way to incredible smoked-meat and mushroom flavors.

1998 Kanonkop Pinotage, Stellenbosch ♈   ★★★ $$$

Violets come to mind—with intensity—when you take a whiff of this. Other aromas surface as well: carnation, barnyard, plum. In the mouth, this is a delicious, fruity wine with a long finish.

1997 Meerlust Pinot Noir Reserve, Stellenbosch ♈   ★★★ $$$

An intensely bacony wine with tart acidity and notes of baked raspberries and fresh violets.

1997 Warwick Trilogy, Stellenbosch ♈   ★★★ $$

In both taste and body, this is a full wine. There is wonderful complexity with flavors of smoke, truffles, stone, and berries.

1996 Kanonkop Cabernet Sauvignon, Stellenbosch ♈   ★★ $$$

The Kanonkop style tends to be full-bodied and earthy, and so this Cabernet is big on the kind of velvety smooth texture that comes from two years in wood. It's also got some lively bell pepper, a good bit of blackberry, and the kind of acidity than can stand up to spicy food.

1996 Meerlust Rubicon, Stellenbosch ♈   ★★ $$$

This wine could use some time to age. At this point, there's raspberry and strawberry flavor, a touch of tar, and a long finish.

reds south africa

1997 Rustenberg, Stellenbosch ♛   ★ ★ $ $
A medium-bodied wine with a good balance of tannin, acid, and flavor. Green bell pepper, pencil shavings, and dark berries all come through. The wine is 80 percent Cabernet, filled out with bits of Merlot and Cabernet Franc. With twenty months in new oak, this wine is striving towards New World, but it straddles the Old with its subtle complexity.

1997 Simonsig Shiraz, Stellenbosch ♛   ★ ★ $ $
An attractive, full-bodied wine with smokehouse aroma and flavors of chocolate, pepper, and red currant.

1997 Swartland Shiraz, Swartland ♛   ★ ★ $
There's a Pinot Noir-like smoky aroma here. Though lighter in body than one would expect, this wine is still a flavorful drink, full of pepper and red berries.

1998 Cape Indaba Cabernet Sauvignon, Coastal Region ♛   ★ $
Harsh tannin in this wine, with an earthy, bitter edge, lots of tar, and a little charred-steak flavor. The price is great, and the wine will mellow.

1998 Swartland Cabernet Sauvignon, Swartland ♛   ★ $
Here's an earthy wine, with licorice, tar, mint, and plum flavors. Fabulous for the money.

1998 Swartland Pinotage, Swartland ♛   ★ $
With subtle mint and blackberry flavors, this Pinotage goes down easy. It's a perfect choice for everyday meals.

australia

In the late 1980s, Australian wines stormed into the international market with intense fresh-fruit flavors, an impressive range of styles, and, not unimportantly, good prices. With dramatic variations in microclimates across its many growing areas and adventurous, technologically savvy winemakers, Australia continues to offer great possibilities. Meanwhile, consumers can thank reasonable Australian prices for keeping the rest of the world's producers on their toes.

grapes & styles

In general, Australian producers lean toward fruitiness and oakiness. The wines are consumer-friendly and yet capable of great complexity when made by the right hands. Though the creamy, tropical-fruit Chardonnays get the most attention, good Semillons, Rieslings, and, to a lesser extent, Sauvignon Blancs can also be found. Chardonnay and Semillon are blended to make complex, full-bodied, dry wines. Many Australian reds have excellent aging potential; some Shiraz, Cabernet Sauvignon, and blends of the two blossom with ten-plus years in the bottle. Look, too, for Rhône-style wines—usually blends of Grenache, Shiraz, and Mourvèdre—and the emerging Pinot Noirs.

on the label

Australians label their wines by dominant (at least 85 percent) variety. Appellation designation is loose, with most of the wines tagged simply South Eastern Australia. (Soon to come: more precise indication of regions.) Among the regions to look for are Hunter Valley in New South Wales; Barossa Valley, Clare Valley, McLaren Vale, Coonawarra, and Padthaway in South Australia, where nearly 60 percent of the country's wines are produced; and Yarra Valley and Rutherglen in Victoria.

Featured Wine-Growing Regions

Barossa Valley

South Australia

Hunter Valley

Clare Valley

New South Wales

Margaret River District

SYDNEY

McLaren Vale

Victoria

Padthaway

Rutherglen

Coonawarra

Yarra Valley

MELBOURNE

chardonnay

Almost every Australian wine area is rife with Chardonnay vines. The wines made from all those grapes range from briskly acidic, mineral-flavored refreshers to oaky cream-and-vanilla mouthfuls, with all stops in-between. Winemakers' signature versions usually have peaches-and-cream lusciousness with hints of exotic spices and baked pineapple—custom-made for U.S. tastes. But the lemony, unoaked Chardonnays now popular with smaller vintners are making great headway.

at the table

Australian Chardonnays tend to be toasty, oaky things, so aim for smoky grilled shrimp; broiled lobster; grilled full-flavored fish, like salmon, swordfish, or shark; fried, roasted, or grilled chicken; game birds, like quail or partridge; or roasted or grilled turkey or pork. Unless the wine has not spent time in oak, avoid raw shell-fish, mild finfish, Asian cuisines, highly spiced dishes, and anything prepared with chile peppers.

235

the bottom line Bargain-hunters have lots of good deals to choose from. Look for a fine selection under $15, with fewer clunkers than among California wines at this price. But the word is out, and prices are climbing.

recommended wines

1996 Leeuwin Estate, Margaret River ★★★ $$$$
Not your typical Australian Chard, this has a mineral strength that balances its fruitiness and mild oakiness. Spicy zip and persistent length.

1996 Penfolds Yattarna, South Australia ★★★ $$$$
Honey and nut aromas. There's a great balance of tangy acidity with the usual Aussie fruit basket—pineapple, nectarine, lemon—and a yeasty note that goes well with the buttery vanilla flavor from oak.

1998 Clarendon Hills Norton Summit, Adelaide Hills ★★★ $$$
A smoky, pungent, nutty Chardonnay with a velvety texture and a stony finish, much like that of a mineral-laden white Burgundy. Enticing.

1997 Chain of Ponds, Adelaide Hills ★★★ $$
Full-flavored and nicely acidic, this wine has spicy vanilla notes that pair well with the green apple and tropical fruits (especially guava) and the touch of mellow citrus.

1999 Hugo Unwooded, McLaren Vale ★★★ $$
A burst of pineapple and guava aromas. Lots of tropical fruit in the flavor, too, with a welcome lemon-lime acidity for balance. Then a good finish. It's an altogether appealing wine.

1998 Tatachilla Wattle Park, South Australia ★★★ $
Moderately oaked so the fruit flavors—lime, guava, honeydew—shine through. A touch of allspice, too. There's lots going on in the glass, and that's particularly impressive at this price.

1998 Grosset Piccadilly, Adelaide Hills ★★ $$$
A pineapple nose and zippy fruit flavors mark this gently oaked, and therefore not too vanilla-y, Chard. A little pleasant yeast taste.

1997 Howard Park, Western Australia ★★ $$$
With an aroma like a yeasty lemon raisin cake, this wine has complex fruit and yeast interplay on the tongue, and a restrained (for Western Australia) oakiness. This medium-bodied Chardonnay is worth pursuing.

1998 Chateau Reynella, McLaren Vale ♥   ★ ★ $

There's a good balance here between fruitiness and oak character. Pear and nectarine flavors are suffused with a mild spiciness from wood. This is a delicious and refreshing wine.

1997 Lindemans, Padthaway ♥   ★ $ $

In the popular style, this wine is full-bodied and has a fruit-packed appeal that defines the easy-going Aussie Chard. Spicy vanilla-cream flavors complete the picture.

1998 Buckeley's, South Australia ♥   ★ $

A fine balancing act: The taste of spicy oak matches the zingy tropical-fruit flavors here. And this is a great bargain among today's overpriced New World Chardonnays.

1997 Leasingham Bin 37, Clare Valley ♥   ★ $

Snappy acidity, with an admirable balance of apple, honeydew, gooseberry, and lemon. A bargain.

other white wines of australia

Aged Semillon (pronounced SEM-uh-lahn in Australia) can develop a rich nuttiness and an orange marmalade-y toothsomeness that has won it numerous fans. When it's young, the wine has a lemon-butter taste. Unique blends of Semillon and Chardonnay rate high in the popularity polls, too. Now, prodded by New Zealand's success, vintners are beginning to develop good Sauvignon Blancs as well. We also recommend looking for the less-known—and outstanding—Australian Rieslings, strong on citrus and peach aromas and flavors.

the bottom line Aggressive marketing keeps almost all of these whites at lower prices than comparable California or Washington State wines, with many great deals under $15, especially among Rieslings.

recommended wines

1999 Grosset Polish Hill Riesling, Clare Valley 🍷 ★★★ $$$
Lime, slate, and stone flavors in a light-bodied wine. It's bone-dry—and a mouthwatering match for any seafood.

1999 Brokenwood Semillon, Hunter Valley 🍷 ★★★ $$
The abundant pineapple and pine-forest nose leads to citrusy flavors with hints of grass and then a strong finish. A grand Hunter Valley Semillon.

1998 Coldstream Hills Sauvignon Blanc, Yarra Valley 🍷 ★★ $$
Perhaps the best Australian Sauvignon Blanc around, this wine's a classic—aromatic and packed with tropical-fruit flavors.

1998 Knappstein-Lenswood Sauvignon Blanc, Adelaide Hills 🍷 ★★ $$
Intensely flavored and steely, with a good balance of acidity and the spicy creaminess of oak. This is a perfect alternative for jaded Chardonnay lovers.

1998 Shaw and Smith Sauvignon Blanc, Adelaide Hills 🍷 ★★ $$
Jammed with flavors of cooked pineapple, fresh gooseberry, and mellow spices, this wine has a slightly oily texture and ends with clear flavors and great length.

1999 Peter Lehmann Semillon, Barossa 🍷 ★★ $
A nose that jumps with all sorts of tropical fruits and intense orange blossom. Lots of lively fruit repeats in the flavor, including great citrusy puckeriness.

1997 Basedow Semillon, Barossa 🍷 ★ $
A luscious wine, full in body and flavor. Spiced pear and cooked nectarines with smoky notes. It's an excellent bargain.

1999 Hill of Content Benjamin's Blend White Wine, Western Australia 🍷 ★ $$
About half Chardonnay balanced with equal parts Semillon and Sauvignon Blanc, this négociant-blended wine is refreshing and charming, with tasty grapefruit, lime-blossom, and pear flavors.

1999 McPherson Semillon/Chardonnay, Southeastern Australia 🍷 ★ $
Simple, straightforward, and easy drinkin', with a clear, mellow apple flavor. A good choice for parties.

1999 Penfolds Koonunga Hill Semillon-Chardonnay, South Australia 🍷 ★ $
Full-flavored, with peach, melon, and lemon-peel sprightliness. Refreshing.

shiraz

The world now knows Shiraz (shee-rahz), the local term for Syrah, as *the* red Australian grape, especially for drinkers seeking herb, earth, and jammy fruit flavors all in one wine. Though easy drinking is the hallmark of most Australian wines, and the majority are drunk young, the ones with aggressive tannin need aging and can continue to improve for up to twenty years. Look, too, for Shiraz sparklers, which abound in Australia and are beginning to come to our shops.

at the table

Young Shiraz is great for barbecues, hamburgers, grilled chicken, and pork. In general, avoid matching even these simpler Shiraz with fish or shellfish, although a grilled tuna or salmon steak might be nice. With a tannic, ageworthy Shiraz, dig into roast beef filet or other beef steaks, leg of lamb, or grilled chops.

the bottom line
While the best wines carry high prices, there's still a wealth of good Shiraz under $20, and with few exceptions, even those at higher prices offer great value.

what to buy SHIRAZ

1995	1996	1997	1998	1999
★★★	★★★★	★★★	★★★	★★★

recommended wines

1997 Barossa Valley Estate E&E Black Pepper, Barossa ♥   ★★★★ $$$$
An explosion of heady eucalyptus and berry aromas mark this as an Australian powerhouse. It's filled with earth, spice, herb, and ginger-beer flavors. Good acidity and a long finish complete this stellar wine.

1997 d'Arenberg The Dead Arm, McLaren Vale ♥   ★★★★ $$$$
With aromas and flavors of bitter chocolate, caramelized dried fruit, and just-roasted coffee, this may sound like a dessert. But the wine is dry and wonderfully tannic. Worth a search.

1998 Clarendon Hills Brookman's Vineyard, South Australia ♀ ★ ★ ★ $$$$

Spice, smoke, and leather aromas lead surprisingly to full fruit flavor and gentle tannin. The acidity in the wine has a good puckery quality, and there's an ever-lasting finish.

1997 Coriole, McLaren Vale ♀ ★ ★ ★ $$$

Woodsy smoke and eucalyptus aromas merge into enticing fruit flavors—cooked plums and dried currants—balanced by a satisfying astringency.

1997 Peter Lehmann The Barossa, Barossa ♀ ★ ★ ★ $$

Aromas of berries and cherries, an indelible spiciness, hints of earth and leather—all are signs of an excellent Shiraz. At a time when prices are creeping slowly out of sight, this one's a bargain.

1996 St. Hallett Blackwell, Barossa ♀ ★ ★ ★ $$

An abundance of fruit, matched with the Aussie Shiraz trademark "sweaty leather" on the nose. There are a lot of flavors in this challenging wine—bitter chocolate and sour cherries with a hint of clove and cardamom, alternating with cooked plums and some tannic astringency—but Shiraz lovers will tackle it with pleasure.

1996 Barossa Valley Estate Ebenezer, South Australia ♀ ★ ★ $$$

Not the leathery, smoky sort of Shiraz, this wine has a basketful of fruit aromas and flavors—blackberries, black cherries, blueberries—backed by hints of cedar and chocolate.

1997 Elderton, Barossa ♀ ★ ★ $$$

More mellow than many of the Shiraz musclemen, yet the leather, spice, and earth aromas are still strong. It's an easy-to-drink wine, with bitter chocolate and cherry mingling on a fine finish.

1996 Mitchelton Print, Victoria ♀ ★ ★ $$$

A potent little number in which the indigenous Australian Shiraz quality jumps out of the glass at first sniff. A bit of spearmint and coffee on the nose and a hint of cedar as well. Nice blackberry flavor.

1996 Penfolds Kalimna Bin 28 Shiraz, South Australia ♀ ★ ★ $$

An earthy wine, with an intense mix of strong tannin and restrained fruit. Match it with rich, robust foods to tame it now, or age it a few years and it will be even better.

1997 David Traeger, Goulburn Valley ♀ ★ ★ $$

With its shimmering reddish blackberry hue, musty-barnyard and chocolate nose, explosive flavors of fruit and spice, and relatively mild tannin, this is a wine that offers instant rewards.

1998 Wolf Blass, South Australia 🍷   ★ ★ $

A very dense, purple-black-hued wine with a straightforward, spicy Aussie Shiraz nose. It's full-bodied on the palate, with a lingering hint of black currants and coffee.

1996 Wolf Blass President's Selection, South Australia 🍷   ★ $$

Very intense, spicy, Christmas-cookie nose, with a wallop of mint as well. An interesting wine.

cabernet sauvignon

Most Australian Cabernet Sauvignons shout FRUIT and have gentle tannin lurking behind. But there are also dusty, chocolatey, spicy wines of distinction from Coonawarra, and other regions contribute vintages that pulsate with spicy blackberries, peppered black currant, or plum seasoned with anise and bay leaf. Cabernet Sauvignon is the second most planted grape in Australia, after Shiraz.

at the table

The lighter Australian Cabernet Sauvignons suit pasta, roast chicken, and either fresh or smoked pork. Those with more heft are good with roasted or grilled lamb or beef, as well as venison or other game.

the bottom line
There are great values here, especially when you compare them to California's skyrocketing Napa and Sonoma Valley offerings. You should find plenty of good Aussie Cabs at around $15.

what to buy CABERNET SAUVIGNON

1995	1996	1997	1998	1999
★ ★ ★	★ ★ ★ ★	★ ★ ★	★ ★ ★	★ ★ ★

recommended wines

1996 Tim Adams, Clare Valley 🍷 ★★★ $$
A concentrated Cabernet with lush berry and black-currant flavors emerging from a fruity, spicy, and woodsy nose.

1996 Penfolds Bin 407, South Australia 🍷 ★★★ $$
Pungent aromas of herbs and spices lead to complex flavors. A light-bodied Cab to seek out for its intense fruitiness and good tannin. Ready to drink now.

1995 Cape Mentelle, Margaret River 🍷 ★★ $$$
Powerful plum and berry flavors with chocolate and hints of cedar and spice. Assertive tannin and a long-lasting finish promise great things to come with age.

1995 Taltarini, Victoria 🍷 ★★ $$
A refined wine for mature tastes, without the hammerhead of fruit and spice otherwise common in Aussie Cabernets. It's tannic, with the evolved complexity of an Old World charmer.

1997 Wolf Blass Yellow Label, South Australia 🍷 ★ $
Year after year, Yellow Label pleases with flavor and value. There's a hint of mint and a little bit of sweet red pepper on the nose. It finishes with a bit of tar, enough to make it a good food wine.

1996 Wynns Estate, Coonawarra 🍷 ★ $
Lots of bell pepper on the nose, with earth and berry flavors and an excellent finish. A good wine at a decent price.

other red wines of australia

Both the Cabernet-Shiraz and Rhône-style Shiraz-Grenache-Mourvèdre blends show why winemakers combine varieties in the first place; the whole can be greater than the sum of its parts. Merlots and Pinot Noirs, as well as some Australian-Italian styles, are also worth investigating.

the bottom line Good wines at better than average prices, along with the fun of experimenting with unfamiliar blends and styles—how can you go wrong? You'll find lots under $15.

recommended wines

1996 Frankland Estate Olmo's Reward, Western Australia ♥ ★★★ $$$
Green pepper and strong tannin meet lush cherry and violet flavors in a classic Bordeaux-style blend: assertive, woodsy, and flowery all at once. The wine has a good acid/fruit balance, a slight dustiness, and complexity that will prosper in the cellar.

1998 Peter Lehmann Clancy's, Barossa ♥ ★★★ $$$
Packed with a Shiraz tang that is enriched and mellowed by jammy Cabernet and gentle Merlot. Enticingly spicy aroma; full berry flavor. A luscious wine with a good long finish.

1996 Penfolds Bin 389 Cabernet/Shiraz, South Australia ♥ ★★★ $$
A mass of black cherries erupt from this full-flavored wine. Good tannin and full body. Earthy, robust, and rewarding.

1997 Rosemount Estate Traditional, McLaren Vale ♥ ★★ $$
This Cab/Merlot/Petite Verdot blend has vibrant plums seasoned with thyme and pepper. Long finish, good value.

1997 Tatachilla Grenache 80%-Shiraz, McLaren Vale ♥ ★★ $$
There's a bit of prune and other stewed fruits on the nose and a hint of alcohol, underneath which lie powerful flavors of coffee and black pepper. Full-bodied and a tad tarry, with a hint of cinnamon, this wine is succulent.

1998 Lindemans Bin 40 Merlot, Southeastern Australia ♥ ★ $
A refreshing nose with a touch of mint and black pepper in a full-bodied wine with plum and earth flavors. Fine value.

new zealand

Even though New Zealand makes only a miniscule percentage of the world's wine, the nation has earned a big reputation among oenophiles. The maritime climate provides ideal conditions for the production of bracing, penetrating, fruit-filled whites. New Zealand Sauvignon Blanc is world-class, and we can expect more great things to come from the country's cool, sea-breeze-kissed coastal vineyards.

grapes & styles

The moderate New Zealand temperatures favor white wines, and of those, Sauvignon Blanc is already a winner. Chardonnay fills out the majority of the country's production, and while New Zealand's Rieslings labor in Australia's shadow, they're still a stand-out. Among reds, plummy Pinot Noir is generally best—likely to be better than the popular Cabernet Sauvignon and Merlot. Overall, the employment of stainless steel in production and the limited use of oak barrels make for pure, unsullied flavors in New Zealand wines.

on the label

There are eleven growing regions in New Zealand. Marlborough on South Island (where commercial growers first planted in 1973) and Hawkes Bay on North Island remain the best known—the latter primarily for its piercingly citric Chardonnay, the former for its stellar and sought-after Sauvignon Blanc, though Marlborough's Chardonnay and Riesling also shine. Gisborne provides another excellent source for Chardonnay. Look to Martinborough for Pinot Noir.

Northland

Auckland
AUCKLAND •

Bay of Plenty

Waikato

Gisborne

Taranaki

Hawkes Bay

Manawatu-
Wanganui

Martinborough

Nelson

Marlborough

West Coast

Canterbury

Otago

Southland

■ **Featured
Wine-Growing
Regions**

sauvignon blanc

From the zesty type with hints of passion fruit, gooseberry, and
lemon to the earthy sort with its strong herb and vegetable aromas,
New Zealand's cold-fermented Sauvignon Blancs thrill and en-
chant. Those from Marlborough, especially from the pace-setting
Cloudy Bay area, deserve their fame. Wines from the gravel-rich
soils in the Marlborough sub-regions Awatere River Valley and
Wairau Valley are developing good reputations.

at the table

Faced with hard-to-match asparagus or artichokes? New Zealand Sauvignon Blanc's your wine. Perfect with shellfish and lean fish, it has sharp citrus flavors that pair well with tomato-based dishes, vinaigrette-dressed salads, and moderately spicy specialties from Thai, Indian, or Mexican cuisine. Among cheeses, choose chèvre.

the bottom line Cloudy Bay bottles may be hard to find and costly, but most of the other Sauvignon Blancs are bargains. They almost always deliver great flavor and palate-cleansing acidity for under $20, sometimes under $10. Buy 'em by the case.

recommended wines

1999 Kim Crawford, Marlborough ♥ ★★★★ $$
Flavors of lime peel and peach skins, with a sharp and assertive minerality and herbaceous complexity characteristic of New Zealand's best Sauvignon Blancs.

1999 Vavasour Single Vineyard, Marlborough ♥ ★★★ $$$
An aromatic wine with persistent flavors of melon and vibrant lime leaf. This full-bodied wine has a long finish of stone and passion fruit.

1999 Babich, Marlborough ♥ ★★★ $$
First, an aromatic burst of yew tree and candied apricots. Then lots of pine forest, anise, and citrus-fruit flavors, and tangy acidity in the finish.

1999 Cloudy Bay, Marlborough ♥ ★★★ $$
The Sauvignon Blanc that put New Zealand on the map. It's full of grapefruit and melon flavors, with earthiness and grassy herbaceousness. Hard to find.

1999 Sacred Hill Barrel Fermented, Hawkes Bay ♥ ★★ $$
Spicy, with lively acidity and flavors of lime leaf, pineapple, minerals, and yew. This slightly creamy wine has a mellow, long-lasting finish. It's oaked, which is atypical of New Zealand Sauvignon Blancs.

1999 Nobilo Fall Harvest, Marlborough ♥ ★★ $
Forceful aromas of passion fruit and yew, with a punch of flavor—nectarine, grapefruit, and lemon peel—and a tangy finish.

1999 Stoneleigh, Marlborough ♥ ★★ $
This is a great vintage for Stoneleigh. The wine has a core of lime, apricot, and mandarin flavors and a zippy, grassy finish.

1999 Villa Maria Estate Private Bin, Marlborough 🍷   ★ $$

Brisk and refreshing, a citrusy Sauvignon Blanc with a cleansing and lightly peppery finish that lasts and lasts. A great bargain.

chardonnay

New Zealand Chardonnay tends to be light and citrusy, with refreshing tropical-fruit flavors unobscured by vanilla from oak (some producers now opt for oak rather than stainless steel, however). The nation's most widely planted variety, Chardonnay yields definite regional style variations—pineapple peachiness in Gisborne, tangy citrus in Hawkes Bay. In Marlborough, Chardonnay is second in importance only to the region's sterling Sauvignon Blanc.

at the table

Less oak means more versatility, giving New Zealand Chardonnays better range than those from California and Australia. Traditional Chardonnay pairings—grilled or baked medium- to strong-flavored fish, roast chicken, pork, or creamy dishes—go well with lightly oaked versions. Unoaked styles match up with shellfish or Chinese food.

the bottom line Expect to spend $20 or so for New Zealand's quality Chardonnay.

recommended wines

1998 Isabel, Marlborough 🍷   ★ ★ ★ $$$

A nutty, toasty smelling Chardonnay with a peaches-and-cream effect. There is also mild spice, a surprising mouthwatering quality, and a good finish.

1998 Brancott Reserve, Gisborne 🍷   ★ ★ ★ $$

A full-bodied wine packed with spice, lemon, and pineapple flavors, this Chardonnay has a refreshing quality and a subtle, creamy finish. Better than many pricier versions.

1999 Kim Crawford Unoaked, Marlborough 🍷 ★ ★ ★ $$

With a soft buttery feel from 100 percent malolactic fermentation (which converts harsh acids into softer ones for a mellower wine), this is a vibrant Chardonnay with a floral nose; apple, citrus, and vanilla flavors; and a fruity finish.

1999 Saint Clair, Marlborough 🍷 ★ ★ $$

Peaches and cream melded with almond and gentle spice makes this a delicious, crowd-pleasing, classic New World Chard.

1999 Babich Gisbourne, Hawkes Bay 🍷 ★ ★ $

A great bargain. This is a snappy wine with lots of nectarine and apple flavor as well as hints of lemon balm and honeysuckle. It has a refreshing finish.

riesling

Dry and off-dry Rieslings, especially those from Marlborough, offer lime-zest flavor, with tasty notes of tropical-fruit and minerals. The grape does best on the cooler South Island and in the southern part of North Island. In years when botrytis develops, you'll get luscious honey-touched unctiousness in late-harvest bottlings.

at the table

The zingy, minerally flavors of these Rieslings are good with fresh or smoked fish and with sweet, sour, spicy cooking: think Asian. More moderately tangy styles go well with rich poultry, such as roast duck.

the bottom line Not widely exported to the U.S. yet, but easily worth the $10 to $15 price when found.

recommended wines

1999 Grove Mill, Marlborough 🍷 ★ ★ ★ $$

This off-dry version of Kiwi Riesling offers tantalizing, clear citrus and tree-fruit flavors. Refreshing, with a mineral zing.

1999 Isabel Estate, Marlborough ★★ $$
From this single vineyard estate comes a mouthwatering wine with peach and nectarine aromas and a long finish.

pinot noir

Pinot Noir is the most planted red grape in New Zealand. Producers are betting on big things in the next few years and expect their Pinot to take second place only to Burgundy's. Once again, cool Marlborough leads the way with plummy and complex Pinot Noirs hinting at smoke and spice.

at the table

As with U.S. Pinot Noirs, the New Zealand versions go well with salmon, roast chicken, turkey, duck, mildly seasoned pork, low-acid pasta sauces, and moderately hot Chinese dishes.

the bottom line Bargains are hard to find; expect to pay above $20 for the better wines.

recommended wines

1999 Giesen, Canterbury ★★★ $$
With flavors of tart berries, red currants, and spices, this wine's a winner. There are hints of violet in the mouth-filling finish.

1998 Martinborough, Martinborough ★★ $$$
Full flavors of plums, currants, and spices. The texture is luxurious and velvety, and the finish has mild tannin and hints of roses.

1998 Te Kairanga Reserve, Martinborough ★★ $$
Silky and gentle, yet refreshing, this wine has a great blend of blackberries and smoke on the palate. Fine balance of tannin, acidity, and flavor.

argentina & chile

Twenty years ago, when they were first exported, South American wines were more attractive for their price than their quality. It's a different story now—even the Mondavis and the Rothschilds of the world recognize the potential for excellent wines from Argentina and Chile and are buying up land suitable for vineyards.

argentina

The wines of Argentina are diverse, interesting—and frustrating. The country is currently fifth in the world in terms of sheer production, and is on its way to making wine that is not only very good to excellent but also has its own identity, somewhere between New World boldness and Old World finesse. The frustration comes in with the newness of Argentine wine exporting: There just isn't enough of it. So frequently when we find a wine we like, we never see it again.

grapes & styles

Argentina is noted for its red wines, and has success not only with the usual suspects—Cabernet Sauvignon, Merlot, Pinot Noir, and Syrah—but also with some less expected varieties, such as Malbec from Bordeaux, Tempranillo (known in South America as Tempranilla) from Spain, and Bonarda, Sangiovese, and Nebbiolo from Italy. Among whites, it's the flowery Torrontés Riojano that's grown in abundance. Thanks to the presence of Moët &

Chile

Jujoy

Salta

Cafayate

Atacama

Catamarca

Argentina

La Rioja

Coquimbo

San Juan

Córdoba

Casablanca

Maipo

•SANTIAGO

San Luis

Rapel

Maule

Mendoza

BUENOS AIRES •

Southern Region

Neuquén

Littoral

Río Negro

Featured Wine-Growing Regions

Chandon in the country, there is also some good sparkling wine. Argentine styles include both traditional and New World, and slowly but surely the vintners here are finding their own excellent compromise between the two.

on the label

Labeling in Argentina is primarily by grape variety. The country's major wine region for both reds and whites is Mendoza, although the best Torrontés Riojano comes from La Rioja and Cafayate. The up-and-coming spots to watch for are the regions of Río Negro and Neuquén in the northern part of Patagonia at the southern end of the continent; look to these areas for Torrentés Riojano and Semillon.

red wines of argentina

Many of the Argentine red wines are attractively full and earthy, but it's the inky, spicy, and big-bodied Malbec that really gets our attention. Until more wines are exported, though, grab whatever you can get and give it a try.

at the table

Argentina is famous for beef, and makes the wines to go with it. Try these reds with grilled steak or braised short ribs. Pinot Noir, lighter and fruitier than most Argentine red wines, goes well with all of the products of the pig, whether fresh or cured—chops, roasts, ham, sausages, charcuterie. Non-meat-eaters needn't despair, however: You can match any of these reds with marinated and grilled tempeh, meaty fish, or a vegetable cassoulet.

the bottom line
There's a bunch of good reds under $10 in the shops now. And look for top quality, too—the super premiums at the $50 price point are on their way.

what to buy RED WINES

1995	1996	1997	1998	1999
★★★★	★★★★	★★★	★★★	★★★

recommended wines

1996 Cavas de Weinert Gran Vino, Mendoza ▼   ★★★ $$

Allspice, anise, clove, and cinnamon—if you can imagine a Christmas fruit-cake that's somehow been turned into a wine (minus the sugar), this is it. Spicy and fruity, medium-bodied and elegant in structure, the wine has a long, long, tarry finish.

1995 Weinert Malbec, Mendoza ▼   ★★★ $$

Gorgeous, spicy black-cherry aroma, with cranberry, tar, and anise on the palate. This is a complex wine that finishes with a bit of licorice.

1997 Trapiche Iscay Merlot/Malbec, Mendoza ▼   ★★ $$$$

A wine with full aromas of red fruits. It's very meaty and smoky tasting, with an appealing velvety texture.

1997 Catena Alta Malbec, Mendoza ▼   ★★ $$$

This is a full-bodied Malbec replete with plum, cedar, spice, pepper, and lots of new oak. It's New World. It's very tasty.

1996 Finca La Anita Syrah, Mendoza ▼   ★★ $$$

The texture of this wine is immediately appealing—smooth and silky, with a bit of cinnamon flavor.

1997 Etchart Arnaldo B. Etchart Reserva, Cafayate ▼   ★★ $$

Could that be a bit of anchovy on the nose? On the palate, the wine is jammy, tomato-pasty, with licorice and chocolate tastes. A really old-fashioned kind of wine, and a conversation piece.

1995 Navarro Correas Cabernet Sauvignon, Mendoza ▼   ★★ $$

A not-too-aromatic Cabernet, but one that's full-bodied and pleasing to drink. The flavors here come through strong and clear with lots of blackberries and prune and a touch of mint. After all that, the finish is light and lingers cloud-like on the palate.

1997 Santa Julia Malbec Oak Reserve, Mendoza ▼   ★★ $

Restrained at this point, the medium-bodied wine has flavors of baked plums and licorice. It needs some time.

1998 Familia Zuccardi Q Cabernet Sauvignon, Mendoza ♥ ★ $$
Deep red-currant and cherry flavors in a full-bodied wine, with enough tannin to make it serious.

1998 Familia Zuccardi Q Merlot, Mendoza ♥ ★ $$
Some Port-like aromas and a smooth, creamy texture. There's lots of black cherry flavor.

1996 Weinert Merlot, Mendoza ♥ ★ $$
Ripe cherry aromas—almost overripe—lead to fruity charred-plum flavors and a deep taste of hot tar.

1999 Don Miguel Gascon Malbec, Mendoza ♥ ★ $
Plum and a bit of cedar flavor. It's got a full, appealing weight in the mouth and is vinified with a dose of toasty new oak that leaves a lingering almond-vanilla-crunch taste on the finish.

1997 Terrazas de los Andes Malbec, Mendoza ♥ ★ $
Vanilla and cedar aromas that follow through on the palate, along with cherry, plum, tar, and oak. Slight caramel in the finish.

1997 Trapiche Cabernet Sauvignon, Mendoza ♥ ★ $
A subtle aroma of candied violet on the nose and then—ever so subtly—on the palate. A nice, rough finish, with good tannin. Drink this one with a steak.

1997 Trumpeter Malbec, Vistalba ♥ ★ $
Aromas of cherry and cola, with a touch of new leather. The wine itself is fruity and simple. It finishes with sweet and dusty notes.

white wines of argentina

Some of the thin, oxidized wines of the past are still around, but Argentine white wines have come a long way. Aromatic, flowery Torrontés Riojano is worth seeking out, as is Semillon and the occasional Viognier. The Chardonnays and Sauvignon Blancs that make it to U.S. shops excite us less, but some are decent.

at the table

Torrontés Riojano makes a superb and unexpected aperitif. The wine's fullness and floral qualities make it a good companion for difficult-to-match food like vinegary salads, poultry or pork with fruit sauce, and Asian or fusion cuisine. Try Argentine Semillon with vegetarian dishes, with rich fish like salmon and tuna, and with smoked fish.

the bottom line Most whites will be under $10, with a few entries at the $30 point.

recommended wines

1999 Etchart Torrontés, Cafayate ★★ $
Highly aromatic—do we smell lily of the valley or Chanel No. 5? Despite the intense perfume, a vibrant acidity perks this wine right up and makes it almost Viognier-like.

1998 Santa Julia Torrontés, Mendoza ★★ $
The fresh ginger on the nose quickly disappears into the wine's opulent perfume. There's a honeysuckle and jasmine quality that finishes a little peachy. Lovely.

1999 Don Miguel Gascon Viognier, Mendoza ★ $
We've had Torrontés that taste more like Viognier than this wine. Though it lacks the characteristic floral quality, it does have medium body and a strong lemony, guava flavor, with steely acidity.

chile

Remember those $3 Chilean wines? Many consumers found them fruity, tasty, and cheap. We found them a bit dull. Then a few producers opened our eyes and mouths to Chile's potential. Now many of the country's wines, from inexpensive to luxurious, deserve their place on the table.

grapes & styles

Grape varieties abound in Chile: there's Cabernet Sauvignon, Merlot, Pinot Noir, Sauvignon Blanc, and Chardonnay, as well as super-premium Bordeaux blends. Carmenère, which is rapidly being embraced as Chile's own red grape, is an almost extinct Bordeaux variety that makes extraordinarily colored and flavored red wines with an intense perfume. Though it's primarily been used in blends, Carmenère will soon be showing up more frequently as a varietal.

on the label

Varietal labeling is the rule in Chile. Be aware that when Carmenère is sold as a varietal, it is often labeled Grand Vidure. Most of the country's wine-growing regions surround Santiago, the capital. Chardonnay is mostly grown in Casablanca, in the cool area northwest of Santiago. Located to the south of the city are the important red-grape growing areas of Maipo (my-po) and Rapel.

red wines of chile

Cabernet Sauvignon and Merlot rule Chile's red-wine market, but there are also some inexpensive and tasty Pinot Noirs as well as expensive Bordeaux-style blends. If you can find a Carmenère bottled as a varietal, expect unique cinnamon and chocolate richness.

at the table

Most of Chile's Cabernet Sauvignons and Merlots can accompany a simple hamburger or slice of meatloaf quite happily. A Pinot Noir is great alongside roasted red snapper with mango salsa and goes with richer fish, too, including salmon, the perennial Pinot Noir match. Many of the blends taste like mature Bordeaux. With these, braised or stewed meats are fine. Simply prepared red meats—roasted prime rib or rack of lamb, pan-seared steak or lamb chops—are even better.

the bottom line Although in recent years prices have climbed, most of Chile's wines are still under $10. A $50 category has emerged, and these bottles are being snapped up as soon as importers release them.

recommended wines

1997 Montes Alpha M, Colchagua ♀   ★ ★ ★ $$$$
After a mouthwatering nose of blackberry, cassis, and smoke, the wine washes over the palate with a full fruitiness, and then leaves behind lingering notes of berry and tar.

1997 Almaviva Puente Alto, Maipo Valley ♀   ★ ★ $$$$
A restrained wine at the moment—the aromas and flavors must be coaxed out by aeration. There's chocolate and subtle black currant. The tannin is already smooth, but time will make this one even better.

1998 Santa Rita Medalla Real Special Reserve Cabernet Sauvignon, Maipo Valley ♀   ★ ★ $$
The wine seduces with violet, black currant, and smoke on the nose, then strikes with cascades of more currants and cocoa on the palate.

1999 D. Bosler Pinot Noir, Colchagua Valley ♀   ★ ★ $
We were so surprised by the deliciousness of this wine that you could have knocked us over. It has refreshing cherry flavor and a silky texture.

1998 Caliterra Merlot, Central Valley ♀   ★ ★ $
Here's a flavorful, medium-bodied wine that's packed with blackberries and black pepper.

1999 Casa Julia Merlot, Colchagua Valley ♀   ★ ★ $
There's a bit of earth and herb on the nose, with tar and tobacco. The wine then explodes in the mouth with zingy, clear fruit flavors and a touch—just a touch—of vanilla in the end.

1997 Don Melchor Private Reserve, Maipo Valley ♀   ★ $$$
The herbal quality in this wine (and we're talking Provençal herbs) is its most prevalent feature. Underneath is cranberry and a touch of cassis.

1998 Santa Laura Laura Hartwig Cabernet Sauvignon, Colcagua Valley ♀   ★ $$
A nicely made wine that, with its tartness and oak-finessed blackberry flavor, really needs food to make it work.

white wines of chile

There are some excellent everyday table wines to be had among the Chilean whites, especially the snappy Sauvignon Blancs and tasty Chardonnays.

at the table

Let's not think too hard here. Match these fairly simple wines with informal food. Think fried chicken with Sauvignon Blanc or Chilean seabass and grilled corn with Chardonnay.

the bottom line
Most white wines from Chile will—and should—cost under $10. The best values among these wines are around $8.

recommended wines

1999 Santa Rita Sauvignon Blanc Rapel Medalla Real Special Reserve, Rapel Valley ▼ ★ ★ $ $
A typical grassy Sauvignon Blanc nose leads to a little bit of nectar flavor in a medium-weight wine. It's like biting into a guava that's been set out in newly cut grass.

1999 Casa Lapostolle Sauvignon Blanc, Rapel Valley ▼ ★ ★ $
An aroma of grass introduces a wine that's bursting with kiwi, lime, and melon. A terrific deal.

1999 Undurraga Chardonnay, Maipo Valley ▼ ★ ★ $
Complex aromas of melon, anise, and spearmint highlight a wine that has zippy acidity and a nice creamy mouth-feel—not to mention an unbeatable price for the quality.

1996 Casa Lapostolle Cuvée Alexandre Chardonnay Reserve, Casablanca Valley ▼ ★ $ $
Full oak flavors that have deepened with a few years of age highlight this full-bodied wine. If this is your style, it'll hit the spot.

1999 Concha y Toro Casillero del Diablo Sauvignon Blanc, Maipo Valley ★ $

Faint apple-orchard aromas and a taste that perks up the mouth with typical Sauvignon Blanc acidity and a hint of faint green grassiness. A good hot-weather choice.

1998 Errazuriz Chardonnay, Casablanca Valley ★ $

Almost subtle for a New World Chardonnay, with a bit of gentle, toasty almond on the finish.

1999 Santa Rita Chardonnay Reserve, Maipo Valley ★ $

An easy-to-drink crowd-pleaser with a really nice green-apple aroma.

champagne & other sparkling wines

We think that the pop of a perfectly opened bottle of sparkling wine is one of the sweetest sounds in life. Although Americans tend to reserve that happy noise for special occasions, Europeans seem to require only the tiniest excuse. Whether it's French Champagne, Italian Spumante, or Spanish Cava, sparkling wine from South Africa or from Down Under, a wine with bubbles can make an ordinary moment sing. Whichever kind you prefer, always keep a bottle on call; there's nothing better to put in the hands of a guest than a glass of sparkling wine.

at the table

Of course, you can drink sparkling wine as an aperitif, and in fact it is ideal with rich, salty preprandial nibbles like nuts, caviar, or shavings of Parmesan. But don't stop there. Bubbly wines are exemplary companions for difficult-to-match fusion cuisine. Choose a Brut sparkling wine for a perfect sushi accompaniment. And don't forget about brunch: Any egg dish will make a good pairing. Full-bodied sparklers will stand up to roasted birds, even the stronger ones, like duck. And a pink sparkler is great with salads or salmon.

champagne

The climate can be quite chilly in Champagne, the northernmost wine region of France. As a result, the grapes retain an enormous amount of acidity, one reason for the wine's longevity. In Europe, only wine made in this region by the strictly controlled process called *méthode champenoise* can be called Champagne.

grapes & styles

Champagne is usually a blend, and Chardonnay, Pinot Noir, and Pinot Meunier are the only grape varieties allowed. If Chardonnay alone is used, the result is called Blanc de Blancs (white wine from white grapes). When the red grapes Pinot Noir and Pinot Meunier are used—either together without Chardonnay or individually—the wine is called Blanc de Noirs (white wine from black grapes). Rosé Champagne is traditionally made by leaving the juice in contact with the grape skins just long enough to extract some of the color, but the method used more often these days is to just add some red wine to the Champagne at blending time.

on the label

Nonvintage Champagne is made by blending the wine of several vintages to make a consistent house style. This combination can generally be drunk earlier than vintage Champagne, which may take a decade to blossom.

The sweetness of Champagne depends on the *dosage*—that is, the amount of sugar added. If a wine is labeled Extra Brut it can have no dosage or a very small dosage. Brut Champagne, the driest widely available category, usually has a tad of sugar added to soften the acidic bite. Progressing upward on the sweetness scale are Extra-Dry, Sec, Demi-Sec, and, the sweetest of all, Champagne-Doux, which is seldom seen in the U.S.

the bottom line Producing Champagne is a labor-intensive enterprise, and thus the wine is expensive. Nonvintage generally falls in the $18 to $40 range, though it can go higher (the divine multi-vintage Krug retails for about $110). Vintage Champagne runs from $30 to $90 as a rule, and, again, can easily top $100.

sparkling wines **champagne**

what to buy VINTAGE CHAMPAGNE

1986	1987	1988	1989	1990
★★	nonvintage	★★★★	★★★	★★★★

1991	1992	1993	1994	1995	1996
★	★★	★★	★★	★★★	★★★★

recommended wines

1973 Dom Pérignon, Épernay ♟ ★★★★ $$$$
Remarkably fresh, with only a touch of honey on both the nose and the palate to reveal its age. There are floral and fruit, especially peach, flavors as well, with just a slight bit of toast on the finish.

1985 Dom Pérignon, Épernay ♟ ★★★★ $$$$
Great buttery, yeasty aromas on the nose, like those of just-baked brioche. There's a waft of lemon, too. Earthy and mushroomy on the palate. The bubbles melt cloud-like in the mouth.

1988 Dom Pérignon Rosé, Épernay ♟ ★★★★ $$$$
Everyone who can afford it drinks Dom Pérignon, but hardly anyone seems to know how terrific the rosés are. Here's a lovely one with a tad of age-related tawny color, aromas of raspberry, strawberry, and dried figs, and a lingering, tart, lemon-peel kind of finish. Delicious.

1990 Dom Pérignon Rosé, Épernay ♟ ★★★★ $$$$
Full-bodied, with a knockout fragrance of apricots and plums and a slight bit of yeast bread.

Krug Grande Cuvée, Reims ♟ ★★★★ $$$$
We love the satisfying, complex aromas and tastes of this wine. It seems to have a little bit of everything—apple, butterscotch, a touch of five-spice powder, brioche, even a hint of melon.

1993 Pol Roger Brut, Épernay ♟ ★★★ $$$$
Toasted yeast-bread aromas and then a lemony, grapey flavor. An impressive wine with good acidity.

1993 Ruinart "R" Brut, Reims ♟ ★★★ $$$$
This is an excellent wine that has lots of typical yeasty, nutty, toasty aromas. Then in the mouth it melts into delicacy; the flavors repeat the aromas but with more subtlety, and with a little creaminess at the end.

ARTISINAL CHAMPAGNE

Champagne is going the way of Burgundy (see "The Négociant and the Farmer in Burgundy," page 51). Some growers who have in the past supplied the big Champagne companies with grapes, or the base wines with which to make the house Champagnes, have started to make their own wines from start to finish. These so-called "grower Champagnes" are usually handcrafted wines made in teensy quantities, and Champagne lovers are going crazy over them.

One of the hottest additions to wine lists around the country is a "Grower Champagne List." Part of the thrill is the romance of the artisinal, the notion that the wine was made by a person who cared about it, not a corporation. The other part of the appeal is that, in fact, many of these Champagnes are excellent, complex wines. You can recognize them by the initials RM on the label, for *récoltant-manipulant* (translating literally as *harvester-operator*). Though thousands of grower-producers exist, some of the best names around include:

Henri Billiot	**René Geoffroy**
Chartogne-Taillet	**Pierre Gimonnet**
Fleury Père & Fils	**Jacques Selosse**

Billecart-Salmon Brut Rosé, Mareuil-sur-Ay 🍷 ★ ★ ★ $$$

A wine that makes a lot of top ten lists—and with good reason. It's great with or without food, and its full-bodied creaminess and complex, nutty, caramel, and strawberry aromas and flavors make it a real winner.

Bollinger Special Cuvée, Ay 🍷 ★ ★ ★ $$$

For the Champagne lover who likes it powerful and full-bodied. It's a generous wine with touches of caramel-accented buttered toast on the nose and pear and ripe-fig flavors.

1991 Demière-Ansiot Côte des Blancs Brut Grand Cru, Oger 🍷 ★ ★ ★ $$$

This is made in tiny quantities, so if you happen to find it on a wine list or a wine-shop shelf, buy it. It's positively yummy, delicate on the palate, with a tart orange finish.

Gosset Grande Réserve, Ay ☻   ★★★ $$$

An unusual champagne—a touch of caramel fragrance, yet extremely dry and lemony, with a lingering hazelnut finish. There's a great smokiness on the nose as well.

Charles Heidsieck mis en cave 1996, Reims ☻   ★★★ $$$

Yes, it's nonvintage. So, you ask, what's with the date? It's the year the bottle, containing a blend of vintages, was set down in the caves to age, and this dating system is now used on all Charles Heidsieck's nonvintage wines. They're as good as ever, date or no. This young wine could use a bit of age, but right now it has a great aromatic lemony freshness and a slight brioche-like quality on the nose. There's a gentle effervescence in the mouth, with a bit of peach flavor, and it finishes with a touch of almond.

Henriot Blanc de Blancs Brut, Reims ☻   ★★★ $$$

It's been off the shelves for years, but now Henriot is back, and it's a good thing. We love this full-bodied wine, a combo of Pinot Noir and Chardonnay with a lush texture and ripe fruit flavors.

Bruno Paillard Première Cuvée, Reims ☻   ★★★ $$$

Medium-bodied and moderately complex, with aromas of apple, citrus, freshly baked bread, and vanilla leading to spice, apple, nut, and vanilla flavors.

Pol Roger Brut, Épernay ☻   ★★★ $$

Here's a Champagne of substance. It has toasty aromas, vibrant acidity, and a lingering finish.

Laurent Perrier Ultra Brut, Tours-sur-Marne ☻   ★★ $$$$

Those of you who think you love dry champagne should give this a try. It's lemony, sandpaper-dry, and not for sipping on its own; pair it with Beluga on toast points.

Piper-Heidsieck dressed by Jean-Paul Gaultier
Bottle Special Cuvée, Reims ☻   ★★ $$$$

You see this bottle tarted up in a red-vinyl wrapping and think it can't possibly be any good—but it is. There's subtle lemon butter and toasted almonds on the nose. On the palate, it's a lively wine with a fair amount of pear flavor and perhaps a-bit-too-big bubbles.

Paul Drouet Special Réserve Alain Ducasse, Reims ☻   ★★ $$$

Brioche and bread-bakery aromas. A medium-bodied wine with lemony tang and nuttiness on the palate. Satisfying.

Pommery Brut Champagne Royal Apanage, Reims ☻   ★★ $$$

Assertive aromas of toast in a full-bodied Champagne, leading into flavors of fruit and spices that linger enticingly on the finish.

Taittinger Brut Champagne La Française,
Reims 🍷 ★ ★ $$$

We always think of this as a good wedding wine. It's got nice small bubbles and enough vanilla-and-fruit flavor to make it perfect for toasting the occasion.

Veuve Clicquot Ponsardin, Reims 🍷 ★ ★ $$$

One of the world's favorite Champagnes for a reason. A somewhat affordable wine that has pear, lemon, and subtle toasty aromas and flavors, and a creamy texture.

Nicolas Feuilatte Rosé 1er Cru, Épernay 🍷 ★ $$$

Frankly, if you had your eyes closed you might think that this was a white champagne, but it is indeed rosé—an almost neutral one, with the slightest hint of strawberry on the palate and a fine texture.

IF YOU'VE GOT LEMONS

The cold region of Champagne could never grow lush red grapes, and even its white wines were, to put it kindly, bracingly acidic. But add some bubbles and a bit of sugar and you have something else again. Folklore has it that the 17th century monk Dom Pérignon of Reims, having tasted Champagne, declared, "I'm drinking the stars." The birth of Champagne some 300 years ago—and its immediate smash hit with the smart set—must be one of history's most successful turning-lemons-into-lemonade stories.

other sparkling wines of france

Since the name Champagne can't be used for French sparkling wines made outside of that region, the words you will most often see on these labels are *crémant* (kray-mahn) and *mousseux* (moo-seuh). Alsace makes its excellent Crémant d'Alsace. The Loire Valley turns some of its Chenin Blanc grapes into Crémant de Loire, and, within the same region, Vouvray produces Vouvray Mousseux and Saumur, Saumur Mousseux. In the Southwest, Limoux offers its spectacular full-bodied sparkler, Blanquette de Limoux, at an unusually inexpensive price. Mauzac is the traditional grape there, often blended with a good deal of Chardonnay and Chenin Blanc.

recommended wines

Domaine Frédéric Lornet Arbois Brut Rosé, Jura 🍷 ★★ $$
A lovely color and a lovely wine. This rosé offers wild strawberry and raspberry flavors and snappy acidity. The bubbles are small, as they should be, giving a gentle feeling of effervescence in the mouth.

1995 Saint Hilaire Blanquette de Limoux, Limoux 🍷 ★★ $
Limoux claims to have discovered bubbly wine centuries before Champagne was invented, and there's a great deal of pride in their wines. This one is consistently impressive. It's got bigger bubbles than we like, but it's full-bodied and has touches of vanilla and toast flavors.

Lucien Albrecht Crémant d'Alsace, Alsace 🍷 ★ $$
A spicy vanilla nose with some tropical-fruit flavors and a touch of toffee on the finish.

Domaine Collin Blanquette de Limoux Cuvée Prestige, Limoux 🍷 ★ $$
Though it's rather aggressively bubbled, this wine nonetheless has lots of redeeming qualities, including a light, citrusy aroma and a stony minerality on the tongue.

Domaine de Provence, Bau de Muscat 🍷 ★ $$
We'd describe this sparkler from Provence as a delightful, gentle froth of fruit salad. In a word, the wine is charming. It makes a perfect offering when guests arrive at the cocktail hour.

Charles de Fère Brut Reserve, France 🍷 ★ $
Not a bad sparkler, and it's great for the price. This one has a nice vanilla-scented nose with a touch of pine and almond.

Domaine du Vieux Pressoir Saumur Brut, France 🍷 ★ $
Chenin Blanc from the Loire can make lovely and brisk sparklers, and here's a good example. The wine's honeyed aromas are a touch musty and almond-y, and the wine is very, very dry.

sparkling wines of italy

Many fine sparklers made by the exacting *méthode champenoise* come out of Italy. The area of Franciacorta produces sparkling wines made from Pinot Noir, Chardonnay, and sometimes Pinot Bianco using the *metodo classico* (the same as *méthode champenoise*). The northern areas of Trentino and Piedmont also produce bubbly wines. Prosecco, the sparkling, fruity wine from the Veneto, is an immensely popular quaffer that is not required to follow the classic Champagne method in its production.

the bottom line Franciacortas weigh in between $25 and $50. Metodo Classico wines from the north can be had for under $30. For the best value in Prosecco, look for bottles that go for less than $12.

recommended wines

Soldati La Scolca, Piedmont 🍷 ★★ $$$
Made from the same grape as Gavi (Cortese), this is a refreshing and zesty wine that has a little apple on the nose, and is beautifully dry in the mouth, with pepper and spice flavors. It has a nutty finish. A great party wine with simple shellfish.

Banfi Metodo Tradizionale Classico Brut, Strevi 🍷 ★★ $$
There's a lot of subtle complexity in this lemony and light-bodied sparkler. It's not too complex, but has a lovely touch of attention-getting nutmeg.

1999 Saracco Moscato d'Asti, Piedmont 🍷 ★★ $$
A very nice wine, with an assertive peach flavor that's slightly honeyed.

1999 Cascinetta Vietti Castaglioni Moscato d'Asti, Piedmont 🍷 ★★ $
A sparkling wine that smells like beer and tastes like lightly sugared cherries. It all works harmoniously. Absolutely yummy.

Ca'del Bosco Brut, Franciacorta ⚲ ★ $$$$
More minerals than fruit. There's some limestone and citrus on the palate and assertive bubbles.

1999 Batasiolo Moscato d'Asti, Piedmont ⚲ ★ $
Don't get too serious here; just pour some of this delightful pineapple-juice-like nectar and enjoy.

Nino Franco Rustica, Veneto ⚲ ★ $
A simple wine, and there's nothing wrong with that. Floral and peachy.

Zardetto Prosecco, Veneto ⚲ ★ $
An easy to drink, under-$10 sparkler is always welcome. We like this one because it's full-bodied and has a lovely touch of melon flavor. Just what's called for in the late afternoon.

sparkling wines of spain

Catalonia is prime Cava territory, though a small amount of these Spanish sparklers is produced in other regions as well. The traditional grapes are Macabeo, Parellada, and Xarel-lo. Chardonnay is now also being used with good results. Though Cava used to seem more like seltzer than sparkling wine, quality is on the upswing.

the bottom line There are a few exceptions, but generally the best thing about Cava is the price. Stay under $15.

recommended wines

Cava Avinyo, Catalonia ⚲ ★★ $$
Subtle aromas of peach and acacia in a deliciously refreshing and citrusy wine. A very pleasant bubbly.

Parxet Cava, Catalonia ♈ ★★ $$

Here's a sophisticated Spanish sparkler that's dry and almond-tinged, with an assertive fizz.

Paul Cheneau Cava Brut Blanc de Blanc, Spain ♈ ★ $

Though the bubbles are a bit too assertive, there's enough apple, toast, and spicy caramel taste going on here to keep us interested.

Cristalino Brut, Penedès ♈ ★ $

Excuse me? It costs how much under $10? A few years back, we didn't care much for this Cava at any price, but this year is a different story. The first whiff brings some hard-cider aromas, and then the flavor is gently floral with a hint of honey.

sparkling wines of the u.s.

The debate is over. America can definitely make first-class sparklers, and, though Oregon and New Mexico make good examples, all eyes are on California. There the French model is followed—using the three Champagne grapes and the traditional method. While Champagne is the template, California's warm climate, soil, and winemaking styles give its sparklers a completely different, fruitier personality.

the bottom line Prices for American sparklers have been slowly climbing. Look for the best from California to range between $18 and $30.

recommended wines

1994 Iron Horse Russian Cuvée, Sonoma County ♈ ★★★ $$$

This is a sparkler with substance. It's got a lot going on taste-wise, with summer and fall tree fruits as well as a refreshing tinge of citrus.

Roederer Estate Brut, Anderson Valley ♀   ★ ★ ★ $$

This is consistently one of California's most complex sparklers, with full, toasty aromas followed by a mixture of pear, limes, and grapefruit.

1996 Schramsberg Blanc de Blancs, Napa Valley ♀   ★ ★ $$$

Refreshing, with a lemony, floral quality and vanilla and herbs in the finish.

1996 Pacific Echo Brut Rosé, Mendocino ♀   ★ ★ $$

Here's a fairly subtle wine that is at first reminiscent of strawberries, and then the flavor turns nutty.

1996 Domaine Carneros Brut, Carneros ♀   ★ ★ $

Very easy-drinking, with light apple and grassy aromas and flavors and honeyed melon in the finish.

Chandon Blanc de Noirs, Carneros ♀   ★ $$

A light-bodied, dry, and assertively bubbled wine with a touch of strawberry in the aroma and a nut-like finish.

Gloria Ferrer Brut, Sonoma ♀   ★ $$

We like this one for a simple everyday sparkler. It's both peachy and tart, with a lingering lime-like aftertaste. It's a fine party choice, too.

Gruet Brut, New Mexico ♀   ★ $$

This New Mexican sparkler is consistently good. It has a creamy texture and a bit of lemon in the flavor.

sparkling wines from other countries

Excellent sparkling wines come from South Africa as well as Australia and New Zealand. From Europe, seek out *méthode champenoise* sparklers, called Sekt, made with Riesling grapes in Germany or Austria.

recommended wines

1993 Georg Breuer Brut, Germany ★★★ $$$$
Appealing floral, lime, and apple accents decorate this rivetingly tart wine. Refreshing and food-friendly.

1993 Seppelt Salinger, Australia ★★★ $$
A complex sparkler that really is attention-getting. Beautiful aromas of fresh-baked brioche and flavors of nuts, figs, and plums. The texture is silky, the fizz quite gentle.

Schlumberger Cuvée Klimt Brut, Austria ★ $$
Though it's already fruity with a touch of tart apple, we really like this wine best with a teensy drop of elderberry liqueur for an extra dimension. The two marry beautifully. Of course, you can also use créme de cassis and make it a traditional Kir Royale.

Chandon Brut Fresco, Argentina ★ $
Here's a good one for a hot afternoon or an everyday aperitif. It's got lots of tropical-fruit flavors that are balanced by a touch of dried herb and refreshingly snappy acidity.

Seaview Brut, Australia ★ $
One of our standard "big party" staples. This is a dry and nutty sparkler, with some tart apple and herb flavors. Refreshing.

dessert wines

Dessert wines tend to be expensive, but their lusciousness makes them worth every penny, and when you consider how they're made, it's easy to see why the cost is high. The best ones are made from grapes that are allowed to ripen well past the normal picking point, or they're allowed to dry on the vine or even freeze in the field. Harvesting methods are labor-intensive; sometimes the grapes are hand-picked, one by one. Add to that the relative scarcity of locations where great sweet wines are made, the low production volumes, and the perpetually risky nature of making wine under unusual conditions, and the prices begin to make sense. But there are some inexpensive beauties you can enjoy on a regular basis without breaking the bank, and they'll whet your appetite for the great ones.

grapes & styles

The world's classic sweet wines are made from a variety of grapes, with those that are botrytised (see "Noble Rot," opposite) being the most sought after. In Bordeaux, botrytis-shriveled Sémillon and Sauvignon Blanc grapes bring us Sauternes. In the Loire, Chenin Blanc is favored. Other grapes (Vidal in Canada, a variety of Muscats in the U.S.) yield pleasant and refreshing sweet wines. In Germany and Austria, a number of varieties become Beerenausleses and Trockenbeerenausleses (see "On the

Label," page 159), including Riesling, Scheurebe, and Silvaner. The trick for all of these dessert wines is high acidity to balance the sweetness. Far from being cloying, good dessert wines are actually refreshing.

at the table

Sauternes's traditional matches—Roquefort cheese and foie gras—show the flexibility of sweet wines. The unctuousness of the wine matches that of the food, and the sweetness of the wine versus the flavor of the food makes an exciting contrast. But, in general, sweet wines are offered with dessert. A good rule is to make sure the wine is at least as sweet as the dessert served. Fruit desserts are the safest partners; chocolate-based treats are a tough match. The finest (and dearest) sweet wines, however, may be best treated as the dessert course, served solo so that you can savor their beauty uninterrupted by other flavors. Or have the best of both worlds by serving dessert first and then the wine.

NOBLE ROT

We have a vampirish fungus to thank for some of the world's best sweet wines. Botrytis cinerea (known as noble rot) usually strikes in the fall and literally sucks the water from the fruit, leaving behind shriveled and ugly grapes with extremely concentrated sugar and flavor. Relying on the fungus is a game of chance, but when botrytis attacks and the resulting grapes are carefully hand-gathered and fermented, the result is splendid indeed. That gambling factor—Will the fungus strike? Will animals get the grapes that have been left so long on the vine? Will autumn rains ruin the entire crop?—and the labor-intensive nature of the wine's production mean costs are generally high.

The pace-setting sweet wine regions—the Sauternes area of Bordeaux, the Loire Valley, and parts of Germany, Hungary, and Austria—all offer ideal fungus-inviting autumn conditions, with cool, damp mornings leading to warm, dry afternoons. Riesling, Sémillon, Chenin Blanc, Gewürztraminer, and Furmint are the most likely grapes to succumb to the rot.

dessert wines of france

As Champagne is to sparkling wines, Sauternes is to sweet ones—the best-known and arguably the world's greatest. But Sauternes has some late-harvest rivals, not only outside the borders of France, but also within the country in the regions of Alsace and the Loire Valley, both of which produce ravishingly exquisite dessert wines.

dessert wines of alsace

To make Alsace's sweet Vendange Tardive (late harvest) wines, grapes are picked when overripe. The wines are made from a single variety, and it's always one of the region's best—Gewürztraminer, Muscat, Pinot Gris, or Riesling—which are the only grapes allowed by law for use in Alsace late-harvest wines. They tend to have full, inviting aromas and great depth of flavor. Some of the late-harvest wines are vinified to be absolutely dry, and since the labels don't indicate sweetness, it's hard to know whether a given bottle is really a dessert wine or not; you just have to rely on your wine merchant.

   Less common than the Vendange Tardive category is Sélection des Grains Nobles (selected noble grapes), the sweetest and most expensive of Alsatian wines. This special sweet wine is also produced from one of the four approved grapes, which, in this case, are usually not only harvested late but also botrytised (see "Noble Rot," page 273). Due to limited production, Sélection des Grains Nobles wines can be difficult to find, but they are worth the search.

the bottom line Be prepared for glorious wines and high prices. Alsace dessert wines are rare and priced accordingly, with the best ones starting at $55 a bottle.

recommended wines

1997 A. Thomas Gewurtztraminer
Quintessence 🍷　　　　　　　　★ ★ ★ ★ $$$$
A powerful wine that should be laid down for a while. Right now it's got a mineral taste as well as a honeyed, spicy lychee fruit flavor. It's succulent, but needs at least five years to reach its full complexity.

1998 Domaine Weinbach Gewurztraminer Altenbourg
Quintessence Sélection de Grains Nobles 🍷　　★ ★ ★ ★ $$$
An enveloping nose of toffee and buttered rum, with hints of licorice and chocolate, then a complexity of dessert and spice flavors in an all-out sweet wine.

1990 Hugel Alsace Gewurztraminer
Vendange Tardive 🍷　　　　　　　　★ ★ ★ $$$$
Enticing, with the aromatic enchantment of spices, roses, and papaya. Fruit and acid are well-balanced. It's a luxurious wine, yet subtle for a Gewürztraminer.

1998 Domaine Weinbach Tokay Pinot Gris Altenbourg
Sélection de Grains Nobles 🍷　　　　★ ★ ★ $$$$
A lush nose of rhubarb and ginger. Intense flavors of plum, raspberry, mandarin orange, and kumquat, with strong acidity for balance.

1997 A. Thomas Riesling Cuvée Particulière 🍷　　★ ★ $$
This is fine right now as an aperitif, or save it for a few years. Its mineral flavors offset the ever-so-slightly viscous fruity sweetness.

dessert wines of the loire valley

A few small areas in the Loire possess the perfect microclimate for developing botrytised (see "Noble Rot," page 273) Chenin Blanc grapes. In Anjou, the Layon Valley (Coteaux du Layon) is known for producing sweet wines of medium weight and intensity. Bonnezeaux and Quarts-de-Chaume like to think of themselves as Sauternes's equal. In the Touraine area, Montlouis and Vouvray produce good sweet wine (labeled Moelleux) from Chenin Blanc. Unsung in the U.S., these wines offer the powerful sugar-acid balance demanded of the best sweet wines, and can rightly be compared to good German Trockenbeerenausleses (see "On the Label," page 159).

the bottom line You're more likely to get a bargain from the Loire Valley than from Sauternes—that is, if you can find a store that stocks the sweet wines of the region. Top-notch entries like Bonnezeaux and Coteaux du Layon will run as high as $50 or more, but other Loire Valley dessert wines can be had for $15 to $25.

what to buy LOIRE VALLEY CHENIN BLANC

1990	1991	1992	1993	1994
★★★★	★	★	★★★	★

1995	1996	1997	1998	1999
★★★★	★★★★	★★★	★★★	★★

recommended wines

1997 Château de Fesles, Bonnezeaux ♥   ★★★ $$$$
Botrytis-induced muskiness bursts from this marvelous, sweet Chenin Blanc. There are also intriguing musty forest-floor notes of damp earth and mushrooms as well as sweet honeysuckle and the concentrated aroma and flavor of cooked apricots. It's a complex dessert wine that has some mineral tang and a mellow finish.

1998 Domaine Ogereau St. Lambert, Clos des Bonnes Blanches, Coteaux du Layon ♥   ★★★ $$$$
Aromas of cinnamon, brown sugar, nuts, and baked peaches lead to loads of flavor, yet very little unctuousness. It's a rather light-bodied and refreshing glass of nectar.

1998 Château Pierre-Bise Clos de la Soucherie, Coteaux du Layon-Beaulieu ♥   ★★★ $$$
This is golden in color and luscious in taste, with lemon-peel and honey flavors dominating and hints of candied apricot. There's a fine balance of sweetness and acidity. This one will only get better over the next ten years in the bottle—if you can wait.

1997 Domaine du Clos Naudin Demi Sec, Vouvray ♥   ★★ $$
Apples, honey, and earthy mushrooms mingle on the nose, and then honey, lemon, and the apple-pie flavors of cooked fruit, cinnamon, nutmeg, and cloves emerge on the palate. There's also enough acidity to make this wine refreshing and satisfying.

1995 Vincent Raimbault Moelleux, Vouvray 🍷 ★★ $$

A light-bodied Vouvray highlighted by intense mineral flavors. It's an easy-drinking wine that has honey-accented, lemony acidity, and a more nectar-like texture than heavy viscosity.

1998 Domaine Roullet, Coteaux du Layon 🍷 ★★ $

A woodsy and mushroomy nose with a honeysuckle background leads to a mouthful of sweet cooked fruit and hints of tangerine, lemon peel, and spices. The wine is light-bodied.

1998 François Chidaine Clos Habert, Montlouis 🍷 ★ $$

Mineral smells and distinct citrus aromas, and then hints of quince, lime peel, mint, and rhubarb. There's a good balance of flavors and acidity and a fine, delicate finish.

sauternes

Honey-sweet and nutty, with dessert flavors of butterscotch, toffee, tropical fruits, apricots, citrus zest, and spices—the list of descriptors for the complex wines of Sauternes (so-tairn) are endless. In perfect years, the wines are dazzling. Many of them can mature well past forty years, and some Sauternes have been known to last up to a hundred.

Five communes—Sauternes, Barsac, Bommes, Preignac, and Fargues—within the Graves district of Bordeaux are entitled to use the appellation Sauternes on their labels. Barsac may also be bottled under its own name.

Sémillon and, to a lesser degree, Sauvignon Blanc and Muscadelle grapes are used, and the wine is generally aged in oak for one-and-a-half to three years. Sauternes delivers sumptuous sweetness, viscosity, and flavor, with great acidity for balance and a high percentage of alcohol. When young, the wine leans toward honey and citrus; when aged, dried fruit, toasted nuts, and spices come in.

the bottom line No bargains here; this is, after all, Bordeaux. In good years, the wines are snapped up quickly by professionals, so you can expect to see more Sauternes available in restaurants than retail shops. If you can find it, expect to pay a minimum of $50.

what to buy SAUTERNES

1989	1990	1991	1992	1993
★★★★	★★★★	★	★	★

1994	1995	1996	1997	1998
★★	★★★	★★★	★★★	★★★

recommended wines

1998 Château Lafaurie-Peyraguey, Sauternes ♟   ★★★★ $$$$
A complex wine that features a great concentration of spiced-pear, apple, apricot, nut, cooked-pineapple, and toasty-oak aromas, all of which follow through on the palate. The result is a luscious, medium-bodied Sauternes with a long finish.

1998 Château Sigalas-Rabaud, Sauternes ♟   ★★★ $$$$
Well-balanced and elegant, with an appealing spiced pineapple and peach character. A full-bodied and medium-sweet Sauternes with a very long and zesty finish.

1998 Château d'Arche, Sauternes ♟   ★★★ $$$
Aromatics of butterscotch, lemon, honey, and spices grace this Sauternes that is full-bodied and has a luscious texture. There's a good burst of acidity on the sweet finish.

1998 Château Coutet, Barsac ♟   ★★★ $$$
In this Barsac, there are plentiful and delightful aromas of honey and citrus, with baked pineapple and spiced tropical fruits to add complexity. The Sémillon-Sauvignon Blanc combination yields a medium-bodied, medium-sweet wine with a spicy finish.

1998 Château de Rayne-Vigneau, Sauternes ♟   ★★★ $$$
Here's an exciting wine with honey and vanilla aromas on the nose and a flavor like pears cooked with spices and lemon zest and served with whipped cream. There are dried-fruit flavors as well. All these tastes are balanced by lively acidity in a medium-to-heavy-bodied Sauternes that ends with a long, lush, sweet finish.

1998 Château Suduiraut, Sauternes ♟   ★★★ $$$
Full-bodied and subtle, with a floral quality on the nose as well as a baklava-like honey-and-nut rush alternating with dried apricots on the palate. A very sweet Sauternes.

vins doux naturels

Vins Doux Naturels (van doo nah-too-REL) are actually fortified wines, made by adding alcohol to the fermenting grape juice. Often made with Muscat, the resulting wine is generally strong and sweet, with much of the floral, citrusy, aromatic quality of the grape itself. The huge Languedoc-Roussillon region produces whites from Muscat and reds from Grenache, while Muscat de Beaumes-de-Venise from the Rhône is arguably the best affordable French sweet wine. It's refreshing and fruity, offering citrus, peach, honey, and floral characteristics.

the bottom line Given quality-to-price ratios, there can be some serious bargains in this category. There is also a great range of prices as well, starting at about $15 for the basic stuff and going up to $85 or so for some of the more complex older vintages.

recommended wines

Mas Amiel 10 Year Old, Maury ♥ ★ ★ ★ ★ $$$
Sun-drenched-plum, fig, raisin, prune, and licorice flavors combined with a little smokiness lead to a finish that won't quit. The wine of choice for hard-to-match chocolate.

1998 Mas Amiel, Maury ♥ ★ ★ ★ $$$
The deep purple hue announces a complex and luxurious dessert wine—a mad amalgam of cocoa, cedar, coffee, black raspberries, tar, and black cherries. It's thick and has a long, multi-flavored finish.

1998 Domaine de La Rectorie Leon Parcé, Banyuls ♥ ★ ★ ★ $$$
This baby is a knockout, with super-concentrated flavors of plums and logan-berries. These intense flavors are beautifully brought out and balanced by good acidity.

1998 Domaine Sarda-Malet, Muscat de Rivesaltes Blanc ♥ ★ ★ ★ $$
From a producer who specializes in intense wines, here's one packed with flowery aromas and flavors, and refreshing acidity.

1998 Paul Jaboulet Aîné, Muscat de Beaumes-de-Venise 🍷 ★ ★ $$

A full-bodied wine filled with aromas of field flowers and a hint of honey, along with a basketful of fruit flavors—tart apples, ripe peaches, and grapes. Delightful finish.

1998 Vidal-Fleury, Muscat de Beaumes-de-Venise 🍷 ★ ★ $$

A touch of spiced orange peel on the nose and luxurious flavors of peaches with hints of rose geranium give this Muscat-based wine a lively, refreshing quality. Good acid-fruit balance in a yummy sweet wine.

1998 Les Clos de Paulilles, Banyuls 🍷 ★ ★ $

Black grapes, plums, and raisins fill up the glass. The wine beautifully balances alcohol, flavor, and body. In the long finish, there are touches of caramel, black tea, and orange peel.

dessert wines of germany

Thrilling acidity and tropical-fruit sweetness balance perfectly in the dazzling dessert wines of Germany. These wines are sweet, yes, but not syrupy—they're delicate, flowery, and restrained, especially when compared to Sauternes. Beerenauslese (BEAR-en-OWSE-lay-zuh) is made from grapes that are late-picked and usually botrytis-affected (see "Noble Rot," page 273), and ranks among the most intensely luscious dessert wines anywhere. Trockenbeerenauslese (TRAH-ken-BEAR-en-OWSE-lay-zuh) comes from grapes that have been dried to raisins by botrytis, and this type of dessert wine is even more honeyed. Eiswein (ICE-vine), which is made from grapes that have been left on the vine so late that they freeze, tends to have a fresh- rather than dried-fruit flavor.

the bottom line Since all three types of German dessert wine are costly to produce, bargains are rare. Expect to pay $40 and up—way up.

what to buy GERMAN DESSERT WINES

1990	1991	1992	1993	1994
★★★★	★	★★	★★★	★★★★

1995	1996	1997	1998	1999
★★★★	★★★★	★★★	★★	★★★

recommended wines

1998 St. Urbans-Hof Ockfener Bockstein Riesling Eiswein, Ruwer ▼   ★★★★ $$$$
There's a burst of orange-zest and apricot aromas here that lead to a powerful and unctuous mouthful of lemon, caramel, nuts, and spices to make a stunning Eiswein.

1998 Balbach Nierstein Oelberg Eiswein, Rheinhessen ▼   ★★★ $$$$
The concentrated flavors of lemon, lime peel, vanilla, baked pineapple, and creamy caramel combine to make this a luscious, mouth-filling dessert all on its own. It's a delicious Eiswein with a citrusy zip for balance and a smooth, long-lasting finish.

1997 Reichsrat von Buhl Forster Ungeheuer Riesling Beerenauslese, Pfalz ▼   ★★★ $$$$
An entirely inviting wine. Stewed peaches seasoned with brown sugar and cinnamon come to mind with the first taste, yet the sweetness on the palate is balanced by a lively citrus acidity. There's a smooth finish with a flash of refreshing minerality.

1998 Selbach-Oster Bernkastler Badstube Eiswein, Mosel ▼   ★★★ $$$$
The mouthful of sugared grapefruit, tangerine peel, and sautéed, caramelized pears is a batch of flavors that are nevertheless nicely balanced. This is an Eiswein of complexity and excitement, a thoroughly delightful dessert wine with a long-lasting finish.

1998 Robert Weil Kiedrich Gräfenberg Beerenauslese, Rheingau ▼   ★★★ $$$$
Despite ownership of the winery by a huge Japanese company, this is an absolutely classic Rheingau Beerenauslese (perhaps because Wilhelm Weil remains as director). It has exquisite fruit flavors—nectarines, peaches, and lemons—supported by harmonious balance between sweetness and acidity.

dessert wines of austria

The Austrian makers of Beerenauslese, Trockenbeerenauslese, Eiswein, and the Sauternes-like Ausbruch (OWZ-brook) have bounced back from a reputation-smearing additive scandal in the mid-1980s. Now, the botrytis-friendly climate (see "Noble Rot," page 273) all over Austria—including the Neusiedlersee and Neusiedlersee-Hügelland areas of Burgenland—and a strong commitment to quality result in fine, reasonably-priced dessert wines. Unfortunately, they're often hard to find in the U.S. Generally, these sweet wines follow the German style: aromatic, fruity, and low in alcohol.

recommended wines

1998 Knoll Grüner Veltliner Beerenauslese Loibner, Wachau 🍷 ★★★ $$$$
The nose is perfumed with a bit of apricot, lime zest, and honey. Yet, despite the honeyed start, the wine is a relatively light Beerenauslese. It has an unusual balance of flavors, body, and acidity that leaves the mouth satisfied but refreshed.

1999 Heidi Schrock Ausbruch Muskateller, Ruster 🍷 ★★★ $$$$
This is an intensely sweet wine. It has flavors of orange peel and white raisin and also a gingerbread sort of spiciness that lasts through the long finish. Sticky and full-bodied.

1995 Ernst Triebaumer Ausbruch, Ruster 🍷 ★★★ $$$$
A mouthful of peach jam studded with golden raisins and hints of ginger and honeysuckle, this Ausbruch (between Beerenauslese and Trockenbeeren-auslese in sweetness) possesses lively acidity and, for all its exuberant sweet-ness, a surprising medium-bodied mouth-feel.

1999 Mantlerhof Grüner Veltliner Eiswein, Kremstal 🍷 ★★★ $$$
This is slightly smoky, yet exploding with sweetness and lemony acidity. The wine has refreshing hints of minerals and spices etched along a finish that just doesn't quit.

dessert wines of hungary

Tokay (Tokaji in Hungary) has for hundreds of years been considered a classic dessert wine, but lack of investment during the Communist era created hard times in the hilly vineyards in northeast Hungary. The wine industry is now back on its feet, which is great news for lovers of this golden nectar with its luscious, intense apricot flavor, dried-fruit notes, and surprising acidity. Tokay is made by adding mashed botrytised grapes (see "Noble Rot," page 273) to barrels of dry white wine. It's measured with *puttonyos*, a system of sweetness ratings ranging from one to six. Esszencia, made only in the best years with grapes from the top vineyards, is the sweetest, rarest, and most expensive Tokay.

recommended wines

1993 Chateau Pajzos Tokay Esszencia 🍷 ★★★★ $$$$
Extremely rare; made from the minuscule amount of free-running juice from the shriveled grapes. The wine is pure sweetness without being syrupy.

1997 Chateau Pajzos Sarga Muskotaly Tokay Late Harvest 🍷 ★★★ $$$$
Sweet and tart, with apricot and a touch of plum, offset by vibrant acidity.

1993 Chateau Pajzos Tokaji Aszu 5 Puttonyos 🍷 ★★★ $$$
Just becomes more beautiful the older it gets. Right now, there are slight nutty and oxidized aromas of age on the nose. But the acidity is still zippy enough to keep the concentrated, honeyed apricot flavor refreshing.

1994 Oremus Tokaji/Tokay Aszu 5 Puttonyos 🍷 ★★ $$$
Glorious hue, with flavors of orange marmalade, honey, walnuts, and minerals. A mouth-filling wine with a nice bitter-almond note on the finish.

1996 Oremus Furmint Tokay Late Harvest 🍷 ★★ $$
Caramel and lemon on the nose, quince and marmalade on the tongue. There's a snap of citrus along with hazelnut and burnt-almond in the finish.

dessert wines of italy

In addition to regular late-harvest (*Vendemmia Tardiva*) wines, there are a couple of special categories in Italy that account for many of its entries into the dessert category: *Passito* and its subclassification, *Recioto*, refer to Italian dried-grape wines. The best known of these is Recioto della Valpolicella, which is made from the usual Valpolicella grapes—Corvina, Molinara, and Rondinells—left to dry for a few months before fermentation.

recommended wines

1996 Marco de Bartoli Moscato Passito di Pantelleria Bukkuram, Pantelleria ♥   ★ ★ ★ $$$

A delightful, concentrated *passito* with a rusty, sunset hue and intense flavors of caramel, clove, golden raisins, cooked apricots, and honey. A tiny bit of refreshing bitter-almond comes out on the wine's lengthy finish.

1998 Feudi di San Gregorio Fiano di Avellino Pietracalda Vendemmia Tardiva, Campania ♥   ★ ★ ★ $$$

Unusually light-bodied for a late-harvest wine. But there's no mistaking the classic dessert wine's baklava honey-and-nut intensity paired with a crème brûlée finish. With its great acid zip, this wine will only continue to improve with time in the bottle.

1996 Salvatore Murana Martingana Moscato Passito di Pantelleria, Pantelleria ♥   ★ ★ ★ $$$

The perfume of dried fruit—dates and apricots—wafts from a glass of this *passito*. The wine's sweetness is balanced by good acidity, and the flavor is lush and full. A characteristic hint of bitterness leads into a medium-long, fig-accented finish.

1997 Botromagno Gravisano Vino Passito, Apulia ♥   ★ ★ ★ $$

A sweet honey nose with a touch of oxidation and some jasmine perfume. This dessert wine has a refreshing lime accent along with a lingering, toasted-almond finish.

1996 Colosi Malvasia delle Lipari Passito di Salina, Salina ♀ ★★ $$$$

Springtime aromas of apple blossom and phlox leading to a lemon-honey tang on the palate and lots of fresh floral flavors. It's a full-bodied dessert wine with a sweet finish.

1998 Maculan Moscato Dindarello, Veneto ♀ ★★ $$

Straw-colored, with a potent Moscato apricot, honey, and floral nose, the wine is luscious, creamy, and full-bodied in the mouth. A good balance of fruit and acid leads to an exceptional finish.

1996 Castello Banfi Moscadello di Montalcino Vendemmia Tardiva, Tuscany ♀ ★ $$

Zippy, with flavors of lemon peel, honeycomb, and nectarine. Charming, medium-bodied wine with a raisiny finish.

1994 Di Majo Norante Passito Apianae, Molise ♀ ★ $$

A lush basketful of fruit and flower aromas, with a splash of honey to boot. The wine is medium-sweet and luscious, with a punch of cinnamon and lemon peel in its medium finish.

dessert wines of the u.s. & canada

Most winemakers in the United States seem uninterested in devoting much vineyard space to Riesling and Gewürztraminer, the two varieties that are most likely to produce good dessert wines here. But there are numerous decent sweet wines to be found, and some outstanding ones, too—generally nicely fruity, though disappointingly low in acidity. Most hail from Washington State's Yakima Valley, New York's Finger Lakes region, and the cooler parts of California.

Canada's outstanding late-harvest and ice wines from the Niagara Peninsula in Ontario, generally made from Riesling and Vidal grapes and sometimes Gewürztraminer, are fine examples of what can be done in North America.

recommended wines

1998 Inniskillin Riesling Ice Wine, Niagara ♥   ★ ★ ★ $$$$

A beauty of a Canadian, with intense flavors, vibrant acidity, and a touch of honey and apricot on the palate. Delicate yet persistently long on the finish, this wine's a winner.

1998 Inniskillin Vidal Ice Wine, Niagara ♥   ★ ★ ★ $$$$

Clear fruity aromas and flavors abound. Nectarines, peaches, and apricots fairly gush from the glass, and the intense flavors are offset by a tree-full of good, citrusy acidity.

1998 Arrowood Hoot Owl Creek Vineyards Late Harvest Special Select White Riesling, Alexander Valley ♥   ★ ★ ★ $$$

Intensely sweet, with a lush texture and a wide array of fruit flavors—melon, peach, and nectarine, to name a few.

1997 Chateau Ste. Michelle Late Harvest Reserve, Columbia Valley ♥   ★ ★ ★ $$

Potent, honeyed lusciousness in a spicy and citrusy wine. There are also flavors of figs, apricots, herbs, and honeysuckle.

1997 Navarro Anderson Valley Late Harvest Cluster Select Very Sweet White Riesling, Mendocino ♥   ★ ★ $$

Pure sweetness, with peaches, apricots, caramel-tinged apple-pie flavors, and nougat on the palate. This is a Riesling that's so lush and full that one glass will be all you need.

1998 Wagner Finger Lakes Riesling Ice Wine, New York ♥   ★ ★ $$

A good example of New York dessert wine, with subtle floral and fruit aromas and an added whiff of damp forest. Full-bodied and refreshing with a bit of stony mineral flavor.

1998 Hogue Late Harvest Riesling, Columbia Valley ♥   ★ $

A very sweet late-harvest wine with notes of lemon-spritzed nectarines and apricots. There's a good balance between sweetness and acidity—and the wine is a bargain to boot.

1998 Quady Orange Muscat California Electra, California ♥   ★ $

Lively and slightly effervescent, with characteristic Muscat grape flavors of clementine, peach, and cantaloupe, as well as hints of freesia and lime blossom. The wine is medium-bodied. It's a great bargain from a dedicated dessert-wine maker.

CLASSIC PAIRINGS REVISITED

The top-10 classic food-and-wine pairings, with alternative wines to try.

Food Caviar
Classic companion Champagne
Alternative California Sparkling Wine (Brut), page 270

Food Oysters
Classic companion Chablis
Alternative Muscadet, page 66

Food Foie Gras
Classic companion Sauternes
Alternative Alsatian Dessert Wine, page 275

Food Sashimi
Classic companion Saki
Alternative German Riesling (Kabinett), page 158

Food Shellfish
Classic companion Vinho Verde
Alternative New Zealand Sauvignon Blanc, page 246

Food Grilled Pork
Classic companion Rioja
Alternative Washington State Chardonnay, page 215

Food Choucroute Garnie
Classic companion Pinot Gris
Alternative California Gewürztraminer, page 189

Food Rack of Lamb
Classic companion Bordeaux
Alternative California Cabernet Sauvignon, page 192

Food Chèvre
Classic companion Sancerre
Alternative New York State Chardonnay, page 224

Food Stilton
Classic companion Port
Alternative Australian Shiraz, page 239

vintage chart

Is that 1995 Opus One you bought while touring Napa a couple of years ago ready to drink? And why is your favorite restaurant selling that 1987 Bordeaux for what seems to be a pittance?

	1983	1984	1985	1986	1987	1988	1989
Bordeaux							
Right Bank	☆☆☆	★	★★★★	☆☆☆	★	★★★	☆☆☆☆
Médoc	☆☆☆	★	★★★★	☆☆☆☆	★★	☆☆☆	☆☆☆☆
Red Graves	☆☆	★★	★★★★	☆☆☆☆	★★	☆☆☆	☆☆☆☆
Burgundy							
Red	☆☆	☆	☆☆☆☆	☆☆☆	☆☆	★★★	★★★
White	☆☆☆	o	☆☆	★★★	★★	★★	★★★
Loire							
Chenin Blanc	★	★	★★	☆☆☆	★	★★★	☆☆☆
Cabernet Franc	★★	o	★★★	☆☆	★	★★★	★★★★
Rhône							
Northern Red	★★★★	☆	★★★★	★★★	☆☆	☆☆☆☆	☆☆☆☆
Southern Red	☆☆☆	☆☆	★★★★	★★	★★	★★★★	☆☆☆
Italy							
Barolo & Barbaresco	☆☆	☆	★★★★	★★	☆	★★★★	☆☆☆☆
Chianti	★★	o	★★★★	★★★	☆☆	★★★	★★
Spain							
Rioja	☆	o	★★★★	★★	★★★	☆	★★★
Ribera del Duero	★★★	★	★★★	o	★★★	☆☆	★★
Germany							
Mosel-Saar-Ruwer	★★★★	★	★★★	☆☆	☆☆	★★★	★★★
Rhine Regions	☆☆☆☆	★	☆☆☆	☆☆	☆☆	★★★	☆☆☆
California							
Cabernet Sauvignon	☆☆	★★★★	★★★★	★★★★	★★★★	☆☆	★★★

o = Very bad vintage, a disaster
★ = Poor to average vintage, only the best wines are good quality
★★ = Good to very good vintage
★★★ = Excellent vintage
★★★★ = Outstanding vintage

This chart answers such questions for wines that are commonly aged. The quality of the wine is indicated by the number of stars, just as in the "What to Buy" sections of this book. The color of the stars tells where the wine is most likely to be in its progress from "not ready" through "well past peak." For example, ★★ indicates a good wine at peak, and ☆☆☆ an excellent wine whose time has almost passed.

1990	1991	1992	1993	1994	1995	1996	1997	1998	1999
☆☆☆	O	☆	☆☆	☆☆☆	☆☆	★★★★	☆☆	★★★★	★★★
☆☆☆☆	★	★	☆☆	★★★	★★★★	★★★★	☆☆	★★★	★★★
☆☆☆	★	★	☆☆☆	☆☆☆	★★★	★★★	☆☆☆	★★	★★
☆☆☆☆	☆☆	☆☆	☆☆☆	★★	☆☆☆☆	★★★	☆☆☆	★★★	★★★
★★★	☆☆	★★★	★★	★★★	☆☆☆☆	★★★★	☆☆☆	☆☆☆	☆☆☆
★★★★	O	★★	☆☆☆☆	☆☆☆	★★★★	★★★★	☆☆☆	★★★	★★
★★★★	O	O	☆☆☆☆	★★	☆☆☆☆	★★★★	☆☆☆	☆☆☆	☆☆
★★★★	☆☆☆☆	O	★★	☆☆☆	★★★★	☆☆☆	☆☆☆	★★★	★★★
☆☆☆☆	☆	☆	★★	★★	☆☆☆☆	☆☆	☆☆☆	★★★★	★★★
☆☆☆☆	★★★	★★	☆☆☆	☆☆	★★★★	★★★★	★★★★	☆☆☆	na
★★★★	☆☆☆	☆☆	★★★	★★★	★★★★	★★★	★★★★	☆☆☆	na
☆☆☆	★★★	★★	★★	★★★★	★★★★	★★★	★★★	☆☆☆	na
★★★	★★★★	★	☆☆	★★★★	★★★★	★★★★	★★★	★★★	★★★
☆☆☆☆	☆☆	★★	☆☆☆	☆☆☆☆	☆☆☆☆	★★★★	☆☆☆	☆☆☆	☆☆☆☆
☆☆☆☆	★★	★★	★★★	☆☆☆	☆☆	★★★	☆☆☆	☆☆☆	☆☆☆☆
★★★★	★	★★★★	☆☆☆	☆☆☆☆	☆☆☆	★★★	★★★	★★★	★★

★ = Not ready, needs more time
☆ = Can be drunk or held
★ = At peak, perfect for drinking now
☆ = Past peak but still enjoyable
★ = Well past peak
na = Not yet available

289

food & wine pairing chart

Legend:
- ▼ (green) = white wine
- ▼ (red) = red wine
- ▼ (rosé) = rosé wine

	barolo/ barbaresco	beaujolais	bordeaux, red	bordeaux, white	burgundy, red	burgundy, white	cabernet franc	cabernet sauvignon	chardonnay	
cheese, mild		red					red	red		
cheese, strong								red		
creamy sauces & soups				white					white	
fish, lean					red				white	
fish, rich			red		red		red		white	
game	red				red		red	red		
garlicky dishes						white				
meat, red	red		red				red	red		
pork		red	red		red		red	red	white	
poultry, chicken & other light		red		white	red	white	red	red	white	
poultry, duck & other dark	red				red		red		white	
shellfish				white		white			white	
veal			red		red		red			

Perhaps inflexible rules are for fools—at least when it comes to wine—but a bit of guidance doesn't hurt. Here's an at-a-glance look at some food and wine matches that have been suggested in this book. For more detail, look to the "Food & Wine Pairing Index," page 293, where you'll find listings of specific wines and the pages to turn to for descriptions of them.

chenin blanc	gewürztraminer	merlot	pinot blanc	pinot gris	pinot noir	riesling	rosé	sauvignon blanc	sémillon	sparkling	syrah	zinfandel	
	🟢							🟢					
	🟢	🔴						🟢		🟢	🔴		
				🟢	🔴	🟢		🟢	🟢	🟢	🔴	🔴	
🟢		🔴		🟢	🔴	🟢	🌸	🟢	🟢	🟢			
🟢		🔴			🔴	🟢	🌸	🟢	🟢	🟢	🔴		
					🔴						🔴		
											🔴		
		🔴		🟢	🔴		🌸				🔴	🔴	
		🔴	🟢	🟢	🔴		🌸				🔴		
🟢	🟢	🔴	🟢	🟢	🔴	🟢	🌸				🔴	🔴	
		🔴			🔴	🟢				🟢			
🟢	🟢		🟢	🟢			🌸			🟢			
		🔴		🟢							🔴		

291

pairing wine with food

The best way to discover terrific matches is to experiment—with both the suggestions we've offered throughout the book and other possibilities. Taste and learn. If you make an uninspired food and wine pairing, the wine police will not come to get you. Though no one should get overly dogmatic about rules, here are a few ideas to keep in mind when making your choices.

1. Opposites attract. Rich food is good with wine that contains healthy acidity to cut through the fat and cleanse your palate. Salty or spicy food tastes good with wine that has some complementary sweetness.

2. Great minds think alike. Matching attributes can work as well as contrasting them. Rich food pairs as well with rich as with acidic wine. With hearty food, you don't have a choice; it needs full-bodied wine. Similarly, a delicate dish requires light wine, and food with lots of acidity needs equally zesty wine.

3. Double your pleasure. Mirroring the keynote flavor of food can make a fine pairing. Does the dish have cilantro? Think of herbal-tasting wines like Loire Sauvignon Blanc or Chenin Blanc. Is it peppery? Perhaps a spicy Rhône wine would work. Does it have a fruit sauce? A fruity Zinfandel might do the trick.

4. Tannin needs taming. Wines such as young Bordeaux or Barolo need protein and fat to counteract their puckeriness.

5. There's wisdom in tradition. Choosing a wine from the same country or region as the cuisine you're serving will put you on the right track.

6. Red and white rules are silly. Remember, salmon and Pinot Noir are a classic match, and pork is great with Pinot Gris. However, do bear in mind that tannic reds taste intensely metallic when drunk with oily, fishy fishes such as mackerel, sardines, or bluefish. For these, choose reds that are low in tannin and high in acidity.

food & wine pairing index

A perfect marriage between food and wine makes a whole that's greater than the sum of its parts. Though the possibilities of such delicious matches between food and wine are endless, the following index lists the ones that have been mentioned in this book as particularly felicitous.

cheese, mild
WHITE
California
  Fumé Blanc, 185
France
  Gewurztraminer, 26
  Sauvignon Blanc, 37, 67
New Zealand
  Sauvignon Blanc, 246
RED
California
  Cabernet Franc, 191
  Cabernet Sauvignon, 191
France
  Bandol, 73
  Beaujolais, 53

cheese, strong
WHITE
California
  Fumé Blanc, 185
  Sauvignon Blanc, 185
France
  Gewurztraminer, 26
  Pinot Blanc, 26
Italy
  Amarone della Valpolicella, 123
  Valpolicella Superiore, 123
RED
France
  Bandol, 73
  Côtes-du-Rhône, 82
Italy
  Brunello di Montalcino, 114
  Chianti, 111
Spain
  Ribera del Duero, 138
Washington State
  Cabernet Sauvignon, 218
  Merlot, 218
SPARKLING
white wine, 260

creamy sauces & soups
WHITE
France
  Graves, 37
  Riesling, 25
Germany
  white wine, 161
New Zealand
  Chardonnay, 247
Oregon
  Pinot Gris, 210
RED
California
  Pinot Noir, 198
Italy
  Barbera, 107
  Dolcetto, 107

fish, lean
WHITE
Argentina
  Semillon, 255
Australia
  Chardonnay, 235
Austria
  Grüner Veltliner, 172
California
  Chardonnay, 182
  Fumé Blanc, 185
France
  Chenin Blanc, 64
  Muscadet, 65
  Riesling, 25
  Sauvignon Blanc, 37
Germany
  white wine, 161
Greece
  Assyrtiko, 156
Italy
  Aristos, 98
  Chardonnay, 98
  Gavi, 109

food & wine pairing index

Greco di Tufo, 93
Pinot Grigio, 98
Roero Arneis, 109
Tocai Friulano, 98
white wine, 98
New York
white wine, 224
New Zealand
Riesling, 248
Sauvignon Blanc, 246
Oregon
Pinot Gris, 210
Portugal
Vinho Verde, 150
Spain
Rioja, 134
Switzerland
white wine, 178
Washington State
Chardonnay, 214
Sauvignon Blanc, 216
RED
California
Merlot, 196
Chile
Pinot Noir, 256
France
Burgundy, 43
Italy
Nebbiolo-Based, 106
Spain
Rioja, 134
ROSÉ
Italy
Apulia, 93
Spain
Rioja, 134
Switzerland
rosé wine, 178
SPARKLING
Brut, 260

fish, rich
WHITE
Argentina
Semillon, 255
Australia
Chardonnay, 235
Austria
Grüner Veltliner, 172
California
Rhône-style, 187
Sauvignon Blanc, 185
Chile
Chardonnay, 258
France
Chenin Blanc, 64
Riesling, 25
Sauvignon Blanc, 37
Germany
white wine, 161
Greece
Assyrtiko, 156

Italy
Fiano di Avellino, 93
New Zealand
Chardonnay, 247
Riesling, 248
Portugal
Vinho Verde, 150
South Africa
Sauvignon Blanc, 230
Spain
Rioja, 134
Washington State
Chardonnay, 214
Sauvignon Blanc, 216
RED
Argentina
red wine, 252
Australia
Shiraz, 239
California
Merlot, 196
Pinot Noir, 198
Chile
Pinot Noir, 256
France
Bordeaux, 32
Burgundy, 43
Southwest, 87
Italy
Nebbiolo-Based, 106
New York
Cabernet Franc, 226
Merlot, 226
New Zealand
Pinot Noir, 249
Oregon
Pinot Noir, 212
South Africa
Pinotage, 232
Switzerland
Gamay, 178
Pinot Noir, 178
ROSÉ
France
rosé wine, 76
Spain
Rioja, 134
SPARKLING
Brut, 260

game
WHITE
Italy
Amarone della Valpolicella, 123
RED
Australia
Cabernet Sauvignon, 241
California
Cabernet Franc, 191
Cabernet Sauvignon, 191
France
Bandol, 73
Burgundy, 43

names you can trust

A number of committed importers consistently bring into the country the best wines they can find from their areas of specialization. If the name of one of these companies is on the label, you can bet that the wine is good for its type and price range.

Cape Classics Wines from excellent South African estates.

Cellars International Elite-estate wines from Germany.

Robert Chadderdon High-quality French wines.

Chartrand Imports Organic wines.

Classical Wines Fine wines of Spain and Germany. Some stunning bargains.

Marc de Grazia Modern-style wines from Piedmont, Tuscany, and Southern Italy.

Robert Kacher French wines, especially Burgundies.

Leonardo LoCascio Selections Italian wines, true to their regions and at good prices.

Louis / Dressner Selections Complex French wines at bargain-basement prices.

Kermit Lynch Gem-like traditional wines from France.

Jorge Ordonez Excellent values from Spain.

Eric Solomon European Cellars Wines from traditional regions of France, Italy, and Spain. Good prices.

Terry Theise Champagnes and Austrian and German wines from small, but first-rate, growers.

P. J. Valckenberg Both great values and top-estate wines from Germany.

Vin Divino Outstanding Austrian and classic Italian wines.

top wine shops

These fine stores were chosen based on diversity of wine selection, services offered, and knowledgeability of the staff.

ALABAMA

Classic Wine Company
1920 29th Ave. S., Birmingham
205-871-9463

Overton & Vine
3150 Overton Rd., Birmingham
205-967-1409

ALASKA

Brown Jug Liquor Store M
8840 Old Seward Hwy., Anchorage
907-349-3286

Downtown Wine & Spirits
930 W. Fifth Ave., Anchorage
907-258-0930

ARIZONA

Red Kangaroo Wines M
10625 N. Tatum Blvd., Phoenix
480-951-9486
www.redkangaroo.com

Sportsman's Fine Wine & Spirits M
3205 E. Camelback Rd., Phoenix
602-955-7730

A.J.'s Fine Foods
23251 N. Pima Rd., Scottsdale
602-563-5075, 888-563-5039
www.ajsfinefoods.com

Plaza Liquors
2642 N. Campbell Ave., Tucson
520-327-0452

The RumRunner
3200 E. Speedway Blvd., Tucson
520-326-0121

ARKANSAS

Colonial Wines & Spirits
11601 W. Markham, Little Rock
501-223-3120
www.colonialwineandspirits.com

The Grape Vine Wine & Spirits
10901 Rodney Parham Rd., Little Rock
501-227-6009

Heights Fine Wines & Spirits
5012 Kavanaugh Blvd., Little Rock
501-664-9463

Popatop, Inc.
1901 S. University Ave., Little Rock
501-663-3276

CALIFORNIA

Kermit Lynch Wine Merchant M
1605 San Pablo Ave., Berkeley
510-524-1524

North Berkeley Wine M
1505 Shattuck Ave., Berkeley
510-848-8910, 800-266-6585
www.northberkeleyimports.com

The Wine Stop M
1300 Burlingame Ave., Burlingame
650-342-5858, 800-283-9463

Enoteca Wine Shop
1345 Lincoln Ave., Ste. C, Calistoga
707-942-1117, www.neteze.com/enoteca

Duke of Bourbon
20908 Roscoe Blvd., Canoga Park
818-341-1234, 800-434-6394
www.dukeofbourbon.com

Hi-Time Wine Cellars O
250 Ogle St., Costa Mesa
949-650-8463, 800-331-3005
www.hitimewine.com

Valley Wine Company M
417 G St., Davis, 530-758-9463

Red Carpet Wine & Spirits Merchants
400 E. Glenoaks Blvd., Glendale
818-247-5544, 800-339-0609
www.redcarpetwine.com

Wally's Liquors M, O
2107 Westwood Blvd., Los Angeles
310-475-0606, 888-992-5597
www.wallywine.com

The Wine House M, O
2311 Cotner Ave., Los Angeles
310-479-3731, 800-626-9463
www.winehouse.com

Beltramo's Wines & Spirits
1540 El Camino Real, Menlo Park
650-325-2806, 888-710-9463
www.beltramos.com

Draeger's Epicures O
1010 University Ave., Menlo Park
800-642-9463, www.draegers.com

Wine Exchange M, O
2368 N. Orangemall, Orange
714-974-1454, 800-769-4639
www.winex.com

O = on-line retail   **M** = mail order

top wine shops

Vin, Vino, Wine
437 California Ave., Palo Alto
650-324-4903

Corti Brothers M
5810 Folsom Blvd., Sacramento
916-736-3800, 800-509-3663

David Berkley Fine Wines & Specialty Foods M
515 Pavilions Ln., Sacramento
916-929-4422

St. Helena Wine Merchants M
699 St. Helena Hwy., St. Helena
707-963-7888, 800-729-9463
email gsmith@napanet.net

San Diego Wine Co.
5282 Eastgate Mall, San Diego
858-535-1400, 888-650-9463
www.sandiegowineco.com

PlumpJack Wines
3201 Fillmore St., San Francisco
415-346-9870, 888-415-9463
www.plumpjack.com

The Wine Club
953 Harrison St., San Francisco
415-512-9086, 800-966-7835
www.wineclub.com

The Wine House M
535 Bryant St., San Francisco
415-495-8486, 800-966-8468
www.winehouse-sf.com

The Wine Rack
6136 Bollinger Rd., San Jose
408-253-3050
www.wineracksanjose.com

Draeger's Epicures O
222 E. 4th Ave., San Mateo
650-685-3700, 800-642-9463
www.draegers.com

Wine Cask M, O
813 Anacapa St., Santa Barbara
805-966-9463, 800-436-9463
www.winecask.com

Prima Trattoria & Negozio di Vini M, O
1522 N. Main St., Walnut Creek
925-945-1800, 800-707-7462
www.primawine.com

Woodland Hills Wine Company M, O
22622 Ventura Blvd., Woodland Hills
818-222-1111, 800-678-9463
www.whwineco.com

COLORADO

LiquorMart M, O
1750 15th St., Boulder
303-449-3374, 800-597-4440
www.liquormart.com

Vintage's Wines & Spirits M
9 S. Tejon, Colorado Springs
719-520-5733
email vintageswine@msn.com

Wines off Wynkoop
1610 16th St., Denver
303-571-1012
email WOWwines@aol.com

Tony's Wines & Specialty Beers
4991 E. Dry Creek Rd., Littleton
303-770-4297, www.tonysmeats.com

CONNECTICUT

Nutmeg Discount Liquor
279 Greenwood Ave., Bethel
203-743-4945

La Vinothèque
206 Main St., Farmington
860-677-9224

Horseneck Wine & Liquor
25 E. Putnam Ave., Greenwich
203-869-8944, www.horseneck.com

Spiritus Wines O
367 Main St., Hartford
860-247-5431, www.spiritus.com

M&R Liquors
120 Tolland Turnpike, Manchester
860-643-9014, www.mandrliquors.com

DELAWARE

Greenville Wine & Spirit Company O
4025 Kennett Pike, Wilmington
302-658-5939
www.greenvillewines.com

Kreston Liquor Mart O
904 Concord Ave., Wilmington
302-652-3792, 800-752-8110

FLORIDA

The Wine Club M
645 Atlantic Blvd., Atlantic Beach
904-246-6450
email markclub@aol.com

Wine Watch O
901 Progresso Dr., Ft. Lauderdale
954-523-9463, 800-329-9463
www.winewatch.com

Broudy's
353 Marshlanding Pkwy., Jacksonville
904-273-6119

Riverside Liquors & Village Wine Shop
1035 Park St., Jacksonville
904-356-4517

Foremost Sunset Corners
8701 Sunset Dr., Miami
305-271-8492, email mbwine@aol.com

Crown Wine & Spirits
12555C Biscayne Blvd., N. Miami
305-892-9463, www.crownliquors.com

ABC Fine Wine & Spirits
530 Sawgrass Village Dr.
Ponte Vedra Beach
904-285-5760, 800-942-9463
www.abcfinewineandspirits.com

Pic Pac Fine Wines & Spirits
6609 Central Ave., St. Petersburg
727-347-0743

J.D. Ford, Purveyor of Fine Wine & Spirits M, O
1925 S. Osprey Ave., Sarasota
941-362-9463, 800-361-9463

Bern's Fine Wine & Spirits M
1002 S. Howard Ave., Tampa
813-250-9463
www.bernssteakhouse.com

Vintage Wine Cellars
3629 Henderson Blvd., Tampa
813-879-2931, email vintwine@gte.net

Wine Warehouse
3310 W. Bay to Bay Blvd., Tampa
813-839-5601

GEORGIA

Ansley Wine Merchants
1544 Piedmont Rd. NE, Atlanta
404-876-6790

Buckhead Fine Wine
3906 Roswell Rd., Atlanta
404-231-8566
email bwine@mindspring.com

Peachtree Wine Merchants
3891 Peachtree Rd. NE, Atlanta
404-237-7128

HAWAII

R. Field Wine Company
Foodland Supermarket
1460 S. Beretania St., Honolulu
808-596-9463, 800-524-4275
email rfield@aloha.net

Fujioka's Wine Merchants
Market City Shopping Center, Lower Level
2919 Kapiolani Blvd., Honolulu
808-739-9463, www.fujiokawine.com

Vintage Wine Cellar
1249 Wilder Ave., Honolulu
808-523-9463

IDAHO

The Boise Consumer Co-op M
888 W. Fort St., Boise
208-342-6652, www.boisecoop.com

Ericson Fine Wine
3220 E. Chinden Blvd., Ste. 120, Eagel
208-938-3698

The Wine Company of Sun Valley
360 N. Leadville Ave., Ketchum
208-726-2442

ILLINOIS

Gold Standard Chalet M, O
3000 N. Clark St., Chicago
773-935-9400

Sam's Wines & Spirits M, O
1720 N. Marcey St., Chicago
312-664-4394, 800-777-9137
www.sams-wine.com

Mainstreet Wines & Spirits
5425 S. La Grange, Countryside
708-354-0355, 888-354-0355
www.mainstreetwine.com

Knightsbridge Wine Shoppe, Ltd. M
824 Sunset Ridge Rd., Northbrook
847-498-9300
www.knightsbridgewine.com

Schaefer's Wines, Spirits & Gourmet Foods M, O
19965 Gross Point Rd., Skokie
847-673-5711, 800-833-9463
www.schaefers.com

Convito Italiano M
1515 Sheridan Rd., Wilmette
847-251-3654

INDIANA

Hamilton Beverage
2290 E. 116th St., Carmel
317-844-0872

John's Spirits, Fine Wines & Decanters
25 N. Pennsylvania, Indianapolis
317-637-5759

Kahn's Fine Wines
5369 N. Keystone Ave., Indianapolis
317-251-9463, 800-621-8466

IOWA

Ingersoll Wine & Spirits
3500 Ingersoll Ave., Des Moines
515-255-3191, www.ingersollwine.com

J.T.'s Fine Wine & Spirits M
5010 E.P. True Pkwy., W. Des Moines
515-224-2997

The Wine Experience
7696 Hickman Rd., Des Moines
515-252-8798

KANSAS

Jensen Liquor
620 W. 9th St., Lawrence
785-841-2256
email elff@sunflower.com

Rimann Retail Liquor Store
15117 W. 87th St. Pkwy., Lenexa
913-492-1604
email rimannliquors@planetkc.com

O = on-line retail   **M** = mail order

top wine shops

Lukas Liquors
7541 W. 119th St., Overland Park
913-451-8030, 800-436-3519
www.lukasliquor.com

Larry Evers Wine & Spirits
7728 E. Central Ave. Ste. B, Wichita
316-685-6868

Rossiter Retail Liquors
4808 E. Central Ave., Wichita
316-686-6921

KENTUCKY

The Party Source
95 Riviera Dr., Bellevue
606-291-4007
www.thepartysource.com

**Liquor Barn,
The Ultimate Party Source**
3040 Richmond Rd., Lexington
606-269-4170, www.liquorbarn.com

Tates Creek Spirit Company
Tates Creek Center, Lexington
606-273-4242

Liquor Outlet
1800 S. Hurstbourne Ln., Louisville
502-491-0753

The Party Source
4301 Towne Center Dr., Louisville
502-426-4222

LOUISIANA

Bottavino World Wines
8966 Interline Ave., Baton Rouge
225-201-9080

Martin Wine Cellar
714 Elmeer Ave., Metairie
504-896-7300, 800-298-4274
www.martinwine.com

Martin Wine Cellar
3827 Baronne St., New Orleans
504-899-7411, 800-298-4274
www.martinwine.com

MAINE

Aurora Provisions
64 Pine St., Portland
207-871-0201
www.auroraprovisions.com

**R.S.V.P. Discount Beverage &
Redemption Center**
887 Forest Ave., Portland
207-773-8808

The Market Basket
223 Commercial St., Rockport
207-236-4371

MARYLAND

Mills Wine & Spirit Mart O
87 Main St., Annapolis
410-263-2888, 800-261-9463
www.millswine.com

North Charles Fine Wine & Spirits
6213 A N. Charles St., Baltimore
410-377-4655
www.northcharlesfinewine.com

Wells Discount Liquors
6310 York Rd., Baltimore
410-435-2700, www.wellswine.com

Calvert Discount Liquors
10128 York Rd., Cockeysville
410-628-2320

State Line Liquors, Inc.
1610 Elkton Rd., Elkton
410-398-3838, 800-446-9463
www.statelineliquors.com

Jason's Wine & Spirits
9339 Baltimore Nat. Pike, Ellicott City
410-465-2424

MASSACHUSETTS

Brookline Liquor Mart M, O
1354 Commonwealth Ave., Allston
617-734-7700, 800-256-9463
www.blmwine.com

Bauer Wine & Spirits
330 Newbury St., Boston
617-262-0363

Federal Wine & Spirits
29 State St., Boston
617-367-8605, email fedwine@aol.com

Martignetti's
1650 Soldiers Field Rd., Brighton
617-782-3700, www.martignetti.com

Best Cellars
1327 Beacon St., Brookline
617-232-4100, www.bestcellars.net

Busa Wine & Spirits
55 Bedford St., Lexington
781-862-1400, email busabros@juno.com

Marty's Fine Wines
675 Washington St., Newton
617-332-1230

Table & Vine M, O
122 N. King St., Northampton
413-584-7775, 800-474-2449
www.tableandvine.com

The Wine Cask
407 Washington St., Somerville
617-623-8656

MICHIGAN

Merchant of Vino
2789 Plymouth Rd., Ann Arbor
734-769-0900

Village Corner
601 S. Forest, Ann Arbor
734-995-1818, www.villagecorner.com

Merchant's Cellar Collection M
254 W. Maple St., Birmingham
248-433-3000

Merchant's Fine Wine M
22250 Michigan Ave., Dearborn
313-563-8700
www.merchantsfinewine.com

MINNESOTA

France 44 Wines & Spirits M, O
4351 France Ave. S., Minneapolis
612-925-3252, 800-416-3582
www.france44.com

Haskell's Wine & Spirits M
81 S. 9th St., Minneapolis
612-333-2434, 800-486-2434
www.haskells.com

Hennepin Lake Liquors
1200 W. Lake St., Minneapolis
612-825-4411

Surdyk's Liquor M
303 E. Hennepin Ave., Minneapolis
612-379-3232

The Cellars Wines & Spirits M, O
859 Village Center Dr., North Oaks
651-483-1767, 888-351-4222
www.thecellars.com

West Side Discount Liquor
45 N. Waite Ave., Waite Park, MN
320-253-9511

MISSISSIPPI

Briarwood Mart Liquor & Wine
4949 Old Canton Rd., Jackson
601-956-5108

Wine & Spirits Discount Center
1855 Lakeland Dr., Ste. A-10, Jackson
601-366-6644, email wsdc@netdoor.com

Terra Nova Wines & Spirits
1074 Hwy. 51 N., Madison
601-853-1533
www.allaboutterranova.com

MISSOURI

The Wine & Cheese Place M
7435 Forsyth Blvd., Clayton
314-727-8788
www.wineandcheeseplace.com

The Wine Merchant M
20 S. Hanley Rd., Clayton
314-863-6282, 800-770-8466
www.winemerchantltd.com

Gomer's Midtown
Fine Wines & Spirits
3838 Broadway, Kansas City
816-931-4170, www.gomers.com

Meiners Sunfresh
14 W. 62nd Terr., Kansas City
816-523-3700
email meinerssunfresh@aol.com

Red-X Fine Wines
2401 W. Platte Rd., Riverside
816-741-2171

**Brown Derby International
Wine Center M, O**
2023 S. Glenstone, Springfield
417-883-4066, 800-491-3438
www.brownderby.com

MONTANA

The Wine Merchant
2720 2nd Ave. N., Billings
406-252-8050

NEBRASKA

Meier's Cork 'N Bottle
1244 South St., Lincoln
402-476-1518, email vindene@aol.com

Spirit World
11424 Davenport St., Omaha
402-334-7123

Spirit World
7515 Pacific St., Omaha
402-391-8680

The Winery M
741 N. 98th St., Omaha
402-391-3535, 800-884-9463

NEVADA

Spirits Plus Liquor Store
4880 W. Flamingo Rd., Las Vegas
702-873-6000

**The Wine Cellar at
The Rio Hotel M, O**
3700 W. Flamingo Rd., Las Vegas
702-252-7777

NEW HAMPSHIRE

The Wine Cellar
650 Amherst St., Nashua
603-883-4114, www.winecellarNH.com

Ceres Street Wine Merchants
65 Ceres St., Portsmouth
603-431-2640, www.cereswine.com

NEW JERSEY

Carlo Russo's Wine & Spirit World O
102 Linwood Plaza, Fort Lee
201-592-1655, 800-946-3276

Sparrow Wine & Liquors
1226 Shipyard Ln., Hoboken
201-659-1501

Carlo Russo's Wine & Spirit World O
626 N. Maple Ave., Ho-Ho-Kus
201-444-2033, email russowine@aol.com

Moore Brothers Wine Company O
7200 N. Park Dr., Pennsauken
856-317-1177, 888-686-6673
www.moorebros.com

**The Princeton Corkscrew
Wine Shop M**
4-6 Hulfish St., Princeton
609-430-1200
www.princetoncorkscrew.com

O = on-line retail   **M** = mail order

top wine shops

The Wine Emporium
25 Valley St., S. Orange
877-505-9189

NEW MEXICO

Kelly Liquors
2226 Wyoming Blvd. NE, Ste. A
Albuquerque
505-296-7815

Kokoman Fine Wines & Liquors
34 Cities of Gold Rd., Pojoaque
505-455-2219
email kokoman@nets.com

Kokoman-Circus
301 Garfield St., Sante Fe
505-983-7770

NEW YORK

Mount Carmel Wines & Spirits M
612 E. 187th St., Bronx
718-367-7833
email carmelwine@aol.com

Skyview Discount Wines & Liquors
5681 Riverdale Ave., Bronx
718-601-8222
www.skyviewkosher.com

Heights Chateau Wines & Spirits
131 Atlantic Ave., Brooklyn
718-330-0963
email htschateau@aol.com

Scotto's Wine Cellar M
318 Court St., Brooklyn
718-875-5530

Tops Wines & Spirits Merchants M
2816 Ave. U., Brooklyn
718-648-7300, email topswines@aol.com

Premier Wines & Spirits
3445 Delaware Ave., Buffalo
716-873-6688, 800-666-6560
www.winedeals.com

Crazy Billy's M, O
1887 Deer Park Ave., Deer Park
631-667-8070, www.crazybillys.com

Wine & Spirit Company of Forest Hills
108-50 Queens Blvd., Forest Hills
718-575-2700

Pop's Wines & Spirits M, O
256 Long Beach Rd., Island Park
516-431-0025, www.popswine.com

Young's Fine Wines & Liquors
505 Plandome Rd., Manhasset
516-627-1234

Acker Merrall Condit Co. M
160 W. 72nd St., New York
212-787-1700

Astor Wines & Spirits M
12 Astor Pl., New York
212-674-7500, www.astoruncorked.com

Best Cellars M
1291 Lexington Ave., New York
212-426-4200, www.bestcellars.net

Cork & Bottle
1158 First Ave., New York
212-838-5300

Crossroads
55 W. 14th St., New York
212-924-3060

Garnet Wines & Liquors M, O
929 Lexington Ave., New York
212-772-3211, 800-872-8466
www.garnetwine.com

The Italian Wine Merchant
108 E. 16th St., New York
212-473-2323
www.italianwinemerchant.com

Morrell & Company M, O
One Rockefeller Plaza, New York
212-688-9370,www.winesbymorrell.com

Park Avenue Liquor Shop M, O
292 Madison Ave., New York
212-685-2442, www.parkaveliquor.com

Sherry-Lehmann M
679 Madison Ave., New York
212-838-7500
www.sherrylehmann.com

Vintage New York
482 Broome St., New York
212-226-9463

Century Discount Liquor & Wines M
630 Ridge Rd. W., Rochester
716-621-4210, 800-992-7651

House of Bacchus, Inc.
1050 E. Ridge Rd., Rochester
716-266-6390, email bacchus@eznet.net

Zachys Wines & Liquors M
16 E. Pkwy., Scarsdale
914-723-0241, 800-723-0241
www.zachys.com

Stone Ridge Wine & Spirits
Stone Ridge Towne Centre, Rt. 209
Stone Ridge
914-687-7125, email tswee@aol.com

Post Wines & Spirits
510 Jericho Turnpike, Syosset
516-921-1820, email postwine@aol.com

Brighton Liquor M
930 Brighton Rd., Tonawanda
716-833-2606

The French Wine Merchant
1504 Old Country Rd., Westbury
516-832-1990, 800-946-3496

NORTH CAROLINA

The Wine Merchant
4240 NW Cary Pkwy., Cary
919-469-1330
www.thewinemerchantinc.com

Arthur's Wine Shop M, O
4400 Sharon Rd., Charlotte
704-366-8610
email arthurswine@msn.com

Reid's M
707 Providence Rd., Charlotte
704-377-5467, 800-998-9855
www.reids.com

Southend Beverage M
1443 South Blvd., Charlotte
704-335-0600

The Wine Vault M, O
813 Providence Rd., Charlotte
704-334-9463, email wineladyNC@aol.com

Carolina Wine Company
6601 Hillsborough St., Ste. 118, Raleigh
919-852-0236, 888-317-4499
www.carolinawine.com

The Wine Merchant
1214 Ridge Rd., Raleigh
919-828-6929
www.thewinemerchantinc.com

NORTH DAKOTA

Bernie's Wines & Liquors
1557 S. University Dr., Fargo
701-232-3434

Happy Harry's Bottle Shop M
2051 32nd Ave. S., Grand Forks
701-780-0902, www.happy-harrys.com

OHIO

Papa Joe's
1561 Akron Peninsula Rd., Akron
330-923-7999, www.papajoes.com

Village Bootlegger
8945 Brecksville Rd., Brecksville
440-526-5885

Chuck's Cheese & Wine Unlimited
23 Bell St., Chagrin Falls
440-247-7534

The Wine Merchant
3972 Edwards Rd., Cincinnati
513-731-1515

Western Reserve Wines M
34101 Chagrin Blvd., Cleveland
216-831-2116, email wrwines@aol.com

The Andersons General Store
7000 Bent Tree Blvd., Columbus
614-766-9500

Carnardo Wine & Cheese M
1735 W. Lane Ave., Columbus
614-486-7474, email CarnWine@aol.com

Gentile's, The Wine Sellers O
1565 King Ave., Columbus
614-486-3406, www.gentiles.com

Grapes of Mirth
59 W. Spruce St., Columbus
614-221-9463

Hill's Market
7860 Olentangy River Rd., Columbus
614-846-3220

Spagio Cellars
1291 Grandview Ave., Columbus
614-486-1114
email spagiocellars@hotmail.com

Dorothy Lane Market O
6177 Far Hills Ave., Dayton
937-434-1294, www.dorothylane.com

Jungle Jim's International Market
5440 Dixie Hwy., Fairfield
513-829-1919, www.junglejims.com

Regency Wine Store
117 Merz Blvd., Ste. 112, Fairlawn
330-836-3447

Maumee Wines
2556 Parkway Plaza, Maumee
419-893-2525

Pat O'Brien's Fine Wines & Gourmet Foods M
30800 Pinetree Rd., Pepper Pike
216-831-8680

Hinman's
19300 Detroit Rd., Rocky River
440-333-0202
email hinmans@nacs.net

OKLAHOMA

Edmond Wine Shop
1532 South Blvd., Edmond
405-341-9122
email thewineshop@msn.com

Beau's Wine Bin & Spirit Shoppe
2810 W. Country Club Dr.
Oklahoma City
405-842-8866

Parkhill's Liquors & Wine
5111 S. Lewis Ave., Tulsa
918-742-4187

Ranch Acres Wine and Spirits
3324-A E. 31st St., Tulsa
918-747-1171
email Ranchacreswine@aol.com

The Wine Rack
6953 S. Lewis Ave.
Lewis Crossing Center, Tulsa
918-492-1220

OREGON

Great Wine Buys M
1515 NE Broadway, Portland
503-287-2897, 888-717-9786
www.teleport.com/~winebuys

Liner & Elsen Wine Merchants M
202 NW 21st Ave., Portland
503-241-9463, 800-903-9463
www.linerandelsen.com

O = on-line retail   **M** = mail order

top wine shops

Mt. Tabor Fine Wines M
4316 SE Hawthorne Blvd., Portland
503-235-4444
www.mttaborfinewines.com

Portland Wine Merchants M
1430 SE 35th St., Portland
503-234-4399, 888-520-8466
www.teleport.com/~drvino

PENNSYLVANIA

Liberty Bell Wines & Spirits Shoppe
401 Franklin Mills Circle, Philadelphia
215-281-2080

RHODE ISLAND

Gasbarro's
361 Atwells Ave., Providence
401-421-4170

Town Wine & Spirits
179 Newport Ave., Rumford
401-434-4563

SOUTH CAROLINA

Harris Teeter Grocery Store
290 East Bay St., Charleston
843-722-6821, 800-432-6111

The Wine Shop
3 Lockwood Dr., Charleston
843-577-3881
email debbiewine@awod.com

Frugal MacDoogal's
3630 Festival Dr., Fort Mill
803-548-6634
www.frugalmacdoogal.com

SOUTH DAKOTA

Kessler's
525 S. State St., Aberdeen
605-225-2440

Madison Discount Liquors M
123 NW 2nd St., Madison
605-256-6870

Once Upon a Vine
507 6th St., Rapid City
605-343-7802

Regal Liquors
2022 S. Minnesota Ave.
Sioux Falls; 605-335-3918

TENNESSEE

Arthur's Wine & Liquor
964 June Rd., Memphis
901-767-9463

Buster's Liquors & Wines
191 S. Highland Ave., Memphis
901-458-0929
www.bustersliquors.com

Nashville Wine & Spirits
4556 Harding Rd., Nashville
615-292-2676
email nashwin@aol.com

West End Discount Liquors & Wines
2818 West End Ave., Nashville
615-320-1446

TEXAS

The Austin Wine Merchant
512 W. 6th St., Austin
512-499-0522
www.theaustinwinemerchant.com

The Cellar M
3520 Bee Caves Rd., Austin
512-328-6464
www.citysearch.com/aus/thecellar

GrapeVine Market
7938 Great Northern Blvd., Austin
512-323-5900
www.grapevinemarket.com

Twin Liquors
5408 Balcones Dr., Austin
512-323-2775

La Cave Warehouse M
1931 Market Center Blvd., Dallas
214-747-9463
www.lacavewarehouse.com

Marty's O, M
3316 Oak Lawn Ave., Dallas
214-526-7796, www.martysdfw.com

Pogo's Beverages
5360 W. Lovers Ln., Ste. 200, Dallas
214-350-8989
email grandcru@pogoswine.com

Red Coleman's #14
7560 N. Greenville Ave., Dallas
214-363-0201, www.redcoleman.com

Sigel's Beverages, L.P.
2960 Anode Ln., Dallas
214-350-1271, www.sigels.com

Bourjalais Beverage Emporium
2720 N. Mesa St., El Paso
915-542-2658
email bourjalais@aol.com

Lomart Fine Food & Wine
6600 N. Mesa, El Paso
915-584-3731

Lukas Liquors Superstore M, O
11621 Katy Freeway, Houston
281-531-7727, 888-545-7727

Richard's Liquors & Fine Wines
5630 Richmond Ave., Houston
713-783-3344
www.richardsliquors.com

Spec's Liquor Warehouse
2410 Smith St., Houston
713-526-8787, 888-526-8787
www.specsonline.com

Wines of America M, O
2055 Westheimer, Ste. 155, Houston
713-524-3397
www.houstonwines.com

Joe Saglimbeni Fine Wines
638 W. Rhapsody, Ste. 1, San Antonio
210-349-5149, www.jsfinewine.com

State Liquor Store #34
1901 Sidewinder Dr., Park City
435-649-7254

Utah State Wine Store
255 S. 300 E., Salt Lake City
801-533-6444

Cheese Outlet Fresh Market
400 Pine St., Burlington
802-863-3968, 800-447-1205
www.cheeseoutlet.com

Bon Vivant
21 Essex Way 210, Essex Junction
802-878-1097

Wines by George
345 Center Hill Rd., Manchester Center
802-362-4936

TJ's Wines & Spirits
1341 Shelburne Rd., South Burlington
802-658-9595
www.tjswinesandspirits.com

Arrowine M
4508 Lee Hwy., Arlington
703-525-0990, www.arrowine.com

Tastings M
502 E. Market St., Charlottesville
804-293-3663, www.tastingsofcville.com

West Side Wine Shop
4702 Hampton Blvd., Norfolk
757-440-7600

Corks & Kegs
7110 A Patterson Ave., Richmond
804-288-0816

Taste Unlimited
638 Hilltop West Shopping Center,
Virginia Beach
757-425-1858

Best Cellars
224 Parkplace, Kirkland
425-576-0770

Best Cellars
University Village, Seattle
206-527-5900, www.bestcellars.com

Larry's Markets
10008 Aurora Ave. N., Seattle
206-527-5333

McCarthy & Schiering Wine Merchants O
6500 Ravenna Ave. NE, Seattle
206-524-9500
email mfrav@sprynet.com

Pike & Western Wine Shop M
1934 Pike Pl., Seattle
206-441-1307,www.pikeandwestern.com

Ace Beverage M
3301 New Mexico Ave. NW
202-966-4444

Bell Wine Shop M
1821 M St. NW, 202-223-4727

Calvert Woodley M
4339 Connecticut Ave. NW
202-966-4400
www.calvertwoodley.com

MacArthur Beverages M
4877 MacArthur Blvd. NW
202-338-1433, www.bassins.com

Morris Miller Wine & Liquors M
7804 Alaska Ave. NW
202-723-5000
email morrismiller@aol.com

Schneider's of Capitol Hill
300 Massachusetts Ave. NE
202-543-9300, 800-377-1461
www.cellar.com

Wide World of Wines M
2201 Wisconsin Ave. NW
202-333-7500, email estaren@aol.com

The Liquor Mart
1600 Patrick St., Charleston
304-346-6000

The Wine Shop at Capitol Market
800 Smith St., Charleston
304-343-9463

Steve's Liquor & More M, O
8302 Mineral Point Rd., Madison
608-833-5995
www.steveswinemarket.com

Grapes & Grain
11301 N. Port Washington Rd., Mequon
262-240-0206

Heiden's Wine & Spirits M
8510 W. Lisbon Ave., Milwaukee
414-462-0440

Discount Liquor, Inc.
919 N. Barstow St., Waukesha
262-547-7525

Town & Country Supermarket Liquors
614 S. Greeley Hwy., Cheyenne
307-634-3474
www.tcsupermarketliquors.com

index

Specific wine listings are in plain type.
Producers are in **bold**.
General categories are in ***bold italics***.
Countries and Regions are in *italics*.

index

index

index

index

index

index